CONFIRMATION CLASS 1936-37

Christmas '36

Alvin Pfahl

Walter Mahly

Daniel Hinrichs

Anita Krahmer

Margaret Koehnke

Genevieve Weichbrodt

Velda Stark

Florence Meyer

Bernice Meyer

Jeanette Brandaw

John Steele

Franklin Koch

THE STORY OF CHRIST'S PASSION

Told and Explained by
REV. E. E. ORTLEPP, D.D.

IN THREE PARTS

Part Three

BURLINGTON, IOWA
THE LUTHERAN LITERARY BOARD
1928

CONTENTS

_____

	Page
The Harmony: The Death of Jesus	9
The Harmony: The Burial	165

The Death of Jesus

53.	Led Away to Calvary	17
54.	Simon of Cyrene	25
55.	The Daughters of Jerusalem	33
56.	The Crucifixion	46
57.	The Superscription	57
58.	The Parted Garments	71
59.	The Mockery	79
60.	The Repentant Malefactor	97
61.	Mary and John	108
62.	Noonday Darkness	123
63.	The Last Request	138
64.	It Is Finished	152

The Burial

65.	The Signs after the Lord's Death	165
66.	The Witnesses of the Lord's Death	185
67.	The Side Pierced	203
68.	Joseph of Arimathea	221
69.	Nicodemus	239
70.	The Tomb in the Garden	250
71.	The Seal and the Watch	262

FOREWORD

The account of the Lord's Passion is the Holy of Holies in the sublime structure of God's Word; it reflects the light of ancient prophecy, and from its rich fountain flow the waters of life through the golden channel of the Epistles. A careful and detailed study of each scene, of every word, of the least circumstance connected with the sufferings of the Savior, reveals such an abundance of instruction and edification that no earnest reader can fail to find food for mind and soul.

If this "Story of Christ's Passion" serves as a reminder to pay closest attention to every word of Holy Writ; and if it helps to make the Lenten season a favored time of serious meditation at home and in the church, then the book was not written in vain.

E. E. O.

Greenville, O, February, 1909.

(5)

A HARMONY OF CHRIST'S PASSION

According to the Four Gospels

Part Three:

The Death of Jesus and the Burial

THE HARMONY: THE DEATH OF JESUS AND THE BURIAL

THE DEATH OF JESUS

Matt. 27, 31-50   **Luke 23, 26-46**
Mark 15, 20-37   **John 19, 16-30**

"And after they had mocked him, they took the purple robe off from him, and put his own clothes on him. And they took Jesus, and led him out to crucify him. And he bearing his cross went forth into a place called the place of a skull, which is called in Hebrew Golgotha. And there were also two other, malefactors, led with him to be put to death.

"And as they came out, they found a man of Cyrene, Simon by name, the father of Alexander and Rufus, who passed by coming out of the country. They laid hold upon him, and on him they laid the cross and compelled him that he might bear it after Jesus.

"And there followed him a great company of people, and of women, which also bewailed and lamented him. But Jesus turning unto them said, Daughters of Jerusalem, weep not for me, but weep for yourselves, and for your children. For, behold, the days are coming, in the which they shall say, Blessed are the barren, and the wombs that never bare, and the paps which never gave suck. Then shall they begin to say to the mountains, Fall on us; and to the hills, cover us. For if they do these things in a green tree, what shall be done in the dry?

"And when they were come to the place, which is called Calvary, they gave him vinegar to drink, mingled with gall, wine mingled with myrrh: and when he had tasted thereof, he would not drink, he received it not.

"And it was the third hour, and they crucified him. And with him they crucify the two thieves; the one on his right hand, and the other on his left, and Jesus in the midst. And the Scripture was fulfilled, which saith, And he was numbered with the transgressors.

"Then said Jesus, Father, forgive them; for they know not what they do.

"And Pilate also wrote a title, and set up over his head on the cross the superscription of his accusation. And the writing was, Jesus Of Nazareth The King Of The Jews. And it was written in letters of Greek, and Latin, and Hebrew. This title then read many of the Jews; for the place where Jesus was crucified was nigh to the city.

"Then said the chief priests of the Jews to Pilate, Write not, The King of the Jews; but that he said, I am King of the Jews. Pilate answered, What I have written I have written.

"Then the soldiers, when they had crucified Jesus, took and parted his garments, and made four parts, to every soldier a part; casting lots upon them, what every man should take, and also his coat; now the coat was without seam, woven from the top throughout. They said therefore among themselves, Let us not rend it, but cast lots for it, whose it shall be: that the Scripture might be fulfilled, which was spoken by the prophet, They parted my raiment among them, and for my vesture they did cast lots.

"These things therefore the soldiers did. And sitting down they watched him there.

"And the people stood beholding. And they that passed by reviled him, railed on him, wagging their heads, and saying, Ah, thou that destroyest the temple, and buildest it in three days, save thyself. If thou be the Son of God, come down from the cross.

"And the rulers also with them derided him. Likewise also the chief priests mocking him, with the scribes and elders, said among themselves, He saved others; himself he cannot save; let him save himself. If he be Christ the King of Israel, the chosen of God, let him now come down from the cross, that we may see, and we will believe him. He trusted in God; let him deliver him now, if he will have him: for he said, I am the Son of God.

"The thieves also, which were crucified with him, reviled him and cast the same in his teeth. And the soldiers also mocked him, coming to him, and offering him vinegar, and saying, If thou be the King of the Jews, save thyself.

"And one of the malefactors which were hanged railed on him, saying, If thou be Christ, save thyself and us. But the other answering rebuked him, saying, Dost not thou fear God, seeing thou art in the same condemnation? And we indeed justly; for we receive the due reward of our deeds: but this man hath done nothing amiss. And he said unto Jesus, Lord, remember me when thou comest into thy Kingdom. And Jesus said unto him, Verily I say unto thee, today shalt thou be with me in paradise.

"Now there stood by the cross of Jesus his mother, and his mother's sister, Mary the wife of Cleophas, and Mary Magdalene. When Jesus therefore saw his mother, and the disciple standing by, whom he loved, he saith unto his mother, Woman, behold thy son! Then saith he to the disciple, Behold thy mother! And from that hour that disciple took her unto his own home.

"And it was about the sixth hour, and there was a darkness over all the earth until the ninth hour. And the sun was darkened. And about the ninth hour Jesus cried with a loud voice, saying, Eli, Eli, lama sabachthani? which is, being interpreted, My God, my God, why hast thou forsaken me? And some of them that stood by, when they heard it, said, Behold, this man calleth for Elias.

"After this, Jesus knowing that all things were now accomplished, that the Scripture might be fulfilled, saith, I thirst. Now there was set a vessel full of vinegar: and they filled a sponge with vinegar, and put it upon hyssop, and put it to his mouth. The rest said, Let be, let us see whether Elias will come to save him. And straightway one of them ran and filled a sponge full of vinegar, and put it on a reed, and gave him to drink, saying, Let alone; let us see whether Elias will come to take him down.

"When Jesus therefore had received the vinegar, he said, It is finished. And when Jesus had cried again with a loud voice, he said, Father, into thy hands I commend my spirit: and having said this, he bowed his head, and gave up the ghost."

THE BURIAL

Matt. 27, 51-66	**Luke 23, 45, 47-56**
Mark. 15, 38-47	**John 19, 31-42**

"And, behold, the veil of the temple was rent in twain in the midst, from the top to the bottom; and the earth did quake, and the rocks rent; and the graves were opened; and many bodies of the saints which slept arose, and came out of the graves after his resurrection, and went into the holy city, and appeared unto many.

"And when the centurion, which stood over against him, saw that he so cried out, and gave up the ghost, he glorified God, saying, Certainly this was a righteous man. Truly this man was the Son of God. Now when the centurion, and they that were with him, watching Jesus, saw the earthquake, and those things that were done, they feared greatly, saying, Truly this was the Son of God. And all the people that came together to see that sight, beholding the things which were done, smote their breasts, and returned.

"And all his acquaintance, and also many women were there beholding the things afar off, among whom was Mary Magdalene, and Mary the mother of James the less and of Joses, and Salome the mother of Zebedee's children; who also, when he was in Galilee, followed him, which followed Jesus from Galilee, ministering unto him; and many other women which came up with him unto Jerusalem.

"The Jews therefore, because it was the preparation, that the bodies should not remain upon the cross on the Sabbath day, (for that sabbath day was a high day,) besought Pilate that their legs might be broken, and that they might be taken away.

"Then came the soldiers, and broke the legs of the first, and of the other which was crucified with him. But when they came to Jesus, and saw that he was dead already, they broke not his legs: but one of the soldiers with a spear pierced his side, and forthwith came there out blood and water.

"And he that saw it bare record, and his record is true; and he knoweth that he saith true, that ye might believe. For these things were done, that the Scriptures should be fulfilled, A bone of him shall not be broken. And again another Scripture saith, They shall look on him whom they pierced.

"And after this, now when the even was come, because it was the preparation, that is, the day before the sabbath, behold, there came a rich man of Arimathea, a city of the Jews, named Joseph, an honorable counsellor; and he was a good man, and a just: who also himself waited for the kingdom of God: being a disciple of Jesus, but secretly for fear of the Jews. The same had not consented to the counsel and deed of them: He went in boldly unto Pilate, and craved the body of Jesus, and besought Pilate that he might take away the body of Jesus.

"And Pilate marvelled if he were already dead: and calling unto him the centurion, he asked him whether he had been any while dead. And when he knew it of the centurion, Pilate gave him leave, and gave the body to Joseph. Then Pilate commanded the body to be delivered.

"And he bought fine linen. He came therefore and took the body of Jesus down. And when Joseph had taken the body, he wrapped it in the clean linen cloth.

"An there came also Nicodemus, which at first came to Jesus by night, and brought a mixture of myrrh and aloes, about a hundred pound weight. Then took they the body of Jesus, and wound it in linen clothes with the spices, as the manner of the Jews is to bury.

"Now in the place where he was crucified there was a garden; and in the garden a new sepulchre, wherein was never man yet laid. And Joseph laid him in his own new tomb, which he had hewn out in the rock: There laid they Jesus therefore because of the Jews' preparation day; for the sepulchre was nigh at hand, and the sabbath grew on. And he rolled a great stone to the door of the sepulchre, and departed.

"And the women also, which came with him from Galilee, followed after, and beheld the sepulchre, and how his body was laid. And there was Mary Magdalene, and the other Mary the mother of Joses, sitting over against the sepulchre, and beheld where he was laid. And they returned, and prepared spices and ointments; and rested the sabbath day according to the commandment.

"Now the next day, that followed the day of preparation, the chief priests and Pharisees came together unto Pilate, saying, Sir, we remember that that deceiver said, while he was yet alive, After three days I will arise again. Command therefore that the sepulchre be made sure until the third day, lest his disciples come by night, and steal him away, and say unto the people, He is risen from the dead: so the last error shall be worse than the first. Pilate said unto them, ye have a watch: go your way, make it as sure as you can.

"So they went, and made the sepulchre sure, sealing the stone, and setting a watch."

53. LED AWAY TO CALVARY

Matt. 27, 31   **Luke 23, 32**
Mark 15, 20   **John 19, 16-17**

"And after that they had mocked him, they
took the purple robe off from him, and put his
own clothes on him. And they took Jesus, and led
him out to crucify him. And he bearing his cross
went forth into a place called the place of a skull,
which is called in the Hebrew Golgotha. And
there were also two other, malefactors, led with
him to be put to death."

———

One short night sufficing to undo a national favorite and
hero, to frustrate his sublime plans and efforts, to strip him
of the glory as Messiah and put him into the place of a condemned transgressor—that was the highly remarkable
triumph of the priests over Jesus. It requires no great
amount of imagination to appreciate the dejection that must
have lowered upon Jerusalem, as well as the elation among
the rulers, when their victim was at last led forth to death.

"And after that they had mocked him, they took the
purple robe off from him, and put his own clothes on him."
Whereas not a single moment was to be lost, this "mocking" seems to refer to the disgraceful scene following the
scourging, before the sentence was rendered. But since that
happened quite a while ago, it is not improbable that Pilate's
final decision was greeted with derisive shouts against the
Nazarene and that the taking charge of the condemned was
not done without repeated insults, though this form of

mockery caused no delay in the preparation for the last act.
Before leading Jesus through the streets of Jerusalem, the
"purple robe," the soldier's cloak, was exchanged for his
own raiment. What was the object of that change, and
who suggested it? The Roman soldiers certainly would
have welcomed the spectacle of parading the King of the
Jews in ludicrous attire; by no means were they ashamed
to show the public how they treated a Jew. Those hardened
men did not stand in awe of a horrible form of death.
Nor did they dread the mummery because the earnest moment of the execution was so near. It was neither against
the spirit of the age nor against the traditions and customs
of Roman soldiers to torment a dying criminal with ridicule
to the last minute. If the soldiers had been free to act as
they pleased, they would not have foregone the sport of
making this famous Jew a laughing stock before all the
world. Evidently they obeyed orders given by Pilate. The
spiteful procurator may have wished to indicate that not
a mock king, no imaginary king, was to be crucified. The
Messiah of the nation was led forth, just as he had waked
and taught among the masses, just as everyone had known
him by his plain clothes, and whom in this attire they had
hailed as their king. Yet it is doubtful whether Pilate,
with this view in mind, would have chosen this trivial
revenge. He had more drastic means at his disposal to
humiliate the Jews; for instance, the herald could have given
insulting announcements in the streets; and also the superscription, which was later on placed over the cross, afforded
him all the desired opportunity. In all probability the Jewish rulers, through Pilate, demanded that change of clothes,
for "unto them" Pilate had delivered Jesus, wherefore they
had something to say as to details; and, naturally, they
watched that the soldiers carried out the given orders. In

ordering that change the rulers were not prompted by the solemnity of approaching death, nor by a sense of shame which sought to cover their malignant treatment of Jesus; it was rather a precaution suggested by the fear of the people. Large multitudes had to be encountered in the narrow streets, and hosts of friends of the Nazarene could be expected among the spectators. Their compassion must not be unduly aroused, the excitable Galileans dare not be provoked too much—this seems to have been the reason for leading Jesus forth in his well known apparel.

The procession was quickly formed. The crosses were ready. "And they took Jesus, and led him out to crucify him." Without delay the punishment was to be inflicted, no time for appeal granted. Paul protected himself with his right of Roman citizenship when he wisely avoided the prejudiced court of the Jews, saying, "I appeal unto Caesar." Acts 25, 11 As a Jew, Jesus did not enjoy the right of appeal from Pilate to the emperor; or, if there had been any chance of retarding the decision, he refused to profit by it; nor were the rulers inclined to tolerate further delay. Again, with the Romans it was customary to allow about ten days to intervene between the sentence and the execution, though it is uncertain whether that rule was enforced in the provinces or in conquered countries. At any rate, the haste shows that Jesus was definitely delivered unto the rulers, and that the Jewish law applied, which knew of no interval between sentence and death. In the time of Moses already the congregation stoned the culprit immediately after the verdict: "And the Lord said unto Moses, The man shall be Num. 15, surely put to death: all the congregation shall stone him 35, 36 with stones without the camp. And all the congregation brought him without the camp, and stoned him with stones, and he died; as the Lord commanded Moses." Shortly after

the days of Jesus the same procedure still prevailed, as
Acts 7, 57, 58 Stephen's fate proves: "Then they cried out with a loud voice, and stopped their ears, and ran upon him with one accord, and cast him out of the city, and stoned him." Therefore the Jewish legend, that the city of Jerusalem was given public notice during forty days, informing the people that Jesus was to be stoned, and that all who could or would defend him should speak at once, is a senseless invention in more than one respect.

Immediately after his condemnation Jesus was led "out." Both the Romans and the Jews had their places of execution beyond the city limits. The Bible furnishes sev-
Num. 15, 36 eral instances. Thus the sabbath breaker: "And all the congregation brought him without the camp, and stoned him
1 Kings 21, 13
Acts 7, 58 with stones, and he died." Naboth: "Then they carried him forth out of the city, and stoned him with stones, that he died"; Stephen: "And they cast him out of the city, and stoned him." That Jesus died beyond the walls of Jerusalem
Heb. 13, 12 is stated in the Epistle to the Hebrews: "Wherefore Jesus also, that he might sanctify the people with his own blood, suffered without the gate." They "took and led" him; extra precautions for safe keeping were taken, the prisoner marching in the midst of soldiers to prevent any attempt at escape or liberation by friends.

The sombre procession moved in a certain order. A maniple of soldiers, fully armed and headed by a centurion on horseback, marched in the van. The culprit followed, immediately preceded by a herald on foot, and by lictors whose office was in this case assumed by common soldiers, because the mentioned dignitaries were not at Pilate's command. The herald carried a tablet containing the accusation; or he loudly proclaimed the guilt of the condemned, who marched along surrounded by a number of soldiers:

the henchmen who did the bloody work. The condemned man carried his own cross, fitted to his size; the cross was placed upon his shoulders, and the arms were tied to the cross-beams. Sometimes the culprit wore a board hanging from his neck, relating the name and the crime for which he was to die. Evidently the Lord did not carry such placard, as Pilate sent and affixed his superscription after the cross was erected. This neglect was owing not alone to the haste of the preparations, but also to the fact that no one knew whereof to accuse Jesus even after the trial; and thus the omission became another significant, though involuntary, confession that they "found no fault in him." And he bearing his cross went forth." It is simply surprising to see the Lord sustain the weight of the rough tree for any length of time after the mental strain of the previous restless night, and after the weakening maltreatment inflicted on his body. He did not complain, did not ask for relief, but silently and willingly tried to bear the burden, and actually carried the cross quite a distance.

The procession moved on. Tradition pretends to know the route over which Jesus was led, and calls it the *via dolorosa* with its seven stations. Commencing with a narrow zigzag street at the Prætorium of Pilate, near the temple, it descends a short stretch down a hill to where formerly a staircase stood—the one that was transported to Rome and placed beside the church of St. John of the Lateran, the same staircase which in 1510 Luther ascended on his knees and where first the truth dawned upon his penitent soul that the just shall live by faith alone. Some hundred feet further on, the street leads through an ancient arch where Pilate is said to have exclaimed his "Behold the Man." Shortly a church is passed, at which point, according to tradition, Jesus greeted his mother who fainted at the sight of her afflicted son. The juncture of a street entering from the north marks the point where Simon of Cyrene was pressed into service. Where the street turns west, the house of Lazarus is shown. At last it leads through the gate of judgment and ends at the Church of the Holy Sepulchre. Whereas Jerusalem has been destroyed and restored so many times during these two thousand years, it is impossible to discover the original sites, and the Catholic church alone has accepted the tradition of the *via dolorosa,* also using its supposed seven stations in penitential services. The Bible is silent on that subject, as it also fails to furnish the least clue to the numerous legends clustering around the path of sorrows.

The procession moved towards a place beyond the city walls, called Golgotha, the translation of this Hebrew word being "skull." A hill rather than a mountain, its identity has not been indisputably proved to this day. Two sites are generally suggested: the one, where today the Church of the Holy Sepulchre stands, in a westerly direction from the ancient temple; the other, north of the city, near the Damascus gate, where the traveller finds the so-called Jeremiah's grotto. The entire distance, if either point be accepted, could be walked in about 10 to 15 minutes, despite the weakened condition of the Lord and the delay of putting the cross on Simon. The hill Golgatha, or Calvary, was near a public highway. The Romans preferred to have their executions in places where many people could see the warning example. But why was that elevation called "skull?" Because it was from time immemorial the appointed spot for executions where the skulls of criminals were lying about? Against this assumption speaks the fact that Joseph owned a garden close by: A rich Jew would not have his property, whether a pleasure garden or a park for

the family's tomb chiefly, adjoining so ghastly and detested
a place. Again, the Jews would not have permitted to
leave skulls lying around so near to the holy city; the law
did not tolerate such defilement: "If a man have committed _{Deut. 21,}
a sin worthy of death, and he be put to death, and thou ^{22, 23}
hang him on a tree: his body shall not remain all night
upon the tree, but thou shalt in any wise bury him that
day; (for he that is hanged is accursed of God;) that thy
land be not defiled." If the Jews had set aside an official
tract for their executions, the same must rather be sought
in the valley of Hinnom the place of abomination. Probably Calvary resembled the form of a human skull, and
simply because of its close proximity to a main road the
Romans may have chosen that hill for their executions.
Joseph's family may have owned the adjoining garden long
before the pagan oppressors rendered the neighboring tract
obnoxious.

The Lord was the principal person in that sorrowful
procession, but he was not without companions in misery.
"And there were also two other, malefactors, led with him to
be put to death." The worst of the trio, Barabbas, had
been set free, and the presence of the Lord seems to have
benefited even these two wretches. Though in the same
train, the malefactors were marched out apart from Jesus,
for the words "they took and led him" indicate that the
Lord was singled out and specially surrounded by guards.
With the attention of the people riveted on the Nazarene,
the two unfortunate men were at least spared the customary
jeers and taunts of the rabble bordering the road. Another
advantage seems to have been their escape from scourging.
During the negotiations before Pilate these two men were
not disturbed, and as they were hurried out with Jesus,
no time was left for scourging them. During the first

hours on the cross their conversation betrayed more vitality than a severe scourging would have left. Thus already on the way to the cross the Lord appears as he whose stripes spare others, whose sorrows accrue to our benefit. But where is one among the people ready to show favors to the friend of sinners? Not even Simon, who now steps up, does it with a willing heart.

54. SIMON OF CYRENE

Matt. 27, 32   **Mark 15, 21**

Luke 23, 26

"And as they came out, they found a man of
Cyrene, Simon by name, the father of Alexander
and Rufus, who passed by coming out of the country. They laid hold upon him, and on him they
laid the cross and compelled him that he might
bear it after Jesus."

———

Three times the Lord fell to the ground under the
burden of the cross, that is what tradition would have us
believe; the sacred record, however, does not tell of a single
instance, not even in the text before us. It is perfectly
obvious, after the tortures of the preceding night, that the
wounded, weakened body of the Lord failed in strength to
carry the heavy tree the entire distance. It is indeed possible that he collapsed and lay helpless on the ground; that
no whipping or buffeting could bring him to his feet; yet it
suffices to assume that he staggered under the unwonted
weight, that he walked very slowly and at last trembled
and stopped.

"And as they came out, they found a man, who passed
by coming out of the country." From out of the judgment
hall and through the streets Jesus had faithfully borne the
cross; this "coming out," therefore, points to the gate in the
city wall; just as the open country with Calvary came into
view, the cross had to be taken from Jesus. It was no act
of kindness. Neither during the past night nor in the hours
of distress on the cross did the soldiers show any sympathy

with the Lord, so that it is unwarranted to assume any
tender feelings in them on this occasion. Or was it spite?
Did the soldiers recognize Simon as a friend of Jesus, or
did that man offend the Roman by word or act, perhaps
by expressing his sympathy for Jesus? The soldiers had
paid no attention whatever to the followers of the Lord
and were ignorant as to the identity of such friends; Simon,
besides, was a stranger whom they perhaps met the first
time. The unconcerned "passing by" indicates that Simon
took no interest in Jesus, that he paid little attention to the
procession and thus cannot have provoked the anger of the
military escort. Evidently he fell into the hands of the
executioners right at or near the narrow passage of the
gateway where escape was impossible. Evidently Simon did
not know anything of the trial, condemnation, and approaching crucifixion, which, in turn, indicates that he must have
spent the night outside Jerusalem. That he was readily
distinguished as one "coming out of the country" goes to
show that at that particular moment few people, or none
at all, had collected beyond the city walls; the mass of
spectators, after having seen Jesus pass at some open place,
were forced to follow behind, as the narrow streets did not
permit their going along. With large throngs of people
present, Simon could not have "passed by" so easily, and
if he had attempted to force his way through a curious
multitude, he could not have been so quickly singled out
as the man just needed. He was "coming out of the country"—returning from work, or from a walk? It was a holy
day, on which all labor was forbidden, and as a stranger
Simon had no occasion to work on a field. And a conscientious Jew, who travelled hundreds of miles to enjoy the
religious feast of his nation, would neither transgress the
sabbath law by walking beyond the prescribed distance,
nor would he superficially spend that first great day in

sight seeing, or in lonely meditation. Probably this visitor
from abroad had been compelled to lodge outside the city
as on his belated arrival he found no quarters in Jerusalem
itself. In the immediate vicinity rich citizens owned gardens and cottages, like Joseph of Arimathea, the proprietor
of Gethsemane, and Caiaphas. Many such men, who would
not have condescended to entertain common guests, may
have accommodated personal friends or even unknown rich
pilgrims like the one from Cyrene. No doubt, Simon came
from his rural lodging and, the hour of day coinciding, was
probably on his way to the morning service, ignorant of
the events of the past night. A lonely church-goer was he
indeed at that moment when the entire population forsook
the altar to follow the Nazarene and his cross! How con-
venient Simon's coming was to the soldiers is evident from
the remark that they "found" him. This may suggest
that for a while they had been hoping in vain to meet a
suitable person. During the march through the city the
executioners may soon have noticed that Jesus with the
cross was unable to reach Calvary at all or only after much
delay. Yet the whole affair required haste. None of the
proud Romans would condescend to perform the infamous
task of carrying the cross for a Jewish prisoner, therefore a
Jew must be pressed into service. But it was impracticable
to seize the next best spectator, as the multitude and the
rulers might have objected to such defamation of one of
their country men. Friends of Jesus willing to render this
last service had not ventured near the procession at all.
Or, if the Romans by the right of requisition would have
unceremoniously compelled any Jew, none was near enough,
as the narrow streets kept the people in the rear. The
Rulers may not have known of this incident until afterward.
However, the word "found" may also denote a mere unexpected meeting: as the Lord, under the gate, yielded to

sudden and complete exhaustion, Simon opportunely happened to appear on the scene.

"They laid hold upon him, and on him they laid the cross and compelled him that he might carry it after Jesus." The soldiers made use of their right of requisition, which entitled them to press anything or anyone into service when needed. The mere act of "laying hold" upon Simon was notification enough that he had to be at their service for the time being. Obviously, there was no lack of pleadings, protests, and resistance, on the part of the unfortunate pilgrim; for the soldiers not only used force in putting the cross upon him, they also "compelled" him to walk on with the burden: if he refused to proceed, the swords spoke their persuasive language. We dare not blame Simon for objecting to that unpleasant duty, as it was not only a disagreeable task, a kind of infamous punishment in itself, but brought him in contact with condemned criminals, with unclean Gentiles, with the accursed tree, rendering also the bearer unclean. This meant much to a man who came from afar with the intention of joining the holy services and festivities of this glad day. To him the whole feast was now spoiled by this cruel defilement that excluded him from the temple and the company of the brethren. That display of Roman authority was thus a quick illustration of that arbitrary power to which the Jews bowed voluntarily when crying, We have no king but Cæsar!

Simon of Cyrene, the protesting cross bearer, here took the place of Simon Peter, who promised to go into prison and death with the Master, but failed to redeem his word. This interesting substitute of the leading apostle is portrayed in the following words: "A man of Cyrene, Simon by name, the father of Alexander and Rufus." About three hundred years before Christ a colony of Jews settled in Cyrene the capital of Cyrenaica in Libya—a name which

with Homer and Hesiod denoted the whole of Africa excepting Egypt; with others, the country extending from
Egypt and the Arabian gulf westward to Mt. Atlas. Though
the colony grew so rapidly that soon the Jews constituted
one fourth of the population, they were tolerated and in
consequence prospered in their trades and as owners of real
estate. Not only in Cyrene did they use their religious
liberty by living strictly after the ordinances of their religion; they also remembered the temple in the land of their
fathers, and were faithful visitors at the main festivals of
Jerusalem—not only on the Passover did they come, but
even among the wondering people on Pentecost were some
from "the parts of Libya about Cyrene." Retired merchants Acts 2, 10.
who had acquired a competency in the diaspora loved to
spend their easy years in the holy city; aged people feeling
death draw near would piously return home to be buried in
sacred ground. Of such people the Cyrenians had furnished
a constituency strong enough in numbers and finances to
have their own synagogue at Jerusalem. Whether Simon Acts 6, 9.
was born in Cyrene, we know not; but he cannot have been
a retired merchant living in Jerusalem, for in that case the
gospel would not simply call him "a man"; it would consider
his service remarkable enough to distinguish him as prominent and rich, as is done with Joseph of Arimathea and
Nicodemus; and this so much the more as Simon's family
soon became well known in the church. Nor can this
Cyrenean have been an aged person awaiting death; putting
the cross on a feeble old man would not have accelerated
the march as the soldiers desired; either he could not have
sustained the weight at all, or he could have walked only
slowly and with difficulty. Neither as a young man nor
as an old man is Simon represented, but simply as "a man"
in the best years of life, strong enough to carry the heavy
cross quickly. Marked by dress, language and manners

as a stranger, he became the more readily the victim of
the soldiers.

But this arduous task was a blessing in disguise to
Simon and his family. On that short way to Calvary his
heart, first agitated with wounded pride and bitter disappointment, seems to have received a lasting impression
of the Lord's beauty. He seems to have remembered that
peculiar following of the Lamb, seems to have rejoiced in
having rendered that service, seems to have become a
believer in Jesus Himself. When the converted Jews of
Jerusalem "which were scattered abroad upon the persecution that arose about Stephen travelled as far as Phenice,
and Cyprus, and Antioch, preaching the word to none but
the Jews only," it became advisable to preach the gospel
also to the Grecians. Such mission work could be done far
better by converted Jews who for years had lived among
Gentiles, than by believers grown up in the prejudices of
the holy land. Now among others who did such work, perhaps upon invitation, there "were men of Cyrene, which,
when they were come to Antioch, spake unto the Grecians,
preaching the Lord Jesus." So striking a departure in
evangelization would naturally be entrusted to reliable men
only, to men who had distinguished themselves among the
Christians; and who among all Cyrenean converts could
be a better witness than the cross bearer who had spent
the last few moments near the Savior and who, as is but
natural, had related his experiences frequently at Cyrene?

That his sons became believers is evident from the
words which point him out as "the father of Alexander and
Rufus." These two men were not only Christians, but
widely known members of the church. By merely mentioning their names, Mark supposes the Gentile Christians, for
whom he wrote his gospel, to know at once who was meant.
If not at the time of Christ's death, then certainly at the

Acts 11, 20

time when Mark wrote his gospel, the names of the two
brothers must have been household words among the Gentile
converts. If the testimony of the church fathers is correct,
Mark wrote his gospel in Rome, and at that place we find a
Rufus with his mother, whom Paul greets: "Salute Rufus Rom. 16, 13
chosen in the Lord, and his mother and mine." Paul must
have known these people intimately long before he saw
Rome, at a place where they lived and where he also stayed
a longer time. The words "chosen in the Lord" indicate that
Rufus either excelled as a Christian in his works and ways,
or that he was a particular friend of Paul's. His mother
also was known to the great apostle, and respected and
loved by him to such a degree that he called her "Mine own
mother." Who knows what acts of kindness this estimable
Christian lady had done to Paul; during his captivity and
work at Rome he may later have found lodging in her home.
The name Alexander occurs, apart from Mark's gospel,
several times in the New Testament and in each instance,
excepting the one of the kindred of the high priest, it points
to Ephesus. Paul complains to Timothy, who had found his Acts 4, 6
lasting abode and work in Ephesus, of "Hymenaeus and
Alexander; whom I have delivered unto Satan, that they 1 Tim. 1, 20
may learn not to blaspheme." This Alexander is apparently
the same of whom Paul warns Timothy later: "Alexander 2 Tim. 4, 14
the coppersmith did me much evil: the Lord reward him
according to his works: of whom be thou ware also; for
he hath greatly withstood our words." The obstinacy and
spitefulness of this Ephesian point backward to the time
when Paul himself worked at Ephesus, but here all traces of
the excommunicated heretic are lost. For that Alexander Acts 19, 33, 34
who appeared during the tumult of the silversmiths was a
Jew and did not act nor was he hailed as a friend of the
Gentile rabble. "And they drew Alexander out of the multitude, the Jews putting him forward. And Alexander

beckoned with the hand, and would have made his defense
unto the people. But when they knew that he was a Jew,
all with one voice about the space of two hours cried out,
Great is Diana of the Ephesians." This man was rather a
convert, a leader in the congregation, an influential person
of the city, who at the risk of his life faced the excited mob
to defend the Christian faith and the teachings of Paul
who was prevented from personally addressing the people.
The courage, the friendship, of that convert reminds us
vividly of the noble family at Rome: "Rufus chosen in the
Lord, and his mother and mine." It seems very much as if
the Jew, Alexander of Ephesus, was Simon's second son,
and we may now conjecture that Simon was one of those
missionaries who came to preach to the Gentiles of Antioch,
and that he moved his family there. Paul preached a whole
year in Antioch shortly after his conversion, and there the
Acts 11, 26   friendship with Simon and his family had its beginning.
After Simon's early death the mother and Rufus went to
Rome whilst Alexander chose Ephesus, both parties probably acting in the interest of the gospel. Glorious results of
a few dreary moments in which the cross was put upon
unwilling shoulders, on a rebellious heart! Mere chance
conducted Simon to the city gate and made him fall into the
hands of the soldiers at the proper moment. And yet not
chance. The hand of God had taken hold of him to lead him
whither he did not wish to go; the same almighty hand
extended with heaven's greetings to the friends of God, or
stretched forth in wrath over those that do not heed the
invitations, as the Savior now informs the wailing women.

55. THE DAUGHTERS OF JERUSALEM
Luke 23, 27-31

"And there followed him a great company of people, and of women, which also bewailed and lamented him. But Jesus turning unto them said, Daughters of Jerusalem, weep not for me, but weep for yourselves, and for your children. For, behold, the days are coming, in which they shall say, Blessed are the barren, and the wombs that never bare, and the paps which never gave suck. Then shall they begin to say to the mountains, Fall on us; and to the hills, cover us. For if they do these things in a green tree, what shall be done in the dry?"

———

The name of Jesus always was like a powerful magnet in attracting multitudes of people wherever he went. Whether he appeared in obscure villages, on the shores of the lake, or in larger cities, the masses flocked near him to listen to his words, to see his wondrous deeds. During the past week he had been the topic of conversation at Jerusalem, the hopeful, enthusiastic expectation of all. Since now the startling news spread that the same Jesus was condemned to die, was just being led to crucifixion, the agitation in the city must have been a tremendous one. "And there followed him a great company of people." When in the early morning hours the rulers and servants took their prisoner to Pilate, only comparatively few friends of the priests and probably a number of early risers went along. As the word was passed from mouth to mouth, the boisterous and fickle crowd swelled until three hours later a vast concourse of spectators had assembled. By the time Jesus was led forth, all Jerusalem with its hosts of visitors was astir. As the procession emerged from the city gate, the people could spread out and accompany the train on either side. It is unnecessary to assume that the rulers helped to call people together in order to overawe Pilate; their purposes were better served by condemning and putting away Jesus as quietly as possible, for large gatherings involved some risk. No efforts were required to bring the population out. A public execution was in itself an event apt to attract swarms of the curious, and this day three men were to die the slow death on the cross. And the principal figure of that spectacle was to be the famous Nazarene! A great company of people followed "him," his sad fate had brought them together. The execution of the two malefactors was an insignificant episode in comparison with the proposed punishment of Jesus. All the more surprising is the peacefulness and order of those many people; not a single protest, no sign of a threat against the tyrants, not the remotest effort to liberate the Lord. Though the personal friends of Jesus need not be supposed among the surging spectators, yet it is unreasonable to think that no friends, no acquaintances of the Lord at all, no Galileans, were present. Can it be possible that their interest in Jesus had subsided suddenly; that they had forgotten his kindness and greatness; that they were of one mind with the rulers? We must not overlook the fact that no shouts of approval, no outbursts of derision against Jesus are recorded until later under peculiar circumstances. Silently the men walked along, and the rulers had no cause but to interpret that sullenness in their own favor. Nor were those multitudes awed into silence by the detachment of soldiers marching along; even the knowledge that more

troops could quickly be called from the Prætorium would not
have deterred the hot-blooded Jews and Galileans, if their
ire had been aroused to action.   This passive attitude bears
the mark of complete surprise, they looked on as if dazed,
a feeling of helpless wonderment paralyzed the masses.
Conflicting rumors were afloat; the false witnesses, the
fanatic rabble of the morning, the servants, and citizens
in general, gave contradictory versions, hearsay stories, fanciful surmises, until nobody knew what actually had transpired.   The rapid developments of the tragedy afforded no
chance for a discussion of the matter among friends.

While the men labored under the painful uncertainty
as to how this affair should be judged, the more emotional
women dealt with the accomplished fact and did all they
were able to do, opening their hearts to pity.   "There followed him a great company of women, which also bewailed
and lamented him."   These women formed a party by themselves, for the Jews did not deign to be found in the company
of women in public.   The women must have walked very
close to Jesus, that the pitiful condition of the Man of
Sorrows could exert its full force upon the tender hearts,
and that they could hear the words of the exhausted Jesus as
he was passing on.   Their grief found vivid expressions:
they "bewailed" him, beating the breast, with gestures
crying and moaning; they "lamented him," weeping, inton-
ing the regular lamentation for the dead, as if a near
relative or friend were departed from them.   This mani-
festation of sorrow has been considered either as a courageous demonstration in favor of Jesus to shame the
indifference of the men, or as a superficial feeling of grief,
meaningless and rather displeasing to the Lord, a type of
weak sentimentalism with which Christ's Passion is nowadays read by some Christians.   It was neither the one
nor the other.   To find in those tears a public accusation

of the rulers and the men of Jerusalem for crucifying the promised king and national hero, is presupposing a profounder religious insight or a deeper understanding of political questions than the secluded and submissive life of Jewish women warranted. On the other hand, to assume a mere momentary emotion, a cheap display of womanly tenderness, means the ignoring of the great influence exerted by Jesus on all classes. Was there actually nobody among so many people to hold the Savior in grateful remembrance, nobody to show a heartfelt interest in him, nobody beyond the circle of immediate friends to realize the cruel injustice of that execution? Though a public execution may amount to a diversion of the vulgar mind, or may give occasion to the morbidly curious or hysterically sensitive to indulge in sentimentalities, those women show no such symptoms. Not the circumstance that three men at once go to their death, not the sad fate of the two malefactors aroused the complaints of their hearts, but the sight of the maltreated Jesus, the thought of his horrible end exclusively; they bewailed and lamented "him." It was a spontaneous expression of genuine sorrow. Who were those women? Judging from the Lord's address, they cannot have been followers of his, much less close friends like those women who ministered unto him: Mary Magdalene, Joanna, Susanna, and many others. These mourners were exactly what Jesus calls them: "Daughters of Jerusalem," inhabitants of the capital, none of them serious believers in the Messiah, yet all interested in the widely and favorably known prophet of Nazareth. If the common people generally thought highly of Jesus, did not the women of the land have special reason to bewail the death of their best friend and advocate? The Lord's kindness to women and children was surely a topic of conversation with the

Luke 8, 2, 3

mothers; what a light is thrown upon the enthusiasm prevalent in those circles, by that incident so displeasing to the rulers, occurring a few days before: "The children crying in the temple, and saying, Hosanna to the Son of David." Bethany was also near, and the many Jews that "came to Martha and Mary" indicate a large acquaintance which helped to scatter the knowledge of that friendship between Jesus and the sisters. A ray of hope had found its way from the Light of the World to the hidden walks of Jewish womanhood. There was good cause for shedding tears of true affection, and it is a relief to perceive these signs of sympathy after a night of hypocrisy and derision. Thus viewed, the wails of the women are neither a worthless burst of emotion, nor a theatrical display of courage. They are an unconscious, yet none the less effective, testimony to the Master's popularity. The women did not stand in such awe of the rulers as to suppress their kindlier feelings toward Jesus. They did not see in him a hated malefactor who died as a disgrace to his country, who was cast out because God wanted him no longer to defile the face of the earth. "He that hangs on the tree is accursed of God," and any devout Jew would rejoice to see God's glory avenged rather than that he would express pity for a condemned criminal. Therefore the women had not a single kind word for the two malefactors, who died justly. But their spontaneous demonstration announced their conviction that Jesus did not die to satisfy the Law; their helplessness found no better way of telling their opinion than in compassionate words and tears.

Jesus saw the women, heard their complaints, and acknowledged their sympathetic lamentations. "But Jesus turning unto them said, Daughters of Jerusalem, weep not for me, but weep for yourselves, and for your children."

Margin notes: Matt. 21, 15   John 11, 19, 45

Silence

For quite a while the Lord had ceased to speak. Neither Pilate, nor the rulers, nor the soldiers, had received any replies. That the Lord favored the women with any word at all shows that he considered them different from his henchmen. Thanks to Simon's involuntary intercession, Jesus was able to utter a few important truths, the last public address delivered by him. Relieved of the bending weight of the cross, he could turn and speak, though it had to be done in walking along. Short as the address was, it yet meant an extraordinary effort of the exhausted and wounded Lord. It may be that the very sight of the trembling, faltering, bleeding Master, just freed from the cross, had occasioned the outcries of the women.

In general, the speech did not encourage the wails; something was lacking in that sorrow: it was one-sided, born of natural affection only. The women comprehended the cruelty of the doom, the personal injustice perpetrated on Jesus, but failed to grasp the vast import of the crime, the sad consequences involving every citizen of Jerusalem. Their grief had to be turned in the right direction. "Daughters of Jerusalem"—a charming address! It reminded them of the days of the prophets when the proud title "Daughter of Zion" or "Daughter of Jerusalem" opened many a direct message of the God of Israel. Here is more than a prophet, he bears divine information by his own authority, and in his mouth the plural "daughters" becomes full of meaning. Not Jerusalem as the city of God was here addressed. This very procession showed that the Daughter of Zion had rejected the King meek and lowly, that her career in the kingdom of God had ended, that Jesus had finished his sayings to her as a whole. The Lord spoke to individuals who happened to be daughters, inhabitants of the city whose doom was sealed. The address reveals the distance between Jesus and the women: despite their well-meant tears they were not nearer to him than the citizens at large, not daughters of the coming kingdom, but daughters of the old Jerusalem. No message of joy, of invitation, of consolation to the disowned daughter; merely a warning affecting all of her household: "Weep not for me, but weep for yourselves, and for your children." He did not forbid them to weep: They had surely cause for shedding tears; but pitiable as the unnatural and unjust death of Jesus was, their own fate was more fearful. "Weep not for me"—this is not the cold stoic refusal to accept tender sympathy, but the language of the magnanimous heart forgetting its own affairs at the misery of others. "Weep for yourselves"; for this hour does not decide the fate of Jesus only, but that of the whole population, aye, that of future generations: "Weep for your children." At the point of deepest humiliation the Lord was so conscious of his influence, of his mission, of the decisive effect of his crucifixion! The mentioning of the children was evidently an answer to the cry of the fanatics in Pilate's hall: "His blood be on us and on our children." The frivolous request has been granted to the fullest extent. The warning is very specific: instead of saying, Weep not for "us," he says, Weep not for "me." The future is not influenced by the death of the two malefactors, let their punishment be deserved or not; it is not the general impiety of Jerusalem that is so dangerous: it is the singular position of the Lord, the attitude of the people towards him, the import of his death alone, that reaches into coming days and generations.

The consequences of his death, the real cause for grief, are given at once: "For, behold, the days are coming, in the which they shall say, Blessed are the barren, and the wombs that never bare, and the paps that never gave suck." "Behold"—a surprising state of affairs is going to overtake

Jerusalem, and not in the dim, indefinite future. "The days are coming" now already, this hour of death is the beginning of a period of sorrows. Undoubtedly the Lord referred to the day of judgment as predicted by him on his last visit to the temple: "The days shall come upon thee, that thine enemies shall cast a trench about thee, and compass thee round, and keep thee in on every side, and shall lay thee even with the ground, and thy children within thee; and they shall not leave in thee one stone upon another." The time of doom is at hand, the storm clouds are gathering and may momentarily burst upon Jerusalem. It is noteworthy that Jesus did not repeat that threat nor did he denounce the city by adding other dire prophecies; neither did he implore the people to amend their evil ways so as to escape from the disaster; not the slightest effort did he make to win friendship or converts by his speech. For the Lord no longer spoke as the Teacher or Messiah of the nation: this office was ended. He gave a simple statement of the dreadful future, a mere description of the effects of God's judgment which was to come inevitably and could not now be avoided or changed any more with admonitions of repentance. Weeping for themselves and for the innocent children who must suffer for the sins of their fathers, that is all Jerusalem can do now.

So full of bitterness are the coming days that "they shall say, "Blessed are the barren, and the wombs that never bare, and the paps which never gave suck." With these three expressions the Lord emphasized the enormity of the ensuing horror. In Israel children were prized as the gifts of the Lord; no one was happier nor envied more by other women than the mother whom the Lord had blessed with the fruit of her body. It was a source of regret and disgrace to be barren. Rachel bore a son and joyfully cried, "God hath

Luke 19, 43, 44

Gen. 30, 23

taken away my reproach." Hannah "was in bitterness of soul, and prayed unto the Lord, and wept sore" because the Lord had shut up her womb." Elizabeth rejoiced when she conceived, saying, "Thus hath the Lord dealt with me in the days wherein he looked on me, to take away my reproach among men." A certain woman praised the mother Mary by saying to Jesus, "Blessed is the womb that bare thee, and the paps which thou hast sucked." God's denying children to the people is the most awful curse uttered by the prophet Hosea: "As for Ephraim, their glory shall fly away like a bird, from the birth, and from the womb, and from the conception. Though they bring up their children, yet will I bereave them, that there shall not be a man left: yea, woe also to them when I depart from them! Ephraim, as I saw Tyrus, is planted in a pleasant place: but Ephraim shall bring forth his children to the murderer. Give to them, O Lord: what wilt thou give? give them a miscarrying womb and dry breasts." Now, we can understand how in an impious nation the woman may be so corrupt as to despise the duties and privileges of motherhood and consider a childless home the proper thing; but among people whose ardent prayer to God, and whose pride before men, were many children, the change of conditions must be most deplorable if the childless are called happy and blessed. The great amount of misery is the cause; whilst all the inhabitants of Jerusalem have their share of sorrow, the mothers carry a twofold burden; themselves in sore distress, they also see their dearest beings on earth suffer without help, without hope. And to the letter this prediction came true during the siege of Jerusalem by the Romans with all its terrors and despair, in that calamity of such extent as to make the words of Jeremiah applicable: "The hands of the pitiful women have sodden their own children: they were

1 Sam. 1, 10

Luke 1, 25

Luke 11, 27

Hos. 9, 11-14

Lam. 4, 10

their meat in the destruction of the daughter of my people."
Josephus, the Jewish historian, an eye witness of the destruction of Jerusalem, in his account of the fearful famine,
narrates the following incident: "There was a certain
woman from beyond the Jordan; her name was Mary, the
daughter of Eleazar of the village of Bethezob, which signifies the House of Hyssop. She was prominent by birth
and wealth, and had fled to Jerusalem with the other multitude, and with them was besieged. Her possessions which
she had brought with her out of Perea into the city had
been already seized by the tyrants; the treasures, as also
the provisions which she had managed to save, were carried
off by the rapacious guards who daily entered her house
for that purpose. The poor woman was in a state of frenzy,
and with frequent reproaches and curses she sought to
provoke the villains to anger against her. None of them,
however, would kill her either in wrath or in pity with her
condition. She perceived that in seeking food she labored
for others, and it had now also become impossible to find
any food. Hunger pierced her bowels and marrow, but
fiercer than hunger burned her wrath within her. She now
consulted only her passion and the extremity she was in, and
then attempted a most unnatural thing. Snatching up her
son, a child sucking at her breast, she said, 'O thou unfortunate infant, for whom shall I preserve thee in this war,
famine, and sedition? If the Romans permit us to live, we
must be slaves; or ere that slavery comes we are destroyed
by this famine, and the seditious rebels are more terrible
than both. Come, be thou my food—and be an avenging
fury to the rebels, a byword to the world; this is the climax
of the calamities of the Jews.' Saying such words she killed
her son, roasted him, ate one-half, and concealed the other
half. Presently the rebels came in and, smelling that horrid

Jos., De Bell., VI, 3, 4

scent of the roast, threatened to cut her throat if she did not immediately show them what food she had prepared. With the words, 'I have saved a very fine portion for you,' she placed before them what was left of her child. Horror and amazement seized them, and they stood there in dumb astonishment, as the woman continued, 'This is my own son, and this is my own doing; come, eat of this food, for I have eaten of it myself. Do not be more tender than a woman, or more compassionate than a mother. Or if you are afraid, or if you abominate this meat, leave it to me, as I have eaten the other half already.' Trembling with fright the men went out and left the rest of that meat to the mother."

The distress of the mothers and the children indicates the amount of misery which is to befall the entire population. None shall be exempt from suffering at a time when within the famined city opposing parties fill the streets with blood, and when before the gates the Romans plant a forest of crosses for fugitive Jews. Then a swift end will be preferable to the lingering tortures that make the soul weary of life. "Then shall they begin to say to the moun- Hos. 10, 8 tains, Fall on us; and to the hills, cover us." Hosea's prophesy is then fulfilled as repeated here by the Lord. Falling mountains, burying and crushing thousands in sudden destruction, denote the greatest natural calamity imaginable, which quickly ends the terrors of the doom and therefore is welcomed as a relief. These words of Jesus were also literally fulfilled. The subterranean cavities and ducts under the temple were a favorite refuge of the frightened Jews in Jerusalem, and thousands of them found their graves under the falling masses of their hiding places.

However pitiful the fate of the people may be, there is nothing cruel or unjust in it; it is but the logical result of their actions. This the Lord points out in the following words: "For if they do these things in a green tree, what shall be done in a dry?" The green wood, full of sap, is naturally unfit for fuel; but if cast into the fire, and it burns readily, how fierce must be the heat of that fire; and how much more quickly and thoroughly will that fire consume dry and dead wood! Such fire is not extinguished until all the wood is burned away, as Ezekiel describes in his vision

Ezek. 20, 47

of the forest fire: "Behold, I will kindle a fire in thee, and it shall devour every green tree in thee, and every dry tree: the flaming flame shall not be quenched, and all faces from the south to the north shall be burned therein." With the picture of a green tree that must burn whilst it ought to be left standing to grow, to give shadow, to yield fruit, the Savior describes himself and the unnaturalness of his death; he is wantonly plucked from the land of the living, where he was planted to do good. Repeatedly the Bible likens the

Ps. 1, 3

righteous man to the green tree: "He shall be like a tree planted by the rivers of water, that bringeth forth his fruit

Ps. 93, 13

in his season; his leaf also shall not wither." "Those that be planted in the house of the Lord flourish in the courts of

Job 15, 32

our God." The very opposite is true with the godless: "His branch shall not be green"; he is the one who is forced to

Isaiah 56, 3

say, "I am a dry tree." Jesus then is the green tree, the Jews are the dry trees. Jesus, obedient to all authority, must suffer the tortures of the cross: what must be the fate awaiting his persecutors, who are the real rebels against God and the Romans? Jesus, the friend of the Law, ever doing God's will, convinced of no sin, dies like a criminal and blasphemer: What becomes of his foes, who are the real blasphemers and enemies of the Lord? The living God will not be mocked.

How short and yet how impressive this farewell address to the people of Israel! It concludes all the words spoken

by the prophets. It fills the last pages in the history of
Israel as the chosen people of God. From that moment
on the history of the Jewish nation began to be a continuous
record of oppression and contempt, of persecution and sorrow without the hope of glorious restoration. They are
no factor in the religious world, in the progress of God's
kingdom, or in its blessings, until they see, believe, and greet
Him whom they pierced. We are not told how the hearers
received the speech. Sullenly the procession moved on and
presently reached Calvary.

56. THE CRUCIFIXION

Matt. 27,33-34, 38   Luke 23, 33-34
Mark 15, 22, 23, 25, 27, 28   John 19, 18

"And when they were come to the place, which is called Calvary, they gave him vinegar to drink mingled with gall, wine mingled with myrrh: and when he had tasted thereof, he would not drink, he received it not. And it was the third hour, and they crucified him. And with him they crucified the two thieves; the one on his right hand, and the other on his left, and Jesus in the midst. And the Scripture was fulfilled, which saith, And he was numbered with the transgressors.

Then said Jesus, Father, forgive them; for they know not what they do."

Simon of Cyrene was relieved of the cross "when they were come to the place which is called Calvary," but for the Savior the real labor of his Passion commenced. He now stood on the spot which afterwards the ancient Christians reverently considered the center of the earth. Though that was an error as regarding this physical globe, Calvary nevertheless has become the center of the spiritual world. On this spot opens that part of the Passion which, more than any other, makes the name of Jesus unforgotten. In one respect we see here the Lord suffer by virtue of his noblest office: the High priest of our souls ready to ascend the altar to accomplish an everlasting atonement; and yet he steps into surroundings and experiences that mark his

(46)

deepest humiliation, and of which the prophetic word is
eminently true: "He is despised and rejected of men; a man   Isaiah 53, 3
of sorrows, and acquainted with grief: and we hid as it
were our faces from him; he was despised, and we esteemed
him not."

During the short minutes required to dig the holes for
the crosses and to erect the trees, the condemned felt the
last touch of humanity noticeable throughout these hours.
"They gave him vinegar to drink mingled with gall, wine
mingled with myrrh." It was a sour wine which by reason
of its acidity could also be called grape vinegar. This
beverage was mingled with gall, which here is a general
expression signifying a bitter drug, and in this case the
drug happened to be myrrh. Thus there is no contradiction
between the words "vinegar with gall" and "wine with
myrrh." Matthew probably chose the former with reference
to David's complaint: "They gave me also gall for my meat;   Ps. 69, 21
and in my thirst they gave me vinegar to drink." The
bitter ingredient was not added to the sour wine with the
purpose of spoiling it, with the thought that a criminal must
receive only the meanest refreshment. The Lord, just on
the point of tasting the very dregs of misery, would not have
have refused to submit to such little spite work. Since the
previous evening he had been without rest or nourishment,
how gratefully would he have accepted the poorest drink!
Again, that mixture was not intended as a last and specially
prepared relish for the dying man: who among all these
enemies would have thought of showing Jesus such favor?
The ancients, and with them the Jews, were accustomed
to spice the wine with aromatic herbs to procure a pleasant
flavor and taste; if such had been the object here, entirely
different ingredients would have been added. The draught   *Sedative!*
was rather intended as a stupefying potion. The severe
shock and pain incident to the nailing of the body to the

cross was to be tempered by dulling the sensibility of the culprit so that for the first few moments he should hang there half unconscious. To this end incense and wormwood were generally put in the sour wine, but also the bitter and benumbing myrrh, as on this occasion. This Jewish custom resulted, probably, from the Rabbinical explanation of the
Prov. 31, 6, 7 following passage in the Proverbs: "Give strong drink unto him that is ready to perish, and wine unto those that be of heavy hearts. Let him drink, and forget his poverty, and remember his misery no more." The ladies used to have the privilege of furnishing and offering this drink when Christian martyrs were led to execution, their friends were permitted to minister unto them. However, there is nothing to show that the wailing daughters of Jerusalem extended such kindness to the Lord; "they" that led him forth, that now made ready to crucify him, the soldiers, gave the drink.

The Lord took the proffered cup. He would have welcomed a refreshing drink; but "when he had tasted thereof, he would not drink, he received it not." Quickly he discerned the object of the draught, and resolutely he refused to drink. And this, because with a clear mind he wanted to wrestle with pain and death; he "gave" his life away, nobody took it from him. What moral courage and heroism the exhausted sufferer evinced! It is a common experience that not only the weaker minds, but very often just the brightest and strongest among men, who wrestle bravely with open adversity, succumb under the creeping, gnawing affliction that comes upon them. Many a proud spirit of whom nobody would have thought it, has sought refuge from sorrow in drugs and strong drink, or by other means ended his misery in a quick death. Jesus did not want to forget, but with a clear understanding met the pangs awaiting him. Nor did the executioners entreat him long, the refusal was his own concern. Without delay they affixed

him to the tree. "It was the third hour, and they crucified II, 328
him." In another place we have explained that there is
no discrepancy between this statement and the one according to which Pilate sentenced Jesus "about the sixth hour."
About nine o'clock, at the time of the morning sacrifice
in the temple, the world's noblest and most memorable sacrifice was offered on Calvary.

The Evangelists do not describe the details of the exe- *Crucifixion*
cution nor do they give information as to the physical
tortures connected with it: partly, because the first readers
of the gospel lived in an age when crucifixion was of common occurrence, many of them probably having witnessed
similar scenes themselves; and, partly, because the aim of
the gospels is not so much to narrate corporal pains, apt
to awaken sentimental pity, as rather to set forth the
spiritual side and eternal significance of the Master's death.
To us, so remote from and unfamiliar with that kind of
punishment, a thorough appreciation of the Savior's Passion
would be impossible without a study of particulars, however
uninviting the subject may prove to be. Crucifixion was
as horrible as it was simple. Sometimes the culprit may
have been affixed while the cross lay on the ground, and
then the tree erected, but it cannot have been so in the
Lord's case. For with four soldiers bending and working
over him, the first word of Jesus could not well have been
heard by the friends who were certainly at that moment
kept at a distance by the military escort; that first word
must have been uttered while he was being lifted up and
fastened to the cross. And the general mode indeed was
first to plant the cross firmly in the ground, then to draw the
victim up, setting him astride a projecting wooden pin in
the vertical beam, thereby preventing the weight of the
body from tearing the wounds in the hands asunder. The
arms, the limbs, and the body, were secured with ropes

until the long, flat, sharp nails were driven through the hands and feet, the soles of the feet pressed against the tree, the knees bent forward. The cross was generally not very high, the body of the victim being elevated only a few feet above the ground. For extraordinary criminals the crosses were often higher than usual, and it is possible that for the sake of distinction the cross of Jesus was taller than were those of the two robbers; yet he hung low enough that his mouth could be reached by the soldiers using a hyssop reed about one foot long. We will not speak of the disgrace connected with crucifixion, although the ancients knew of nothing more detestable than the cross, the accursed tree; and this perhaps among other reasons also from the circumstance that everything contrived to make the crucified sufferer a most repulsive sight. Let us rather endeavor to imagine the physical pains defying all description, those most terrible tortures ever invented by the evil genius of the ancient world. The unnatural position of the body forced the blood to the head, to the lungs, to the heart. The obstructed circulation of the blood caused fierce headache, congestion, fever, burning thirst. The slightest motion irritated and rent the four wounds in the hands, the feet, and on the body wounded and torn by the scourges. Inflammation and mortification of the wounds set in, and the limbs were paralyzed. With every passing moment the pains increased. No loss of blood hastened the approach of death as the nails and the clogging blood closed the wounds. No merciful oblivion granted relief, for the pains kept the victim conscious until death ended all after six, twelve, twenty-four, or even thirty-six hours of lingering misery. It has happened that culprits condemned to be crucified implored their executioners first to strangle them, some paying immense sums for that dreary privilege which, nevertheless, spared them from ineffable suffering. Constantine the first Christian emperor abolished this form of punishment, which since that time is no longer known in civilized countries: also a pleasing fruit of Christ's Passion.

Jesus was not the only one brought to death on that Friday morning. "With him they crucify the two thieves; the one on his right hand, and the other on his left hand, and Jesus in the midst." This may have been the long appointed day for the execution of those criminals and their leader, Barabbas, whose place was at the last moment taken by Jesus. The apparently indifferent fact that those two unfortunates were hung to the right and left of the Lord is carefully noted by the Evangelists, for there was method and purpose in that arrangement. The leading sinner must occupy the leading place, the daring rebel must have his daring followers at his side, the king must see his attendants near him in pain and death as well as in life. At whose behest was this arrangement chosen? Pilate did not go along to superintend the execution; such details were not worthy the attention of the highest authority; the officers and men knew their duty. The Jewish rulers were present to watch that everything was carried out properly, but they found it hardly advisable to treat Jesus in public as a rebel king, for the assembled spectators and all Jerusalem knew the untruth of such charge. The main argument among the rulers themselves had been that Jesus called himself the Son of God; with this plea they had frightened Pilate and won the wavering multitude to their side, and to spread this accusation as the reason for his death best fitted their plans. If on that account they suggested the central cross, they were willingly accommodated by the Roman soldiers. These were the real authors of the jest, and with them the idea was perfectly natural: Barabbas, "the notable prisoner," would have been thus distinguished, and since Jesus was his substitute, must he not also take his assigned place?

Furthermore, in this manner the soldiers were able to continue their mockery started in the guard room: they have invested and crowned the king of the Jews and have paid him homage, now they put him on the throne with his retinue to the right and left.

This close and systematic proximity of the crosses was no mere chance, neither on the part of man, nor in the providence of God who rules all human affairs. A deeper significance is pointed out: "And the Scripture was fulfilled, which saith, And he was numbered with the transgressors." The prophet Isaiah literally prophesied concerning the servant of the Lord: "He was numbered with the transgressors." Of such weight and import is this short prediction that Jesus recalled it to his disciples as one that cannot be slighted in his sufferings: "For I say unto you, that this that is written must yet be accomplished in me, And he was reckoned among the transgressors." Now it is strictly fulfilled. Not only is he one who happens to die in the company of robbers, however bitter that circumstance in itself is to a pure and noble heart; but he hangs on that central cross singled out as the greatest criminal and leader of rebels.

Jesus seems to have been the first of the three victims to be affixed to the tree, and just as the nails pierced him, he opened his mouth speaking the first of the seven precious words on the cross. A crucifixion, as can be imagined, was a scene of considerable tumult: the curious babble of the spectators, the commanding words of the officers, and the blows of the mallets, were mingled with the implorations, screams, and curses of the culprits. Now while the air was not yet rent with the shrieks of the two thieves, while the expectant multitude stood in momentary silence as they saw the famous Nazarene lifted up, his words could be plainly heard. "Then said Jesus, Father, forgive them; for they know not what they do." That was language

Isaiah 53, 12

Luke 22, 37

First Word

quite unusual. No request for mercy, no cry of agony, no imprecation came over his lips; a tender prayer sanctified the coming hours of woe. In the service of God and for the sake of God Jesus was abased, yet there was no faltering faith, no shaken confidence, no murmur against the Most High who seemed to care so little for his Anointed. In the presence of a fearful death the Master did not doubt his divine mission for a moment, nor was afraid of the judgment of the Holy One in Israel, before whose throne he was soon to appear. No guilt to confess, no errors to repent, the obedient Son comes from the depth of anguish with a child-like trust, saying, Father!

This prayer shines forth in exceptional beauty especially because the Father's name was not invoked for the benefit of the sufferer himself. His own pains were forgotten; in the midst of his misery his heart remembered the need of others, and these others were not dear friends left behind, but enemies engaged in the act of torturing him. A priestly prayer of forgiveness, that is what the Lord addressed to his Father. The question may be raised, why Jesus did not simply in his own authority announce the remission of sins, as he had done on other occasions. The Lord was undoubtedly willing on his own part to forgive the wrong done to him, else how could he have entreated the pardon of the merciful God with a heart refusing to be merciful? His own forgiveness is presupposed. But the Master also knew that the crime being committed on Calvary was not only directed against the Son of Man, but that it also constituted a stupendous sin against the God of Israel who had blessed and sought his people so long, who had so loved the world as to give his own Son, and who in these hours was mocked and insulted by Jew and Gentile. Yet more: by imploring God to be merciful, Jesus issued a final declaration of his love to the people, indicated his sufferings as a great intercession for the world, and attested once more his oneness with the Father who does what his crucified Son demands. Gloriously did Jesus verify the grandest, the sweetest proof of goodness and perfection which Isaiah saw in the Messiah, stating that he even "made intercession for the transgressors" Admirably did he follow his own rule: "Love your enemies, bless them that curse you, do good to them that hate you, and pray for them which despitefully use you, and persecute you." And aptly does Peter describe the nobility of this mediating prayer in that well known passage: "Who when he was reviled, reviled not again; when he suffered, he threatened not; but committed himself to him that judgeth righteously."

That the prayer was in no wise a mere outcry or a pious phrase born of intense pain, but rather a positive and much needed act of intercession, is clear from the fact that the Lord adduced a reason for his petition: "For they know not what they do." So enormous was the crime against God and his Christ that the immediate rejection of the entire chosen nation appeared inevitable, that the judgment of God could be expected to break forth in full force and at once. The prayer of the Lord kept the gates of mercy open a little while longer. That was possible on account of one extenuating circumstance: ignorance, a word which indicates the persons benefited by the prayer. Not each and every sin is committed through ignorance. Judas Iscariot helped to bring Jesus to the cross, and he did it with a firm resolution all the while knowing what he was doing: the prayer was not for this son of perdition. Caiaphas boasted of his keen insight and prudence when he derided his colleagues, "Ye know nothing at all"; he together with his unscrupulous father-in-law cannot have been the object of intercession. Among the priests we may distinguish two classes: the willing and spiteful tools of

Isaiah 53, 12

Matt. 5, 44

1 Pet. 2, 23

John 11, 49

the leaders by right sharing the fate of the leaders; and others who at heart were not hostile to Jesus, although they lacked courage to stand up for him. Pilate, a materialistic pagan, was too superficial than that his casual acquaintance with Jesus should have convinced him of the Lord's divine character. Knowingly he violated his office as judge, though he did not know that he crucified the Son of God. The Roman soldiers who maltreated the Lord in the judgment hall and then were ordered to finish the bloody work, certainly did not know what they were doing; their way of thinking was far too remote from the religion of Israel as to understand the teachings about a divine Messiah. The Jewish people in general as well as the assembled multitudes gazing at the cross, because largely deceived by their rulers, were those in whose interest the prayer for mercy was especially offered.

Was the petition granted by God? Yes, to the fullest extent, if we rightly understand its purport. Asking that God should forgive them, does not mean that he should simply overlook and forget the crime. The plea of ignorance did not excuse the sinners altogether, for the ignorance was very culpable in view of the many opportunities to ascertain the truth. The Holy One cannot and will not leave the crime on Calvary unpunished, the doom comes upon Jerusalem without fail. But a respite was granted, and therein the prayer of Jesus was heard. Forty years elapsed ere the judgments of God began to materialize; and even as "for the elect's sake those days shall be shortened" and the Matt. 24, 22 tribulations made tolerable by the favor of the Lord, so the opportunity for repentance was graciously prolonged through this prayer. This ray of hope was afterwards diligently pointed out by the preaching disciples. Peter said, "And now, brethren, I wot that through ignorance ye Acts 3, 17 did it, as did also your rulers." Paul also said that they

Acts 13, 27
1 Cor. 2, 8
crucified him "because they knew him not"; and to the
Corinthians he wrote of the Wisdom of God: "Which none
of the princes of this world knew: for had they known it,
they would not have crucified the Lord of glory."

The prayer was not without immediate effects. We
may justly assume that the centurion, who afterwards made
a good confession, here received his first deep impression,
as did one of the crucified thieves. The apostles were able
to gather many penitent Jews into Christ's kingdom, on
Pentecost three thousand were won, and later many more
Acts 6, 7
among the lower and higher classes of citizens: "The number of the disciples multiplied in Jerusalem greatly; and
a great company of the priests were obedient to the faith."
Many of them may have realized that they were the
"ignorant" sinners for whom Jesus had prayed. No doubt,
this prayer continues to exert its influence to the end of
days. All who spend their life in thoughtless insult to
the Lord, all who long have rejected their Savior, may know
that he intercedes for them; and at last even Israel, when
their banishment is ended, shall see whom they have pierced,
and love him who pleaded so warmly in their behalf: Father,
forgive them; for they know not what they do.

57.   THE SUPERSCRIPTION

Matt. 27, 37   Luke 23, 38
Mark 15, 26   John 19, 19-22

"And Pilate also wrote a title, and set up
over his head on the cross the superscription of
his accusation. And the writing was, JESUS OF
NAZARETH THE KING OF THE JEWS. And it was
written in letters of Greek, and Latin, and Hebrew.
This title then read many of the Jews; for the place
where Jesus was crucified was nigh to the city.
Then said the chief priests of the Jews to Pilate,
Write not, The King of the Jews; but that he said,
I am King of the Jews. Pilate answered, What I
have written I have written."

———

With the crucifixion ended, it remained that the customary title be affixed; for at executions of that nature it
was the rule that the top of the cross bore a small tablet,
a short description announcing the name and the crime
of the culprit. This was done in the Lord's case. "Pilate
also wrote a title, and set up over his head on the cross
the superscription of his accusation." If the board had
been hanging from the neck of Jesus on the way out, it
would have been unreadable as long as he was stooping
under the heavy cross; but as soon as the Lord was relieved
by Simon, the inscription would have been noticed and
the priests would have entered their protest sooner. Or if
a herald had carried the white board, which seems to have
been the most general custom, its contents would also have
been noted and objected to at once. It is rather trivial to

(57)

assume that the soldiers, during the march, hid the tablet in order to surprise the Jews; though, if they did bring it along, the title may have suggested the placing of the Jewish King in the middle. But it seems that the procession had left the judgment hall ere Pilate had formulated the public accusation. The writing was not done on Calvary, for the governor had not accompanied the train, the tablet was rather sent out to the soldiers just as the nailing to the cross was finished. There was ample time for that: the exhausted Lord had not walked very fast; some delay was caused by substituting Simon; after Jesus himself had been crucified the two thieves had their turn, and the executions in former ages were not done so expeditiously as in our days; finally, with the gathering up of tools and garments belonging to the soldiers, more time elapsed. While the men were working about the crosses, the priests and the people were kept at a distance, and their attention was turned to the three victims as one after the other was lifted to the cross. Not until the military escort retired and the four soldiers sat down to divide the garments, could the priests draw closer and discover the meaning of the letters.

The three crosses now loomed up to uninterrupted view, the central cross naturally attracting the most attention. Nobody in all that surging host had the least idea that before their eyes that invincible sign was erected that overcomes the world. On the contrary, the defeat of the Nazarene seemed now completed, and the rulers triumphed in their victory. But, lo! at the height of their apparent success the first omen of their downfall appeared. Unawares a bitter drop galled their exultation, the hour of rejoicing was spoiled by that objectionable superscription. It was a remarkable piece of writing in many respects.

First of all it furnishes food for thought, because the governor himself composed it. "Pilate also wrote a title."

As the judge who had pronounced the sentence, as the commander-in-chief who had given his orders to the soldiers, he had the right as well as duty to pen the superscription. Ordinarily, this insignificant labor may have been left to one of the officers. We are not told whether the two malefactors also had their titles, and if they had, it is scarcely probable that Pilate himself should have written them since he had more important duties to perform. But he was so peculiarly involved in the Lord's trial that he made a special effort to furnish an appropriate inscription. Not as if he had put down the letters with his own hand; this routine work may have been done by an officer or an educated slave; but the sentence dictated was formulated by Pilate himself, no one had suggested it to him. Pilate "also" wrote a title: this "also" means that the writing formed a distinct and important act following the governor's former acts in the trial and naturally growing out of the judge's attitude.

To find a proper title was not quite easy for him, and it must have required some thinking before the final choice was made. For the "accusation," the cause of that severe punishment was to be given; the sentence then became the public property. Not only thousands of Jews would scrutinize it, but Roman justice demanded also to be reckoned with. An accusation! Pilate personally knew of none, he had no grudge against Jesus. He even "knew that the chief priests had delivered him for envy." Repeatedly he had declared that he found no guilt in him, that, even if the Jews had some cause of complaint, Jesus did not deserve death. Against his convictions the governor had been forced into condemning the prisoner by the threats of the rulers; and that had happened in the presence of Roman officers and soldiers: Pilate's prestige must have suffered in the opinion of his men. We can understand that his search for an accusation was done with bitter feelings against the Jews, and that he eagerly embraced the opportunity to revenge himself. He had the choice among several charges submitted by the priests. He could have called Jesus a common malefactor, imputing on him any vulgar crime; for with quite indefinite statements had the rulers delivered the Nazarene: "If he were not a malefactor, we would not have delivered him unto thee." But with such a cause assigned, Pilate would have pleased the priests, yes, he would have recognized the Sanhedrin as a court to be respected by Rome; and this he was unwilling to do. Or he might call Jesus a rebel who "perverted the nation, stirring up the people, teaching throughout all Jewry, beginning from Galilee to this place, forbidding to give tribute to Cæsar, saying that he himself is Christ a King." In this case, however, he would have written a fine testimonial to the patriotic rulers who were more vigilant than the Roman authorities to whom a sedition of Jesus and his followers was unknown; and the regained friendship with Herod was then endangered: Herod consented that Pilate do with Jesus as he deemed best, but to publish broadcast the insinuation that Herod was unable or unwilling to suppress a rebel in his country was going too far. Finally, that other charge could have been selected, which frightened Pilate so much: that Jesus "made himself the Son of God"; or that he was a false Messiah. Then the governor appeared as the defender of Jewish faith, as the tool of the rulers, an idea both disagreeable to him and contrary to Roman usage which forbade meddling with the religion of subjugated people. Practically nothing remained but to return to that question which Pilate had at once recognized as the fundamental and most important one, and which he as the first one submitted to Jesus: Art thou the King of the Jews? No other accusation could serve the governor's purpose better. It is true that he himself had declared Jesus innocent of just that charge: "I find no fault at all in this man"; but, probably, he argued that since the Nazarene was now on the cross, the lie could not affect his fate. And had not the Jews actually accused him of being a King? Now Pilate could restore his lost prestige and at the same time satisfy his heart's desire of wounding the Jews to the quick! Falsehood mingled with truth always constitutes the most dangerous weapon.

Consequently, "the writing was, JESUS OF NAZARETH THE KING OF THE JEWS." The name is given first; that name so familiar with innumerable men, women, and children throughout the land; that name which had but a few days ago stirred all Jerusalem: Jesus of Nazareth. Why did Pilate select this name in preference to his expression during the trial: "Jesus which is called Christ"? The vague knowledge which the procurator had concerning Jesus of Nazareth was no doubt enhanced by information gained during the trial and by advices coming from Roman officers. Both the character and the popularity of Jesus were seen in a remarkable light, and that was necessary to make the kingship plausible. Any obscure, common criminal might have the title "king" on his cross, and it would be considered an absurd joke at which perhaps the Jews themselves would laugh. But here was the famous Jesus of Nazareth. Incidentally a stinging reproach is expressed by the fact that the Jewish nation has but a disgraceful cross for her greatest and best son. But the main point is that there was nothing incongruous in the assertion that a person like Jesus with his genius, influence, and popularity, should consider himself, or be considered, a king. He was the mental and moral king of the Jews, why should he not be worthy to be their spiritual and political ruler?

"The King of the Jews." As the title reads, it contained no crime, nothing the disappointed rulers could have

used to defame the character and memory of Jesus; in the
eyes of all patriotic Jews it was rather to his credit, for they
all entertained ardent hopes for the long expected king to
come. Or if the words were to express a true accusation,
then all the Jews were involved. Jesus was represented as
being truly the king whom the people had acknowledged as
such, whom they had followed and obeyed; the king not only
of the Galileans, or of "some" misguided rebels, but of all
"the Jews." The meaning then is clear: The Romans as
the lords and masters of the land deem it not only a crime,
but also a reckless folly for the Jews to have their own
king. This cross is a denunciation of every such effort,
a warning and a threat: do not dare to repeat the offense,
the cross is the inevitable end! The people were at liberty
to apply the title either to the spiritual or to the political
king. If to the former, it amounted to a taunt of their entire
religion, of their most sacred national hopes and expectations. How ardently did they look for the glorious son of
David to restore the throne and kingdom of David to which
all Gentiles should be subjected. And here the cross teaches
them that the mere thought along that line is criminal, that
their fond dreams are bound to have an inglorious awak-
ening and are vain forever. Or if they thought of a political
king, of one who tried to liberate his country from the
hated yoke of the Romans, they were here served with public
notice that the powerful conquerer was willing and able to
hold them under his iron yoke. The masses had the choice
also as to whom they wished to blame as the real author of
that humiliating scene on Calvary. If for a moment they
imagined the Romans as having caused the arrest and crucifixion of the Nazarene, they were thereby forcibly reminded of the fact that every step was closely watched and
controlled by the alert servants of Cæsar. But as the

intelligence spread that Jesus had first been condemned by the priests, and by them accused before Pilate of being a candidate for the throne, yes, as being the promised "Christ a King," what must the plain people think of their rulers? Where was the patriotism or their faith in the prophets? Why did they work hand in hand with the governor to expose to ridicule and contempt the whole Jewish nation? The spiritual aristocrats did not have very many friends in the land, and this latest incident did not tend to increase the respect for them.

Pilate had his revenge well planned, and he took care to give it widest publicity. "And it was written in letters of Greek, and Latin, and Hebrew." That several languages were used was nothing extraordinary in itself; the ancients frequently published decrees or wrote inscriptions in two, three, or even four languages. Jerusalem was a cosmopolitan city: on the wall of the forecourt of the Gentiles in the temple notices were posted in Greek and Latin, forbidding Gentiles the entering of the sanctuary. Pilate himself may have acquired a working knowledge of several languages, since his office brought him in contact with people of different nationalities; if he knew Latin only, then skilled interpreters were at his service. Now it is of no consequence at all as to which language stood first and which stood last on that tablet; each class of readers regarded its own as most important. The first person to read the title were necessarily the Roman soldiers, who were closest to the cross until after the crucifixion proper. These read the "Latin" inscription which must have been a source of satisfaction to them. Their tongue was the language of proud Rome and her august courts. It was but natural, it was obligatory, that the Roman governor and judge should use Latin in his official publications—and what publication was this! The soldiers who so cruelly had mocked the Jewish king discovered that Pilate not only did not censure them, but entered into the spirit of their jest, that he took their mockery seriously by incorporating it in that notice. That was a fine compliment to the soldiers; and as warriors always think highly of a general who is "one of them," they were inspired with renewed confidence in their supreme commander. In military circles it was certainly felt as a disgrace that Pilate yielded to the fanatic threats of the Jewish rulers, but now Roman honor was vindicated by defying a whole nation with the crucifixion of their king. The tablet was a testimonial to Roman glory and power, a vote of confidence for the cohorts stationed at Jerusalem during these hazardous hours and days. Pilate and his men were one again, and if anything had happened, the army would have been found at the post of duty with unusual enthusiasm. Not so elated were those, and they constituted a majority, who read the sarcastic letters in the "Hebrew" or Aramaic vernacular spoken in Palestine. Pilate had provoked the Jews often, but never had he flung such bitter insult at them, nor with such audacity. This happened on the great day of the Passover, a day reminding Israel of a glorious past, kindling in them anew the fires of patriotism, reviving the ardent hope of a national independence and glory. On a day when the masses were especially sensitive on political subjects, the governor did not hesitate to challenge them with such effrontery. Strange, indeed, that not the faintest sign of demonstration is discernible. After the rulers had stated their objection and were refused by Pilate, they did not "persuade and move the multitude" to clamor for another title, and the hosts of people remained in passive silence. If that means anything, it signifies that the rulers did not trust the people and were not certain of finding applause for having surrendered the Nazarene. The masses, on their part, realized their helplessness because they were divided: though not many may have rejoiced in the fate of Jesus, the rabble of the judgment hall had also come along and declared themselves against him; and even among the well-meaning spectators much could be said pro and con Jesus as the "Son of God," as the "Messiah" hanging there in his blood. Thousands of the best patriots were thus forced to endure in helpless rage the arrogance of the Romans. The day of joy was turned into a day of gloom for Jerusalem and for distant lands where Jews lived, and for future ages. For the inscription was also written "in letters of Greek," evidently for the benefit of Jewish visitors whose home was in countries where Greek was spoken. When they returned to their own, it was with sad stories of Israel's disgrace. Many Greek traders also frequented the capitol, and on their journeys they will be the news bearers carrying the inglorious report to the uttermost ends of the earth. The Jews had no friends among the ancient nations, but were held in bad repute and treated with contempt almost everywhere. How much must this latest incident teach the world to despise a people that suffered to have their king crucified; So then in three languages Pilate's spite published the title, "Jesus of Nazareth The King of the Jews." In God's providence those very languages became the agents of scattering broadcast the gospel of the same Jesus: Latin, the language of world conquering power, announced the novel force of the cross which overcomes the world; Greek, the language of culture, told of that finer, nobler education which mankind acquires in the school of the Nazarene; Hebrew, the language of religion, bore the germ of the New Testament established on that day so dreary for Israel, so gladsome for the nations of the earth.

"This title then read many of the Jews; for the place where Jesus was crucified was nigh to the city." Calvary being so near Jerusalem, the triple execution attracted not only the sight-seers usual on such occasions, but many more came for the sake of the famous prophet. The multitudes "that passed by" indicate that a much travelled road led by the hill. It seems that the chief priests were not among the first to read the title. Probably they had stood at a dignified distance complacently watching their triumph. But "many of the Jews," the common people, crowded near as soon as the soldiers had finished their work. Through the muttered comments of the disappointed readers, or through the information of friends, the rulers had their attention called to the title. It was too late to prevent the mischief, too many had read the ominous words; and since the people themselves did not cry out against this Roman insult, the priests hastened to avoid further trouble. These astute leaders of men saw no sign in their favor; if the ill will of the people is aroused, it may turn just as well against the rulers as against the Romans. More than the patriotism of the land did their own safety concern them in their present action.

"Then said the chief priests of the Jews to Pilate, Write not, The King of the Jews; but that he said, I am King of the Jews." The war for supremacy between the "King of the Jews" and the "chief priests of the Jews" was not yet ended. As rulers "of the Jews" they are here expressly designated because they, as supreme judges, had brought this disgrace upon the whole Jewish nation and were now expected to correct their mistake and to blunt Pilate's irony. All the chief priests present on Calvary immediately formed or appointed a delegation entreating Pilate to change the title. They were supposed to act in

Matt. 27, 39
Mark 15, 29

the name of all the Jews, but the petition indicates that their own interests came first. No demand for an entirely different superscription was made, but only a very slight addition requested. Thus the public defamation of the popular name "Jesus of Nazareth" was quite satisfactory to them, though they knew that the feelings of thousands of the best citizens were wounded by detracting that honored name. Little did they dream that the intended reproach was quickly to become a name of honor; that after but a few weeks the disciples of the Crucified will dare to preach this very "Jesus of Nazareth, a man approved of God among you by miracles and wonders and signs"; that in the same name wondrous things shall continue to be done. At present they were convinced of having rendered that name an abomination to the world. But the ambiguous title "King of the Jews" must be altered. "Write not, the King of the Jews." No reason for the objection was adduced; Pilate was not accused of having done spite work, nor did they point to the displeasure of the people. A trifle, a mere technicality, the adding of a few letters only, was asked for; and since Pilate had yielded so frequently in much more serious matters, why should he not grant this small favor? Write "that he said, I am King of the Jews." With the insertion of the "he said, I am" the equally easy erasure of the article is suggested, not "The" king, but simply, "a king." The priests could plead that in such form they had accused Jesus before the governor: "We found this fellow perverting the nation, and forbidding to give tribute to Cæsar, saying that he himself is Christ a king." Whilst they cannot deny having accused Jesus of assuming kingship, they will not admit that he was "The" Christ king whom Israel awaited; he was an imposter, a false prophet. Much less was he the political king whom the people acknowledged

Acts 2, 22

Acts, 3, 6; 4, 10

as such; he was a demagogue, a pretender, whose destruction was dictated by the welfare of the nation and the loyalty to Rome. What would have been the result if Pilate had ordered that innocent looking change to be made? The rulers would have returned to Calvary as influential men whom Pilate dare not insult, whose wishes he must respect; and that would have made a deep impression on the masses. Furthermore, Pilate would have admitted his having sentenced Jesus for a crime of which he had declared him innocent, would, after all, have accepted as true the slanders which branded Jesus as a political agitator and rebel against Cæsar. The revised tablet would have borne a fine testimony to the patriotism of the rulers, to their vigilance, to their spiritual insight, which enabled them to detect a supposed Messiah as a dangerous rebel. "He said, I am a king": that would have amounted to a real crime such as the rulers wished imputed on Jesus, while the original text contained no accusation at all.

This visit of the rulers must have been gratifying to Pilate. Their protest showed how well his arrows had found their aim. A few letters will change the whole meaning: this is exactly what he knew, and just for that reason he had omitted them. Should he now relieve the rulers of their perplexity, should he please those men who had so unrelentingly pursued him this morning? Should he again appear as their tool and thereby forego the confidence of his soldiers once more? "Pilate answered, What I have written I have written." Proud words were these: as if Pilate had never modified any of his decrees, as if he would rather die for his convictions. But with this momentary firmness he cannot regain the respect which he forfeited during the morning hours. We remember that just the undecided characters may have fits of stubbornness which they mistake for strength. In all probability Pilate's reply would have sounded different if not everything had been in his favor. As it was, he had the Roman law on his side, which prohibited any alteration of the sentence, or of the title containing the crime, after its publication. Or even if the addition of those few letters would have been permissible, and if the governor's spite had been satisfied with the hitherto success, a personal consideration must have kept his hand from that tablet. His safety, his future, depended partly on that inscription. Had not the desperate rulers in the presence of many witnesses questioned his loyalty to Cæsar, implying a threatened accusation to that effect? Since the revised inscription would have described Jesus as a rebel against the emperor, could not the rulers truthfully boast of having forced the procurator against his will to do his sworn duty? All that was cut off with the title as it read. In three languages the whole world was notified of Pilate's efficency and faithfulness as an officer of Cæsar. Thus the public shame of the Jews was allowed to travel forth from Calvary into distant countries and future ages. Pilate with his personal motives, like Caiaphas, had to prophesy and testify that the innocent king of the Jews must be despised and rejected of men.

The rulers certainly did not forget or forgive that insult. But, as remarked before, they made no effort to incense the masses. If at first they were afraid of the people alone, they had now also cause to fear Pilate. His unexpected resistance must have set them to thinking. They may have suspected his daring provocation as a pretext for the long sought opportunity to take the place of the rulers and their nation at the slightest uprising. No doubt, we see here already one of the beneficial effects of the Savior's prayer, Father forgive them. The hand of God used the misgivings of the rulers to postpone a dire calamity.   For it is clear that there on Calvary a clash between the Romans and the Jews was imminent, and an insurrection on that day would have meant bloodshed the like of which had not been known in Israel.

The rulers had to give some kind of explanation to the people, and it would be interesting to hear what they had to say on their return to Calvary.   We may catch the echo of their words in some of the following events.

58. THE PARTED GARMENTS

Matt. 27, 35-36   **Luke 23, 34**
Mark 15, 24   **John 19, 23-24**

"Then the soldiers, when they had crucified Jesus, took and parted his garments, and made four parts, to every soldier a part; casting lots upon them, what every man should take, and also his coat: now the coat was without seam, woven from the top throughout. They said therefore, among themselves, Let us not rend it, but cast lots for it, whose it shall be: that the Scripture might be fulfilled, which was spoken by the prophet, They parted my raiment among them, and for my vesture did cast lots. These things therefore the soldiers did.

"And sitting down they watched him there."

––––––

The scene described in this passage is in itself brutal, and it seems scarcely worth while to study its repulsive details. Yet three evangelists found the incident worth recording, while St. John even invites us to ponder it, as his thoughts also lingered on that circumstance. For, as often in Christ's Passion, when men appear to follow their own impulses and the Lord is apparently abandoned to their evil ways, the masterly hand of God is discovered in skillful work, strengthening the faith of his own people. Such is the case here.

Four soldiers, so this passage teaches us, had nailed Jesus to the cross. The four men were under the immediate command of a centurion and thus constituted a quaternion,

(71)

the smallest detachment in the Roman army. Prominent prisoners were confided to four guards at a time, the active watch being composed of four such quaternions. Thus Herod, whose military was modelled after that of Rome, did in the case of Peter: "When he had apprehended him, he put him in prison, and delivered him to four quaternions of soldiers to keep him." A single quarternion was sufficient to carry out a crucifixion and keep the watch, especially on a day when the bodies were to be taken down towards evening. The Roman soldiers were generally charged with the executions: in Italy as well as in the provinces; during war, as the siege of Jerusalem shows, as well as in time of peace. They were chosen with a twofold purpose: to illustrate the great power of the ruler, and to overawe people bent on interference. Such executions, with their prolonged torture of the helpless victims, were certainly undignified work for honest and brave soldiers. Yet this does not justify us to assume that the executioners were selected from the coarsest characters of the army. They were taken from the rank and file, and may be considered a fair example of the manhood found throughout the army. The soldiers themselves did not think it a degrading duty. Judging from the eagerness with which those on Calvary mocked Jesus and parted his garments, an execution seems to have been looked upon as a privilege, at least as a pastime, especially when a foreigner was brought to his death. Nothing better could be expected of a troop of hirelings who in no sense were patriotic defenders of home and country, but mere tools effectively used for the glorification of a despot.

These four representatives of the Roman soldiery did what all their comrades would have done: "Then the soldiers, when they had crucified Jesus, took and parted his garments." The personal belongings of the crucified were

Acts 12, 4

the rightful spoils of the executioners, including the commanding centurion. This ancient Roman custom was later abolished by emperor Adrian, but here it was still in use with all its heartless traits. To claim their property was the first thought of the men after finishing their work. The commotion among the Jews and the indignation of the rulers on account of the superscription did not interest them; they took for granted that a subjugated nation must bear every taunt of Rome. Neither had the Master's prayer for pardon, spoken right in their ears, made any impression upon them. It may be urged that as illiterate men they did not understand the language used by Jesus, though later on they do seem to understand; at all events the centurion must be supposed as having known what Jesus said. Right on the spot and without delay the division of the garments was commenced: was this haste meant as an additional insult to Jesus? Apparently they were not so anxious to appropriate the effects of the dying thieves, probably because they were not worth having, disorderly men wear disorderly clothes. Jesus, though a poor man, naturally plain in dress, and constantly wandering up and down the country, was nevertheless clean, decent, and careful in matters of apparel. The circumstantial way in which the soldiers dealt with these clothes, was quite a compliment to the Lord's habits. This, however, does not exclude that the soldiers also continued their mockery of the Jewish king: his possessions become the prey of the invincible Romans, and the subjugated people must silently suffer the dividing of the spoil!

They parted "his garments," not only one piece. The ordinary apparel of the average Jew consisted of the upper garment, or cloak, practically a large square cloth which was wrapped about the body like a tunic; of the coat, or under garment—the one over which the lot was separately cast— which was either worn close to the body or over a linen shirt, the latter worn mostly by the better class of Jews; of the girdle holding the loose clothes together; and of the sandals. The Lord had been arrested in his usual clothes, and these were taken from him when they lifted him to the cross. Only in rare exceptions were people crucified with some or all of their clothes on; the rule was to strip them completely and leave the body hang entirely naked. This was done with the Lord. This exposure, whether intended as such or not, was an additional disgrace if we remember certain customs of Israel, certain utterances of the Old Testament, and the dignity of Him who came to sanctify also the secret life of man. Naked, deprived of his scant possessions, the Master hung on the tree. Poor he entered the world, poor he remained all his life, and poor he departed. As if the world begrudged him even the few modest garments, they were snatched from him and distributed ere his eyes closed in death.

The soldiers "made four parts, to every soldier a part; casting lots upon them, what every man should take." They wanted to deal fairly and squarely among themselves, as becomes comrades. The clothes were divided into four equal parts by ripping the seams of the upper garment. Why not five parts, one for the centurion who was also entitled to a share? Did he get the girdle and the sandals, or was at first the more valuable under garment intended for him? His claim was not at all considered, which indicates that he refused to participate in the spoil. Perhaps the legacy of the Nazarene was too poor to arouse his desires. Or he waived his rights from nobler motives, as we are prone to believe. If the centurion had been so coarse-fibred as to indulge in this inhuman game, he would scarcely have been capable of uttering his glowing tribute to the deceased Master, of which we read later. We presume that at this moment already his heart went out to Jesus,

and beyond his stern duty he would do nothing to aggravate
the pitiful condition of the Crucified. Thus we discover a
tender human trait in the bosom of an officer hardened in
service. It order to avoid all dispute, the soldiers did not
simply select one of the four parts, but decided on "casting
lots upon them, what every man should take." Among the
ancients the casting of lots was a favorite device of gaining
certainty. The Jews used it chiefly to ascertain the will of
God, in the partition of lands, in the granting of offices, in
the assignment of temple duty among the priests, and for
the establishing of right and wrong in court or in private
life. With the Romans, especially among the soldiery, the
casting of the lot was rather a pastime, a game of chance.
However, these four men did not choose the lot to gratify
their gambling passion or to while away tedious hours;
there was too much excitement about the cross, particularly
at the beginning of their watch, to necessitate or permit
a quiet game; they did it business-like with the sole purpose
of doing justice to the comrade. Whether they used the
customary stones of different colors, dice, sticks of wood,
or some guessing contest, cannot be decided.

Among the goods to be disposed of was "also his coat:
now the coat was without seam, woven from the top
throughout." Unlike the cloak, this coat, or under garment,
could not be parted in the usual manner, for it was "without
seam," and ripping the fabric would have rendered it
entirely useless. The garment was a work of art, made
without needles, in one piece, the weaving commencing
"from the top," with the opening for the neck, continuing
down to the hem. The silken shirts worn by the priests
were of similar workmanship. In our days that kind of
weaving is an almost forgotten and very expensive art, but
in Palestine it was well known, so that even people of mod-
erate circumstances could afford to own coats of such make.

This would explain why the poor and plain Jesus possessed
a coat like that, except we assume that it was the work and
gift of loving hands, perhaps of women like those that
Luke 8, 3 "ministered unto him of their substance." As practical
men the soldiers realized that the rending of this coat would
spoil it altogether. "They said therefore among themselves,
Let us not rend it, but cast lots for it, whose it shall be."
Rather than take worthless fringed pieces, the coat was to be
chanced off as a whole. That the three losing soldiers were
willing to yield their shares in it without any compensation,
is evidence that the coat was of no extraordinary value.

"These things therefore the soldiers did"—with these
words John, who himself saw much in it, invites us to pay
close attention to this scene. And indeed, as we look up to
the dying Jesus and down to the gambling group of soldiers,
how vast a contrast meets our eye! On the cross hangs
the perfect man, the fairest among the mortals, and near
him stand men devoid of every fine, true and noble instinct
of human nature; as if we were to view the gulf existing
between man as he came from the hand of God, and man
as he ruined himself in the sins of the world; between man
as he ought to be, and man as he actually is. Ah, if the
crucified Nazarene had been nothing but a model man, who
would deny that he has still a great mission in our own
day, and for ages to come, among his depraved brethren?
On the cross a heart expires and a mind departs that blos-
somed with holiest love, with eternal thoughts, with heavenly aims; and close by human nature displays its selfish,
unthinking, brutal side, with no interest in the Son of
man but his garments. Who must not pity mankind that
in its history so dreary a spectacle was possible? Or who
doubts that the great Jesus, who knew what was in man,
had not love, courage, and determination enough, to make
himself a sacrifice for this degenerate race of men? On the

cross dies he who aimed at the salvation of the world, and
near him assemble a few soldiers: representatives of numberless hosts of men who are no better or even worse than
they.   Here we realize that none but a divine Redeemer
could, under such circumstances, dare to foster plans of a
divine kingdom on earth, and nothing short of power divine
can raise and regenerate mankind fallen so low; and we
conclude that the Lamb of Calvary must still be preached
to the people just because and just while so many cannot
recognize or refuse to accept him as their Savior king.

But deeper than our reflections and more important are
the aspects of this scene as given by the Evangelist: to him
the hand of God was visible in those details; he saw the
soldiers unwittingly fulfilling a word of Holy Writ. "That
the Scripture might me fulfilled, which was spoken by the
prophet, They parted my raiment among them, and for my
vesture they did cast lots."   David was that prophet, and
his saying is found in the psalm particularly distinguished ^{Ps. 22, 19}
as messianic.   Israel as a political community loved to remember David the king; but Israel as the chosen nation of
God revered David the sweet singer of psalms, the royal
prophet, the ancestor of the Messiah.   With such appeal the
apostles gained the ear of devout Jews: "Men and brethren, ^{Acts 2, 29, 30}
let me freely speak unto you of the patriarch David, that
he is both dead and buried, and his sepulchre is with us unto
this day.   Therefore being a prophet, and knowing that God
had sworn with an oath to him, that of the fruit of his loins,
according to the flesh, he would raise up Christ to sit on his
throne."   The same David, though a man of many afflictions
has described his soul's manifold suffering in pictures so
vivid, in terms so peculiar, that they become inapplicable
to his own experiences, and the thought of a meaning reaching far beyond himself is at once suggested.   Now after a
thousand years the wondering believer finds the solution:

David has depicted the sorrows of the Messiah, the anguish of Him who dies on Calvary. The soldiers are seen literally to inflict the pains, the humiliations upon the Lord, of which David prophesied in the long ago. It is as though we were permitted to cast a glance into the secret cabinet of God; where to our dim vision naught but chance, neglect, or confusion appears, there unexpectedly his skillful hand is discovered at work, his deep plan matured; and not a word shall fail, not a single act shall be done, even by Gentile soldiers, except he knows, permits, and guides it all. Such knowledge relieves the depression with which we view a scene like the present one; we gather hope, trusting that the foes shall not altogether have their own way, that God on high has not yet spoken his last word.

"And sitting down they watched him there." Guards were generally kept near a cross until the victim was dead. The purpose was to prevent friends or any unauthorized persons from taking the body down before death ensued; for under favorable conditions one not crucified too long a time could be restored to life and health. The watch, which otherwise would have been tedious to the soldiers, was here enlivened by the carnival of mockery in which the spectators united.

59. THE MOCKERY

Matt. 27, 39-44   **Mark 15, 29-32**
Luke 23, 35-37

"And the people stood beholding. And they
that passed by reviled him, railed on him, wagging
their heads, and saying, Ah, thou that destroyest
the temple, and buildest it in three days, save
thyself. If thou be the Son of God come down
from the cross.

And the rulers also with them derided him.
Likewise also the chief priests mocking him, with
the scribes and elders, said among themselves, He
saved others; himself he cannot save; let him save
himself. If he be Christ the King of Israel, the
chosen of God, let him now come down from the
cross, that we may see, and we will believe him.
He trusted in God; let him deliver him now, if he
will have him: for he said, I am the Son of God.

The thieves also, which were crucified with
him, reviled him and cast the same in his teeth.
And the soldiers also mocked him, coming to him,
and offering him vinegar, and saying, If thou be
the king of the Jews, save thyself."

———

Four distinct classes are mentioned as having mocked
the crucified Lord: The people in general, the rulers, the
soldiers, and the two dying culprits.

For a while silence reigned among the masses. "The
people stood beholding." The affixing of the three men, the

wrath of the rulers on account of the superscription, and the
parting of the garments furnished food for curiosity. Most
of those silent spectators were no friends, no sympathizers.
It is but natural to assume that the average followers of
Jesus were not numerous in that concourse on Calvary.
When a leader of the people is suddenly arrested, accused of
rebellion and other great crimes, and executed on the spot,
a paralyzing terror befalls his adherents; if they are not
numerous, not organized, not resolute enough, to resent the
injustice by force, they will rather keep themselves in retire-
ment to avoid either the authorities or unwelcome notoriety.
For such reasons most of those citizens of Jerusalem who
believed on Jesus certainly stayed at home or at least in the
back-ground. Those friends who did venture out would
surely not stand in the front ranks to "behold" the details.
To earnest believers the crucifixion meant more than an
occasion for sight seeing: their best hopes were crushed and
ridiculed; their beloved Master was shamefully maltreated,
and the surroundings were such that not even a last farewell
could be extended to him. Thus we find that not until after
the first excitement and this storm of mockery had passed
some friends drew near: Mary and John, who were gradually followed by others. Those spectators, then, were at
least indifferent to the Lord, people who had never been
connected with his cause. And not only that. Jesus was
crucified at the hour of the morning sacrifice, when solemn
service was held in the temple. To forsake the house of
God on this great day to which old and young had looked
forward for months, means that these truants were as much
hardened as their rulers who also forgot the altar of God.
True, as bigoted Jews they could argue that right on Calvary
where the enemy of God and Moses was destroyed they were
rendering service to God; but such excuse would simply
prove our contention that they were no pious children of

Israel. We recognize in these spectators, and the text warrants it, largely the false witnesses and their associates; the people who before Pilate cried out against Jesus and asked for Barabbas; these would naturally be the first ones to follow out to Calvary to see the end of their work; and where so many enemies of the Nazarene assembled, others of their type were attracted until they were in the majority. Everyone in Jerusalem, who had a special grudge against Jesus or his doctrine, may be supposed a member of that queer Good Friday congregation. These people stood "beholding." When the watch sat down, indicating that their task was finished, Jesus became the exclusive center of interest; all were gazing at him, and the more so as his agony was now beginning to be visible in his features. Once more the prophetic psalm was fulfilled: "They gaped upon me with their mouths. Dogs have compassed me: the assembly of the wicked have inclosed me. They look and stare upon me." Ps. 22, 13, 16, 17

The people who viewed with satisfaction the sufferings of the crucified one, cannot be expected to keep silence very long, nor can they stand on one spot all day. Gradually the masses began to move; groups were formed to discuss the situation; or some withdrew from the immediate neighborhood of the cross, others had a chance to draw nigh; and with this going back and forth the derision was commenced. "And they that passed by reviled him, railed on him." Those passers-by were mainly the people that had stood beholding. It is out of place to suppose that they were laborers who on their return from work passed by; labor was forbidden on that day, and even if that had not been the case, the noon intermission when laborers go to their meals, was yet about two hours away. Or were they people who just came from Jerusalem on hearing the news, to take a leisurely walk? They were then informed very late and were slow in coming; and how could they "pass by" through the assembled masses that "stood beholding"? Can these earlier crowds be thought to stand still, allowing others to go up to the cross before them? Perhaps pilgrims were they, of whom many were compelled to live in tents in the vicinity? To them the foregoing arguments would also apply; and, further, in their case it would appear decidedly strange that, at the moment of hearing an accusation of which they had never known anything before, they should instantly turn into bitter revilers of the Lord! No, although different classes with different motives passed by and many came out from Jerusalem during those hours, these present passers-by were principally the people who previously had stood in silence. It is unnecessary to assume that a formal procession passed the cross; but acquaintance was seeking acquaintance, and many who had stood in the rear where they could see and hear little, now came closer as others retreated.

The viewing of the crucified Nazarene was not done in silence. Some of the most hostile and fanatic men made the beginning, others followed: "they reviled him, they railed on him"; literally, they "blasphemed." Their ejaculations were to express their satisfaction, their approval of the punishment that had overtaken Jesus. Bearing in mind that the rulers stood near, hearing it all, we may imagine their delight at this justification of their acts. Nobody criticized them, all agreed that this enemy of God and man should die. What was that, if not a compliment, a unanimous vote of confidence to the rulers for having done their duty? Whence all at once so many outspoken enemies of the Lord, remembering that even the fierce multitude before Pilate wavered now and then, and that on the way to Calvary irresolute silence prevailed? These mockers here were very decided. In their opinion Jesus deserved no sympathy at all; even since judgment has overtaken him, he dare not see the slightest trace of pity, must still be persecuted with bitter insults. In their insensible attacks all limits of propriety were overstepped: they "blasphemed." This is to say, that not only every noble and holy trait in Jesus was held up to ridicule but that their faith in God and everything sacred connected with the Jewish religion was dragged into the dust. Such conduct arouses our suspicion, we are led to ask: How did that mockery actually begin? The text indicates the answer, as we shall see.

Different modes and expressions were employed in their blasphemy. They passed the cross "wagging their heads." This gesture implies denial, disapproval. So Job answered his miserable comforters: "If your soul were in my soul's stead, I could heap up words against you, and shake mine head at you." It also expresses amazement, such as should befall the land of Israel: "every one that passeth thereby shall be astonished, and wag his head." Scorn and contempt is also indicated by it. The boastful Sennacherib, king of Assyria, is not so terrible: "the daughter of Zion hath despised thee, and laughed thee to scorn; the daughter of Jerusalem hath shaken her head at thee." David the prophet complains of such contemptuous treatment: "All they, that see me laugh me to scorn: they shoot out the lip, they shake the head." Thus the wagging of the head by the revilers of Jesus was a combination of disapproval, of mock amazement, and of contempt. No, this man they did not know and did not want as their Messiah. No, they failed to comprehend how this person ever dared to teach, to invite them. No, this wretch hanging in his blood deserves nothing but contempt for his audacious blasphemies.

The scornful gesture was accompanied with biting remarks addressed to the Lord. The first is this: "Ah, thou

Job. 16, 4
Jer. 18, 16
2 Kings 19, 21
Ps. 22, 8

that destroyest the temple, and buildest it in three days, save
thyself." A long drawn "Ah" of profound astonishment
opened their reproaches. Was that surprise genuine? Were
they strangers who had never before seen Jesus? Why
then should they at once fall upon him with invectives? Or
did they just now hear the rumors as to the Nazarene's real
guilt, and did that amaze them so much? By this time everybody in and about Jerusalem, and certainly all those on
Calvary, knew why the rulers had condemned Jesus. The
very words of the revilers betray the fact that the accusation was not entirely new to them, they had already
invented a new title, a nickname, "The destroyer of the
temple." Their "ah" refers therefore to the condition in
which Jesus was found, to the contrast between his fate and
his claims. Here they meet and in such predicament they
see the restorer of Israel, the boastful prophet—is that his
glory, his power, his end? How vain must be his claims
and promises! Their "ah" was uttered in feigned surprise, as an intentional mockery, like all their other words.
As one who wanted to destroy the temple and to rebuild it
in three days, Jesus was mocked. This is highly suggestive.
One would expect them first of all to mention his name, that
famous name "Jesus of Nazareth," in order to ridicule it; or
that the "King of the Jews" in the superscription would be
the butt of their derision. But as by common consent all
avoided that subject. May we not suppose that the rulers
returning from Pilate had given a hint to that effect? Their
mission had failed, the dangerous title was to remain, something had to be done to divert the attention of the masses
from it. Now if the rulers quietly instructed their friends
and followers to ignore Pilate's insult in order to avoid a
clash with his troops; if tacitly that inscription was branded
as a lie and the supposedly real accusation was set afloat
and Jesus rendered ludicrous, then the rulers were safe

once more. Thus we would know what the rulers actually
did after their futile mission to the governor: would understand why all at once so many supporters of the hated
rulers, so many exaggerating enemies of Christ arise in
that hitherto divided and undecided mass of people; would
have it explained how this mockery actually started, why
it so quickly assumed such proportions and then quickly
died out: the rulers had put their adherents at work to
accomplish a certain end. This is not a mere supposition,
but a conclusion justified by the text itself.

For we must remember that the words about destroying
the temple were spoken by Jesus three years before this
event. It is impossible that this host of spectators was
entirely composed of men who themselves had heard the
original utterance of the Lord. Evidently they must have
taken up a rumor originating right on Calvary. It is significant that while the exact words of Jesus were not
repeated, this accusation conformed to the testimony given
by the two false witnesses of the previous night, "I am
able to destroy the temple of God, and to build it in three
days." Those witnesses were confidential men of the rulers;
they would not of their own accord boast of their statements
or divulge the secrets of that session, especially since Jesus
was not condemned on that charge at all. The rulers were
present on Calvary and heard those remarks, yet none
corrected them: we are forced to believe that the report
was started by the false witnesses themselves at the behest
and with the consent of their masters. Once more they
earned the title of false witnesses, testifying now, as they
do, that Jesus was actually condemned as "The destroyer of
the temple." Who among the silent friends of Jesus was
able to contradict that charge? It had been preferred and
tried behind the walls of the priest's palace. And how
readily did that charge silence those half-hearted people

who thought this punishment too severe, who indeed had considered Jesus as a benefactor and prospective king of the nation! If the rulers have not betrayed the national hero into the hands of the Romans; if that superscription rests on Pilate's spite or error; if the real crime was a blasphemy against the temple, they cannot but support the rulers. A more potent factor to arouse the fanaticism of the Jews could scarcely be found: the national sanctuary was their pride and consolation, the visible guarantee of God's presence, the emblem of their peculiar position as the chosen people. Nobody could be a prophet, a Messiah, a friend of the people or of God, who was hostile to the temple. As such arguments were scattered on Calvary and throughout the city, could not many a one recall the gloomy prophecies which Jesus but a few days ago had uttered against Luke 19, 43, 44 Jerusalem, including the temple: "The days shall come upon thee, that thine enemies shall cast a trench about thee, and compass thee round, and keep thee in on every side, and shall lay thee even with the ground, and thy children within thee; and they shall not leave in thee one stone upon another." And had he not predicted a gloomy future for Jerusalem just on the way to Calvary?

We perceive how skillfully the rulers had saved the situation for themselves. The indignation against "the destroyer of the temple" burst forth at once. The sarcasm and resentment of the revilers was given vent in the angry demand, "Save thyself." Why did he want to exert his superhuman power, if he had any, against the temple? Simply because he was dissatisfied with the law of Moses, with the religion of the country! He wanted to improve the conditions of a whole nation, whereas he ought to mend his own ways first. If he wanted to save many people, he ought to commence with one person, with himself. The breaking down has now happened unto him instead of to

the temple; and if any power is left in him, let him begin
with the breaking down of the cross to save himself. Only
three days he pretended to need for the restoration of the
temple, now much less time ought to be required for re-
storing his liberty: right in their presence, at this moment,
he ought to save himself.

With the confidence in Jesus shaken to such extent, it
was easy to proceed another step: "If thou be the Son of
God, come down from the cross." Here again we have an
echo of the trial before Caiaphas. The priests had actually
condemned Jesus because he claimed to be the Son of God.
Moreover, they had a large number of witnesses to testify
that this charge was preferred before Pilate: "We have
a law, and by our law he ought to die, because he made
himself the Son of God." This was the most effective
argument to convince such as had been impressed with
the divine character and teaching of the Nazarene. Supposing that some friends were standing near who would
never believe that Jesus threatened to destroy the temple,
who also suspected the real motives of the rulers, what
could they say against the charge as to his Sonship? Perhaps they had believed it, had themselves cried with the
people of Galilee: "Of a truth thou art the Son of God."
No more plausible reasoning, then, than that his present
condition was unworthy the Son of God. He may have
committed no crime, may not have deserved this punishment, but he hangs on the tree that is accursed, and God
does not come to his rescue. What could such friends do
but waver and doubt, lose hope and surrender the field
to the revilers who had all evidence in their favor? "Come
down from the cross." A sign, a miracle is demanded.
He claims to have done many wondrous things, now let
him do the greatest work worthy of the Son of God and
to his own benefit! It cannot be God's will that his Son

should hang there as a dying criminal; if he then be the Son of God, his own honor and that of God must compel him to step from the cross.

That the rulers were no disinterested or passive listeners we learn presently. "And the rulers also with them derided him." Ordinarily these aristocrats had nothing in common with plebeian crowds, but on that occasion the vulgar throng pleased them. Not satisfied with having inaugurated the mockery they "also" reviled, giving an encouraging example to the people. They had a finer and more effective way, in fact were furnishing the material for further derision. That such was their purpose is indicated by the text. "Likewise also the chief priests mocking him, with the scribes and elders, said among themselves." The three official classes of the Sanhedrin were represented. Why should they be specially mentioned in this connection? We understand that many of the rulers would come out to rejoice in their victory, but to tell us that, their offices need not be pointed out. These officials came with a definite object in view. At the critical moment they were probably summoned by the leaders to make a demonstration to influence the people. Each one was to lend the dignity of his office to convince the masses that the entire court had condemned the Nazarene. And each one of the dignitaries had his friends, his adherents ready to believe and spread every word suggested. These men formed a group, for they were speaking "among themselves." Their remarks were not adddessed to Jesus, nor to the people, but were discussed in their own circle. Naturally the people came as near as propriety would permit; for if the reports of the witnesses, of the servants connected with the court, were so interesting, how much more weighty must be the arguments and opinions given by the judges themselves. And these rulers not only confirmed the re-

ports, but threw ever new light on the subject from every
point of view.

The works of the Lord were their first theme. They
said among themselves, "He saved others; himself he cannot
save; let him save himself." The fame of Jesus on account
of his miracles filled the land. The rulers could not deny
the many good works of the Nazarene, there were too many
witnesses. Many plain people would argue that one who
had scattered so many blessings could be no sinner to deserve crucifixion. This favorable opinion, this belief in the
beneficial power of Jesus was to be obliterated. "He saved
others"; this is a glorious testimony fully deserved by the
Lord, but just his acts of charity and kindness have turned
the rulers into implacable foes, and they here use them
for his undoing. They stood there "mocking him," literally,
"turning up the nose," giving expression to supreme contempt for anything connected with the life of Jesus. No
doubt, a certain twang in uttering their "He saved others"
conveyed their real meaning: Who is so ignorant as not to
know that all his miracles were a fraud, a deception of those
who assert to be profited by them. "Himself he cannot
save." This is their dictum admitting of no doubt. Where
is his miraculous power? It fails just when needed most in
his own behalf. "Let him save himself." This was probably a repetition of the people's "save thyself," to indicate
that the rulers perfectly agreed with the multitude, an
encouraging hint to continue along that line of derision.
They were doing their utmost to persuade the people that
the works of the prophet of Nazareth were all mere imagination. The rulers never believed in him, let the people judge
now whether that was not the right attitude. So completely
is this Jesus annihilated that they will not even condescend
to speak to him directly.

The rulers had other arguments in store. "If he be Christ the King of Israel, the chosen of God, let him now come down from the cross, that we may see, and we will believe him." Here again it is noticeable that the priestly group spoke for the benefit of bystanders, for they enlarged upon the demand of the multitude, "Come down from the cross." That the rulers made rapid progress in turning public sentiment against Jesus is evident from the striking display of confidence: they discussed now that very superscription which at first had annoyed them so much, which had put them in fear of the people, and the effect of which was to be met just by this scene of mockery. Their scheme had worked, they had succeeded in bringing the people once more to stand by them, they could now speak freely. "If he be Christ"—this they had denied all along against the convictions of thousands in the country; they had even dared to arrest and condemn this supposed Messiah of the masses: did not the cross with its helpless victim justify their action? Stronger proofs than mere declarations must be given, if they are expected to believe in him. If he is the promised Messiah, he is of course also "The King of Israel." Carefully did they avoid the word "Jew" used in Pilate's title, for that was a rather contemptuous expression employed by the foes of Israel, and it also savored of political aspirations. As the chosen people of God, Israel did not look for a mere political intriguer, but for the great King promised by the prophets. If Jesus were that king, how would he come to the cross? Would God suffer the glorious Son of David to die like a criminal? On the contrary, the King of Israel must be "The chosen of God." Chosen, not self-established. Chosen from eternity, of extraordinary power and appearance, not a frail man hailed by deluded followers. Chosen of God, not rejected and

accursed by him in death. As long as this Jesus had no
better proofs to offer, the rulers had a right, a duty to treat
him as they did. The people were unjust when accusing the
leaders of hating the Nazarene without cause: they will
gladly believe, if the crucified consents to do a sign worthy
of the Messiah, a sign which necessarily must be demanded
of the King of Israel: "Let him now come down from the
cross, that we may see, and we will believe him." In their
presence the miracle must take place if they are to believe.
With this condition they discredited all reports circulated
concerning this prophet. Those who did believe in him
were deceived by false stories; the rulers never had a chance
to verify the claims of the Nazarene. First seeing, then
believing. Here we have the gist of the religion of those
Jewish rationalists. Notice how widely the piety of the
children differed from that of their fathers: "By faith
Abel offered unto God a more excellent sacrifice than Cain;
by faith Enoch was translated that he should not see death;
by faith Noah prepared an ark to the saving of his house; Heb. 11
by faith Abraham went out, not knowing whither he went,
by faith he offered up Isaac; by faith Jacob blessed both
the sons of Joseph; by faith Joseph made mention of the
departing of the children of Israel; by faith Moses kept
the passover, and the sprinkling of the blood," and whatever other acts of faith are related in Holy Writ. That
grand old faith had dwindled until the rulers sitting in
Moses' chair want to see ere they believe!

So sure of their righteous cause the rulers pretended
to be, that they hesitated not to appeal the case to the highest
court, to the throne of heaven, calling God himself as a
witness. "He trusted in God, let him deliver him now, if
he will have him: for he said, I am the Son of God."
Nothing less than an immediate and direct divine inter-

ference would convince them of the Messiahship of the Crucified.   How well did they describe the Lord's religion, how
closely had they watched his life, how correctly did they
judge his main trait: "He trusted in God."   No detail of
Christ's public ministry had escaped the notice of the spies,
the rulers were thoroughly informed, and so it was not
unknown to them that one of the noblest features in the
Nazarene was his unbounded confidence in God.   The Savior
himself depended on the providence of the Father from
day to day, and he taught his followers to do the same.
However, these rulers must not be considered here as bearing testimony to the fine character of the Lord, they rather
used his truthful faith as an occasion for their sarcasm.
Undoubtedly they referred to such instances of the Master's
reliance on God as had come to their notice since the night
before.   In the presence of Caiaphas Christ had spoken of
the right hand of God exalting, avenging him; in the palace
and in Pilate's Prætorium he had set unbroken silence over
against the wildest insults: the rulers were well aware that
thus he relied on the judgment of God.   Finally, the prayer
on the cross asking the Father's pardon for his enemies also
told the rulers and the people that "he trusted in God."
Then why not submit the whole matter to God, leaving the
decision to him?   "Let him deliver him now, if he will
have him."   With their "now" they discredited future
stories of help, if any should be alleged.   In their presence,
at this moment, the Almighty must show his interest "if he
will have him."   The rulers will not have him, the people
will not have him, if then God discovers anything worth
having in that man, it must be shown plainly.   For Jesus
was not only one who trusted in God, he claimed close communion with heaven, saying, "I am the Son of God."   Once
more we learn that the rulers understood it in the very

highest sense when Jesus called himself the "Son of God," and their indirect appeal to the masses indicates that they knew of people who explained the term in the same manner, for they offer no explanation of the word. Though they used the expression for the purpose of destroying the claims of his Sonship, there was no exaggeration in it. It would have been incongruous to plead that because Jesus, in the ordinary sense, asserted to be a dear child of the heavenly Father, the heavens must necessarily open to save him if they are to believe it. There was much more at stake than an exceptional pity of the Nazarene. The Son of God he claimed to be, and God's direct confirmation of that claim is demanded. But nothing happens, the nails hold him firmly, the cross does its work: what further proofs are needed that God will not have him? Strikingly David's prediction is fulfilled: "All they that see me laugh me to scorn; they shoot out the lips, they shake the head, saying, He trusted on the Lord that he would deliver him: Let him Ps. 22, 7, 8 deliver him, seeing he delighted in him." Whether or not the rulers were conscious of using the very words of the psalm, the fact remains that they were the enemies of God's Anointed described by the prophesy of David.

Thus, without committing themselves or betraying their fear of the people, the rulers were the instigators and the soul of that disgraceful scene. Their success was gratifying, their arguments were plausible and pleasing to all, even to the unfortunate culprits hanging to the right and left of Jesus. "The thieves also which were crucified with him, cast the same in his teeth." The numbing effect of the spiced wine or vinegar, if they had received any, lasted only a short while; afterwards the crucified remained conscious to the end. Generally, crucified criminals gave vent to their wrath in imprecations, denouncing their executioners, or in wild cries and entreaties for mercy. These two also used angry language, but their ill will, instead of turning against their tormentors, was directed against their companion in misery. Why were they so angry as to forget their own sore plight long enough to scold him who had never harmed them? Because they ascribed their execution to the fact that Jesus was crucified with them, that without him they would have remained in prison much longer? But their trial and condemnation must have taken place long before that Friday, and it is probable that Jesus was killed so quickly because the day had been set for the execution of those two thieves. Possibly it was on the cross, through the derision of the priests and people, that the two men learned who the substitute for Barabbas was. Condemned criminals were not formally told in whose company they were to die. Rumors about the famous Jesus may have reached even the shadowed paths of these disorderly characters, but they had not been interested in him or in religion. Unexpectedly they find themselves in his presence, and, lo! he is not better than they are. He is in the same predicament, and worse, for everybody mocks him and upbraids him for many great crimes. And this is the prophet of Nazareth! If there were any power in him to save himself, he would certainly hasten to make use of it. Since Jesus remains in his agony, his claims are vain!

That entire scene proved exceedingly interesting to the four soldiers who, sitting near the cross, had the best opportunity to hear every word. At last their turn came. "And the soldiers also mocked him, coming to him, and offering him vinegar, and saying, "If thou be King of the Jews, save thyself." Did they interrupt priests and people in order to interpose their own jests? They would scarcely disturb the entertaining sight of Jews mocking a Jew. Was it their wish to assist the multitude in ridiculing Jesus? But they had an entirely different view of the matter. To them Pilate's superscription was law. The efforts of the scribes to disown the Nazarene as their king in any sense did not impress them. Stubbornly they adhered to the governor's and their own opinion. As soon as a lull in the tumult permitted, they reminded the Jews that here their king was being killed by Roman authority. This they did not only with words. They arose, stepped up to the cross "offering him vinegar," of the sour wine which perhaps they just had enjoyed. They did not actually give him the cooling drink, but merely held it out to tantalize him. A brutal jest perpetuated on one who suffered severely from thirst, as was the case with every crucified person. Either they acted as if drinking to his health, or, more likely, as if waiting on the exalted king, doing special homage to him. From the general derision they had learned more and more of the powers of this king of the Jews, and put it to use at once: "Save thyself." This is the echo of the Jewish mockery combined with their own ideas of the executed political king. After these final sallies of the soldiers the Jews desisted from further mockery. Why? Because the dinner hour was near and the people returned to the city? A large multitude is not so easily and quickly dispersed on that account. For hours afterwards comparative quiet reigned about the crosses. Evidently the rulers did not want to be insulted by these soldiers. On the one hand the Jews eagerly denying all affiliation with him whom they rejected as king, on the other side the Roman soldiers wounding their pride with "the king of the Jews": that was a moment when the rulers deemed it wise to withdraw with their friends, for their purpose had been accomplished, the priests were once more considered the patrons of Israel's glory.

The Lord hung there in silence, though he was able to speak for hours afterwards. No threat, no sign of indignation escaped him. How great is he in the midst of his revilers, great not only in patience, but great in faith. Through the gloom of his agony he looked forward to the hour when he indeed should save himself, when he did step from the cross and did build the temple of God. A ray of his coming glory shone from him on the cross already in that remarkable incident engaging our attention now.

60. THE REPENTANT MALEFACTOR
Luke 23, 39-43

"And one of the malefactors which were hanged railed on him, saying, If thou be Christ, save thyself and us. But the other answering rebuked him, saying, Dost thou not fear God, seeing thou art in the same condemnation? And we indeed justly; for we receive the due reward of our deeds; but this man has done nothing amiss. And he said unto Jesus, Lord, remember me when thou comest into thy kingdom. And Jesus said unto him, Verily I say unto thee, Today shalt thou be with me in paradise."

————

There is no contradiction in the circumstance that Matthew and Mark report the two malefactors as having mocked the Lord, while Luke tells of only one doing so. Let us but grasp the situation, and quite a difference will be discovered between the first and the second mockery. At first both thieves "cast the same in his teeth." That is to say, they simply repeated the derisive language heard from the rulers and the people, without giving a thought as to whether those attacks were justified and deserved by Jesus, or not. Then the rulers retired. Whatever reason may have driven them so abruptly from Calvary, they may now be supposed preparing themselves for the festive meal, especially since on account of the arrest they had to forego the pleasures of the passover meal the previous evening. With the rulers many of their adherents went away, and comparative quiet ensued about the crosses. During this

(97)

interval, however short or long, the two thieves, with their attention no longer distracted by the people, had time to think of the much reviled Messiah. Now nobody can come into the presence of Jesus, can learn something about him, can use his name in one way or another, without consciously or unconsciously deciding for or against him. The repentant robber, whose name according to tradition was Dysmas and who, supposedly, occupied the cross to the right of Jesus, was through his meditations led to a firm belief in the Lord, he was converted. If this sudden conversion is called an occurence so extraordinary as to defy explanation, then it must be remembered that the perversion of Gestas, as tradition names him, is equally miraculous. The degree of unbelief in the one is just as surprising as the degree of belief in the other. Both culprits started under the same conditions, with the same chance, with the same indifferent attitude toward Jesus; but the one quickly stepped into light and life as a friend of the Lord, while his comrade just as resolutely turned into a convinced enemy, making not only the spite and unbelief of the rulers his own, but surpassing it, making quick progress in his unbelief. From that central cross two ways led in opposite directions, and each robber travelled at once to the end of the way chosen by him. This is exactly what happened.

"And one of the malefactors which were hanged railed on him." He cannot have been so persistent as to continue his mockery uninterrupted even after the multitudes resumed silence. In that case it would have amounted to a mere babble, an insensible raving prompted by furious pain, hardly worth the rebuke of his companion or the perpetuation in the records of the gospel. But it was more, it was a hostile outburst, a deliberate assault, for he did now what neither he nor his companion had done in the first mockery; literally, "he blasphemed." Through the many reproaches of the multitude he had his attention directed to the greatest hopes of Israel, which to some extent were shared by the lowest Jew. Those hopes, however, were closely connected with the terms Messiah, temple, religion, God. Thus the long neglected subject of religion in general was brought back to him, and his conclusion was that no merciful God existed, no glorious Messiah should come, that all religion is vanity. This desperate reasoning was certainly induced by his ever increasing, excruciating pains, by his feeling of utter hopelessness. It is also possible that he was specially irritated because Jesus had not replied to his former taunts and was hanging there so patiently as if he felt no tortures. His wrath found at last expression in a loud proclamation of unbelief.

"If thou be Christ, save thyself and us." It was rather a derisive question: "The Messiah art thou, then?" He meant to say that if any person claims to be the Messiah he deserves to be crucified, for in reality there is none. Thus he went much farther than the rulers and the people who still looked for the true Messiah to come. In the opinion of this agnostic malefactor such hope was sheer superstition. This becomes plainer from his impudent demand: "Save thyself and us." Not only did he agree with the rulers and the people that Jesus was a braggart, but he surpassed their verdict by adding, "save us." The only demand made by priest and multitude was that Jesus should save himself, then they would believe him. They had enough respect for the real Messiah not to expect Jesus, if he proved to be the Son of God, to save people that had treated him as they did. The Messiah belonged to his friends, to the righteous. But now this malefactor published his conviction that he and his companion were good enough to claim the Messiah; if there were any possibilities of Jesus' descending from the cross he must necessarily take his two fellow

sufferers along. A Messiah of condemned criminals! Two
things were implied in that blasphemy: first, Jesus was
declared as being no better than the murderers hanging at
his side; and, secondly, there was never to be any such
Messiah as expected by Israel. That this was not said
merely in the nature of a vulgar jest is clear from his
speaking as the advocate of his companion: save "us." He
took it for granted that any person in his place could not
but throw all religion, all higher hopes, to the winds.

It was such reckless blasphemy which shocked Dysmas
on the right. The hardened sinner had spoken in the name
of his comrade, who immediately entered a protest. "But
the other answering rebuked him, saying, Dost not thou
fear God, seeing thou art in the same condemnation?" A
rebuke, a sharp reprimand, he administered. How could he
have done so, if at first he had also used such blasphemous
expressions, without inviting the retort, "hypocrite"? His
dissent shows that the former mockery of the two was but a
thoughtless repetition of what they had heard. But the
surprising element in the present derision of the impenitent
was the complete lack of reverence for God, as the wondering question indicates: "Dost thou not fear God?" It
appeared not strange to him that under the stress of pain
one might insult Jesus, for he had done the same. But it
was beyond his comprehension how one could go so far
as to lose all fear of God, to throw religion entirely away.
This all the more, because "thou art in the same condemnation." The three crucified persons were rapidly approaching
their end, and even under ordinary circumstances it would
have been senseless to increase each other's tortures with
biting remarks. How much more inopportune to declare
that Jesus deserved to be condemned, when the reviler has
enough of his own guilt and punishment to bear. If nothing
else, he ought to fear God instead of denouncing all that

is holy and good. This earnest answer shows how bitter and great the blasphemies of the impenitent culprit must have been. It also informs us of the thoughts that occupied the penitent man since that first mockery. He had been thinking of his end and of his God. He knew nothing of a merciful God whose pardon could be secured, who ought to be loved as a father. The "fear" of God who punishes the sinners agitated him, though just that was the right mood to learn more of Jesus. While thus under God's judgment one malefactor embittered himself and wilfully turned away from every hope of salvation, the other under and by the same judgment learned to read in his heart and to realize his need of a Savior.

Concerning that condemnation, that punishment on the cross, which all three suffered alike, the penitent had some distinction to make: "and we indeed justly; for we receive the due reward of our deeds: but this man hath done nothing amiss." That was an honest public confession. Convicted criminals generally deny their guilt, asserting that they suffer for crimes not committed by them. Or if their guilt is established beyond a doubt, they insist that the punishment is too severe, out of proportion with the offence. Up to that hour both malefactors may have observed the same tactics. The one now admitted that no injustice was done to either of them. He did not want to appear better than his companion. Both had committed deeds whose "due reward" was that slow, torturing death on the cross; if a milder punishment had been inflicted on them, they would not have paid their full dues. Not every crime was punished with the cross; in times of peace only the most atrocious criminals were executed in that manner. It is therefore possible that these two men had shed blood. This unreserved confession of the malefactor proves that his "fear" of God was genuine. He did not ascribe his downfall to others, did not excuse himself with the bad example or the sins of others who perhaps had greater guilt than he. Simply reading in his own heart and life he acknowledged that neither God nor man had dealt unjustly with him.

The more of just retribution he discovered in his own condemnation, the brighter shone into his soul the innocence of Jesus. "But this man hath done nothing amiss." The same Jesus, whom a while ago he helped to mock, had now risen in his estimation so much as to deserve not only no derision, but also no punishment whatever. Since he addressed his "nothing amiss" to his companion, it meant that Jesus had done no such evil deeds as the malefactors were guilty of. Before men the Lord's life bore quite a different record; not even his fiercest enemies on Calvary have mentioned any such crime as they had committed. But the "nothing amiss" meant also nothing wrong in general, nothing unseemly or unbecoming. Pilate's inscription and the mockery of the soldiers accused him of political ambition. The rulers called him a false Messiah, a destroyer of the temple, a blasphemer of God. In opposition to all that this penitent declared that he believed none of those charges, that before men and even before the tribunal of God Jesus stood innocent, having done nothing amiss. How did he gain such certainty? Had he met Jesus before, had he known his works and words, and did he now testify from experience? Nothing indicates that he ever had come near Jesus; for in that event he would have spoken differently from what he did. As to the alleged crimes, though, he was able to speak from experience. If Jesus had been a demagogue, or if the fanatics had hailed him as one who shortly was to inaugurate a rebellion, then the robbers, the entire lawless element of the highways and mountains would have known it, would have been interested, would have come near; for public disturbances were their harvests. But no such people ever came to the Lord, and these two robbers had probably never heard of him. In this respect he was surely an authority: nothing amiss. But how concerning those religious charges? What did coarse men like these malefactors care for the hopes of the pious Jews, for the views of the rulers, which Jesus was said to have offended? We assume that the exaggeration of the rulers and the multitudes convinced the penitent of the untruth of their charges. He was a Jew and as such had, in his childhood at least, received some instruction in the Word of God, either from his parents or in a synagogue. Then he must have heard something about the expected Messiah. These meager remembrances, the seed sown in youth, now sprang up within him. And with his realization of God's judgment of his sin, of his need of a Savior, and seeing Jesus hang in patience, an ardent faith in the Lord's innocence and greatness began to grow. Just as the other malefactor could not comprehend why in his condition any one should retain the least faith in religion, so this penitent failed to understand how one in his condition should not recognize the innocence of Jesus.

A still greater knowledge had he acquired: in the innocent Jesus he saw the promised Messiah to whom he turned with a request. "And he said unto Jesus, Lord, remember me when thou comest into thy kingdom." He was conscious of a separation having taken place between him and his former companion, for he was aware that he could pray only for himself as he did. Not, remember "us," but remember "me." Thereby he declared his willingness to be known as a friend of the Lord and a believer, his willingness also to be mocked together with Jesus if the people will resume their derision. He addressed the Savior not

with the name "Jesus" or the title "Rabbi"; both were quite
unfamiliar terms to him as regarding his new Lord and,
also, the former he probably did not venture to use because
it was written on Pilate's spiteful superscription. To him
Jesus was the "Lord" with a kingdom, such as was promised by the prophets. His humble and modest request
was the very opposite to the demand of the impenitent:
"Remember me." He believed that a time should come
when Jesus recalled that scene on Calvary, when the hos-
tility of the enemies as well as the prayer of the contrite
sinner were to be remembered. No liberation from the
deserved punishment, no immediate release from the cross
did he ask, but merely a kind remembrance at some future
date: "when thou comest into thy kingdom." His conviction was that the present pain and death were not to
be the end of either the Messiah or himself. Thus far we
have the evidences of a quick, genuine, and unusual conversion, as furnished by the penitent himself. The Bible
relates of no other change so complete and marvellous. In
the history of the martyrs we do meet with instances showing that executioners who just had tortured Christian men
and women turned around, confessing their faith in Christ.
But that was not so very strange since such converts were
influenced by the heroic example of excellent and perhaps
esteemed people. On Calvary there was nothing inspiring,
the Christ was hanging in his deepest humiliation, rulers
and people rejected him, even the apostles were shaken in
their faith, and the dying thief was the last and least whom
one would select as a candidate for Messiah's kingdom.
As said before, no personal acquaintance with Jesus can
explain even part of that conversion, much less the whole
of it. By that time no friends had yet come near to express
their love to the crucified. The silence of the Lord alone

seems to have been the impressive incident which moved the benighted heart and revived early memories clustering around a glorious though suffering Messiah. The Spirit of God worketh when and where and how it listeth. Only this one conversion so near death's door is given in Holy Writ. It is a profound consolation, but also an effective warning. Though the other malefactor was so close to the Savior, heard the admonition of his former comrade, the blessed assurance of the crucified Messiah, and though he ceased his godless speech, we do not read that he sought pardon. Silently, stubbornly, he passed into the night of the great Beyond.

That the conversion of the penitent thief was genuine, though his ideas about Christ and his kingdom may have been confused and vague, is evident from the fact that the Lord did not quench the smoking flax, but gave a glorious answer.

"And Jesus said unto him, Verily I say unto thee, Today shalt thou be with me in paradise." The Lord did not console the penitent by lamenting his cruel fate, or by deploring his early death, or by exonerating his guilt; not a single trait of sentimentality is discernible in those words. There is rather a familiar ring in that phrase, "Verily I say unto thee." In that way he used to open his speeches when he spake with authority and not as the scribes. Here was a reply to the mockery of the multitude, a refutation of all their charges. Without a sign of decreasing faith, of discouragement or of fear of God, as unyielding in his claims and as positive in his promises as ever, Jesus gave that wonderful assurance. "I say"—it is not in the name of God that Jesus decides the future of the convert; on his own authority, as the great High priest, as the King of the coming kingdom, in sovereign power he distributes his

Second word

favors: I say unto thee! And what he says is not the usual word of pardon, "thy sins be forgiven thee." One whose sins are forgiven may again fall into sin, a short while later needing renewed pardon. But unusual as the confession and conversion of this sinner was, so unusual is his reception by his Lord: "Today shalt thou be with me in paradise." This believer shall not relapse into doubt and uncertainty or into condemnation; he shall be preserved to the end then to be safe forever. "Today" his translation shall take place; the agony of death, this earthly life shall pass away with the passing day, for the converted sinner as well as for Jesus. After all is ended here below he shall be "with me," with Jesus. This is the privilege announced to his faithful ones: "Where I am, there shall also my servant be"; this he had asked of the Father in his last prayer: "Father, I will that they also, whom thou hast given me, be with me where I am." Thus the malefactor was accepted as a servant, as a dear friend, as a gift of God—quite a contrast to the religion of the rulers who doubted whether God "will have" this Jesus, and who certainly would not have been willing to have the dying thief as a partaker of their Messiah's kingdom. Where does Jesus want to meet his friend that very day? In or after some purgatory? "In paradise." Not in the immediate presence of God, which we call heaven, but at the place of those departed spirits that are saved, in "Abraham's bosom," as contrasted to the Gehenna the place of spirits not saved, though immediately after his death "he went and preached unto the spirits in prison." Afterwards he would meet his first fruit of the cross in paradise.

A remarkable incident. It was a consoling evidence to the Savior that he did not suffer in vain; his blood, his death, should bear children as the dew of the morning. This first example of the atoning power of the Crucified

Margin notes:
John 12, 26
John 17, 24
Luke 16, 32
1 Pet. 3, 19

has gone into the world as a welcome message to all sinners. But how did the people on Calvary view this conversion? The malefactor's confession was quite an unexpected declaration of the Lord's innocence. And what did they think of the Lord's solemn assurances? The whole scene must have made a deep impression upon the bystanders, for the mockery is not resumed, and a few friends venture near to bid the Lord a last farewell.

61. MARY AND JOHN
John 19, 25-27

"Now there stood by the cross of Jesus his mother, and his mother's sister, Mary the wife of Cleophas, and Mary Magdalene. When Jesus therefore saw his mother, and the disciple standing by, whom he loved, he saith unto his mother, Woman behold thy son! Then saith he to the disciple, Behold thy mother! And from that hour that disciple took her unto his own home."

The edifying incident with the penitent malefactor was not to remain the only consolation refreshing the heart of the great sufferer. Perhaps at a moment when the multitudes withdrew, an opportunity offered itself for a few loving friends to venture near, whose object was to attest their faithfulness and to bid him farewell. "Now there stood by the cross of Jesus his mother, and his mother's sister Mary the wife of Cleophas, and Mary Magdalene." With the exception of the beloved disciple who was standing by, upholding and encouraging the mother of Jesus, none of the Eleven were present. These men had evidently not recovered from their shock and were sitting in disconsolate solitude, scattered like sheep without a shepherd, shaken in the depths of their faith. Women were here in the majority and seem themselves to have suggested the visit to Calvary. They "stood by the cross of Jesus." They had not waited long before the Lord noticed them, for they cannot be supposed as having stood near the cross all

through the previous hour of derision. If they witnessed
that scene at all, they remained at a distance, for even if
they were not apprehensive of personal insult or violence,
they must have felt that there was no place for them among
the excited blasphemers. When the mockery subsided they
drew near and stood "by the cross," very close to it, in
full view of the Lord; for it is unreasonable to assume that
the Master shouted his tender words across intervening
throngs. By standing near the cross they publicly attested
their interest in Jesus, their love to him, their connection
with his cause. That was quite a courageous act. There
were certainly Jews or Galileans on the hill, who recognized
one or the other of the women, especially the mother; and
John himself must have been well known to persons connected with the high priest's palace and to citizens in general. If nothing else, they surely risked to hear the insults
and railleries of some fanatics, especially after the words
of Jesus addressed to them established their intimate re-
lationship to the Crucified One.

Two of the fearless women were members of the Lord's
family, his nearest friends according to the flesh: his mother
and her sister. These were his only relatives to visit him
on Calvary. All through those sad hours we see and hear
nothing of his four brethren or of his sisters so well known
to his countrymen: "His brethren, James, and Joses, and   Matt. 13,
Simon, and Judas, and his sisters, are they not all with   55, 56
us?" If we suppose them as having been in Jerusalem
during the feast, they had apparently not yet renounced
their unbelief of former days when we were told: "Neither   John 7, 5
did his brethren believe in him." If such was the case,
they naturally disliked to be identified with the crucified
prophet, and detested the public disgrace brought upon
their family. Neither do we discover any trace of Joseph,
Mary's husband. We are entitled to conclusion that he was

dead; for Jesus, in placing his mother into John's care, did
certainly not demand a separation from her living husband;
nor did the Lord express thereby an opinion as to Joseph's
unwillingness or incapability of supporting his wife, had
he been yet alive.

Among the "many women which followed Jesus from
Galilee, ministering unto him," some of whom we meet later
on Calvary, the mother of Jesus was the principal person.
Silently, without uttering a single word, she stood there and
silently she departed. What does that mute reserve teach
us? That she was unbelieving, failing to see any divine
mission in the work and death of her son? This suspicion
has been variously advanced just on account of her con-
sistent reticence throughout Christ's public ministry. As
if that noble woman, who tasted the bitterness of life as
no other, could not adduce more valid reasons for her modest
conduct! There was the poverty, the fight to Egypt, the care
of the early years; later she had to wrestle for a subsistence
as a widowed woman, for her husband is not mentioned
again after Jesus was twelve years old; then she had to
suffer under the friction and division in her own household
where some did not believe in Jesus and thereby rendered
the family life unpleasant; and she lived in a village the
populace of which was by no means friendly to Jesus, and
who molested her with disquieting rumors and unkind arguments. Under such circumstances it was rather an evidence
of belief that she was found in the company of her Son
as often as she was. Sometimes one former incident is
pointed out as a proof of her unbelieving attitude: "While
he yet spake to the people, behold, his mother and his
brethren stood without, desiring to speak with him, and
could not come at him for the press; and, standing without,
sent unto him, calling him." This is superficially explained
as an effort, on her part, of dissuading Jesus from his Mes-

Matt. 27, 55

Matt. 12, 46
Mark 3, 31
Luke 8, 19

sianic work and career! As if there were not a vast difference between maternal affection which made her fearful as to the detrimental effect of his unceasing toil, and cold unbelief trying to end his ministry. That she at that time appeared in the company of the unbelieving brethren is but natural, for after Joseph's death they were, of course, her nearest protectors and advisers, and her dependence on them is no indication whatever that she shared their opinions. Her visit on Calvary is in itself a testimony to her faith. Supposing that she had lost confidence in the divine character of Jesus, and that she had endeavored to divert his steps from the path of danger, how must she then have looked upon her crucified son? She would have considered him a wayward child who refused to heed a mother's advice or the dictates of reason; a son who had brought this calamity upon himself by his own rashness, who thereby also disgraced his mother and the entire family. Would this woman, so deeply wounded in her pride, so long neglected and disobeyed by him, have come out to see him once more? Granted that a mother's love is capable of even such a sacrifice of self-denial, she would surely have appeared in different company. She would not have come leaning on the arm of John who, as the closest friend and follower of Jesus, she could have accused of confirming him in his errors, of contributing to his downfall. She would not have stood there with Mary Magdalene, one of the many women "who ministered unto him" and whom she could jealously blame for having kept the son from mother and home. Would she have so readily obeyed the son, who never listened to her, when he told her to make her future home with John? Would she together with the finally converted brethren of Jesus have continued to associate with the circle of disciples and believers as we see her do? For the same Mary whose faith Elisabeth praised many years ago, "Blessed is she that _{Luke 1, 45}

believed," was later a believing and honored member of the young pentecostal congregation: "These all continued with one accord in prayer and supplication, with the women, and Mary the mother of Jesus, and with his brethren." Her silent mourning, then, instead of betraying her unbelief, is the aptest illustration of her insight into the Lord's office and nature. No doubt, in her speechless grief the ineffable distress of a sorely tried mother was momentarily paramount. Mary did not walk on spiritual stilts, ever conscious of her peculiar position; she rather lived the life of the plain, pious woman that she was, attending to her duties as wife and mother, simply knowing that God had specially favored her in that Son. When we remember that even the greatest disciples walked in darkness before the resurrection, we have no right to expect that in those hours she should have grasped the full significance of the Lord's life and death. She had no idea of a speedy resurrection from the dead, and therefore doubly felt the loss of her glorious Son. She had been hailed as the highly favored and blessed among women; other mothers had called her happy on account of that Son; and now that cruel change! It would have been hard for any mother to give up a noble son, to see him die so disgraceful a death. How much more must Mary have realized the injustice the bitterness of that end! Right there Simeon's prophecy was fully accomplished in her: "Yea, a sword shall pierce through thy own soul also." No finer portrait could the gospel have drawn of this afflicted mother than by pointing out her silence. She did not, like the daughters of Jerusalem, wail over the sad fate of Jesus or her own misfortune; she did not indulge in vain complaints against the unjust authorities; she did not attempt to offer consoling words to him who bore a heaven of consolation in himself. We realize how trivial, how absurd in her or her companions, a common conservation,

Acts 1, 14

Luke 2, 35

a show of desolate grief, or even an encouraging talk, in the presence of Jesus would have been! We like her much better for her silence in that solemn moment. Her mute grief shows that she resolutely bore the burden placed upon her shoulders, that she had resigned herself into the will of God who in all her life had strangely and wonderfully led her, who at his own appointed time would also shed his light upon this gloomy hour of trial.

Mary stood not alone in her bereavement. Her "sister" had accompanied her to Calvary. Here the question arises whether that sister was "Mary the wife of Cleophas," so that only three women were present, or whether her name is not given. In the latter case four women would stand there: the mother; her unnamed sister; Mary the wife of Cleophas, and Mary Magdalene. Assuming this latter theory, a speculation ensues forthwith as to who that nameless sister of the mother actually was, and some have conjectured that she must have been Salome, John's mother, simply because later we meet her also on Calvary. This supposition rests on too frail a basis. Therefore we assume that only three women were there: the mother's sister, Mary by name, being the wife of Cleophas. For we fail to understand why that sister should have been left entirely nameless while Mary Magdalene and other women were named. If that sister had been an unbeliever, she would not have come to Calvary, at least not in the company of these women with whom she could not feel herself at home because differing with them in matters of faith. Or if she had tactlessly forced herself as a curious spectator upon the others, her presence would have been too trivial to be perpetuated, without any purpose and without any explanation, in that record which puts so much importance into every word. The presence of that sister was also a heroic act, a sign of attachment not only to the mother of Jesus, but to the Lord himself, whom she not only esteemed as a dear relative, whom she rather revered and loved as the Master of her two sons.   She was the wife of Cleophas who was also known as Alpheus, both names being practically one and the same.   Alpheus and Mary were the parents of the younger James, and Joses.   The former is known to us as one of the twelve apostles, "James the son of Alpheus"; and since his brother Joses is mentioned together with him, we infer that he also was a believer.   Thus Mary the wife of Cleophas stood there as the mother of two distinguished followers and by her presence avowed her own faith in Jesus.   She did not think that Jesus had led her sons astray, or that she and they had reasons to be ashamed of the former Master!   The faithful woman rather declared her allegiance to him to the end.

Matt 27, 56
Matt. 10, 3

If tradition may be trusted, Cleophas was the brother of Joseph, and then we would have the peculiar coincidence that two brothers married two sisters, and the sisters were both called Mary.   It has often happened that brothers married sisters.   Stranger is the circumstance that both sisters bore the same name.   The similarity has been explained in various ways.   In noble families, especially in ruling houses, it was customary to repeat the given names of the children of either sex indefinitely.   Mary was of David's royal lineage; but is it convincing that her parents in their reduced circumstances should have fostered the traditions of their ancient race to the point of such pedantic details?   It is suggested that both Marys were only step-sisters, that perhaps both were brought along from a former marriage when their father and mother married a second time.   This is probably the most plausible explanation, if we will not accept the last, according to which the word "sister" must not be taken literally, but rather as meaning "sister-in-law"; for it is surmised that after Joseph's death

Mary the widow had her household or, at least, occupied the same house, with Cleophas and his wife Mary. Then the word sister would indicate that the two women lived together in sisterly friendship and love so that in the course of time the people overlooked their true relation and simply knew them and spoke of them as "the sisters." John, who was intimately acquainted with the family of Jesus, must then have thought details unnecessary, he considering the broad term sufficiently plain for the readers of his gospel. Whether we adopt the second or third solution, Cleophas' wife conducted herself really as a sister to the bereft mother. The sympathy of that woman, who had her two sons among the believers, must have been a source of consolation to the mother whose own home was overcast with the shadow of unbelief. The constancy of her believing friend was apt to revive or strengthen her confidence that God would turn the hearts of the yet distant brethren of Jesus, even as we find recorded after the resurrection that her hopes had not been in vain. Acts 1, 14

Not less consoling was the presence of the third woman, "Mary Magadelene." This Mary was from Galilee, her residence, it is thought, being Magdala, whence she probably derived her name "Magdalene." She must not be confounded with Mary the sister of Lazarus and Martha in Bethany, nor with that "woman, which was a sinner," entering the Pharisee's house and weeping at the feet of Jesus. Luke 7, 37 Magdalene had followed the Lord to Jerusalem, serving him, but not for the first time in her life. Having been healed by him of a severe affliction, she gratefully devoted her time and means to his service, she being one of a number of pious women who were of the same thought: "And the twelve were with him, and certain women, which had been healed of evil spirits and infirmities, Mary Magdalene, out of whom went seven devils, and Joanna the wife of Chuza Luke 8, 1-3

Herod's steward, and Susanna, and many others, which ministered unto him of their substance." On account of the similar affliction, tradition makes her the daughter of that Canaanitic woman who "cried unto him, Have mercy on me, O Lord, thou Son of David; my daughter is grievously vexed with a devil." We are also told that she went to Rome to accuse Pilate for having condemned Jesus. Finally, she is said to have preached the gospel in Gaul. More important than such legends are the statements made in the Bible concerning her. On Calvary she stood with John, with the mother Mary, and with the other Mary; which means that she belonged to the most intimate circle of prominent believers. She did not leave Calvary until evening, after having witnessed the burial of the Lord. Early on Easter morn she was again at the tomb in the company of other women and later also by herself. She is generally mentioned first among the ministering women, as an energetic leader among her friends. Here in her silence, as well as in her eager activity before and after that hour, she had but one purpose: to manifest her gratitude to him who had done wondrous things to her. How genuine her piety must have been, and how well remembered her visit on Calvary was, is perhaps best seen in the fact that the risen Lord deigned to appear to her. No, in such company the mother of Jesus could not remain inconsolable, could not lose her faith in the Son.

     The crucified Lord quickly noticed the group. "Jesus therefore saw his mother, and the disciple standing by, whom he loved." He did not hang there unconscious or apathetic. Though his heart communed with the Father, nothing on Calvary escaped his eye or ear. What especially seems to have pleased the Lord was that the beloved disciple was "standing by" his mother, probably supporting her. Bearing in mind that John dislikes to mention his own name,

Matt. 15, 22

John 20, 11-18

we are not in doubt as to the identity of Mary's escort.
All night John had been in the high priest's palace and,
presumably, afterwards in or near Antonia. Not until
after Jesus had been condemned to die may he have gone
home to inform and assist the friends, especially the Master's mother. Mary came to Calvary accompanied, assisted
by John, and the care of a better friend she could not possibly have found. Did not John himself suffer a great
loss by the death of the noblest friend ever loved by any
man, by the parting from the adored Master whom he had
gladly served in glorious days gone by? If anyone, John
was the man to understand and console the mourning
mother. How suggestive his "standing by" Mary appears!
Not only in the days of success did he wish to be the friend
of Jesus and of Mary, but also in the hour of direst need he
was ready to reman with them. It seems as if this "standing
by" the mother implied his declaration that, as much as
was in his power, Mary should not be left friendless. And
the Lord accepted that offer of unchanging love and service.
He who was ever grateful for the smallest token of kindness
had a fine reward in store for his faithful servant. When
Jesus therefore saw that scene, "he saith unto his mother,
Woman, behold thy son." With his accustomed tact and
genuine tenderness he addressed the mother first, for she
was the one needing consolation most. His weakened condition permitted the speaking of but a few short words, but
just on that account they are so impressive. They reveal
the fact that his heart and mind were engaged in his usual
occupation: thinking of others. He spoke as if those visit-
ing friends were the real sufferers who needed his attention;
as if he must hasten to show his appreciation, his intention
to requite their good will. Why, then, did he use the rather
formal address "woman," instead of the more endearing
term "mother"? Did he wish to avoid an undue arousing

of painful feelings in the stricken mother? But just such
an attempt would have been quickly noticed by her, and it
would then have stirred the very depths of her sorrow.
Or did he wish to conceal the fact that he was conversing
with his mother in order to spare her possible insults from
godless bystanders? However, the conversation cannot have
been without all witnesses, and even if his words were
not understood by strangers, the mere fact of his speaking to
Mary would have betrayed her identity. We remember that
he addressed her as "woman" ever since his public ministry
began; the first time at the wedding feast of Cana. The
Messiah could not retain the obedient filial attitude distinguishing him in the home of Nazareth. Mary, like all other
believers, had to approach him as her divine Lord. On
Calvary he was shedding his blood also for her sins. Thus
not so much as a son to his mother, but as the Redeemer
to a sinner, as the Lord to a follower, did he speak at
that moment. Therefore, the somewhat distant address
"woman" was not his renunciation of her as his mother
according to the flesh, but it conveyed the effective consolation which that mother just then needed. It was a
recognition of her faith. He still believed in his mission,
and she believed in him. The cross did not disgrace either
him or her. He was not the unfortunate son rejected by
God, but hung there just in the midst of the work assigned
him by the Father. Her Lord and Savior was speaking to
Mary. That human tenderness which the appellation failed
to convey was manifest in what he did say to the "woman."
"Behold thy son." Knowing that henceforth his human
obligations to this earthly life were ended, Jesus made his
domestic testament, as it has been called, giving his mother
into the care of John. We notice that he did not ask for
John's consent. Here we wonder why he did not make this
last preparation a few days before, as soon as he knew

the appointed hour of death. What, if some untoward event had prevented Mary from coming to Calvary? Had the Master quietly made some arrangement with John? Such petty planning and disposing would have been unworthy of him who knew his every step, and his entire future as well, ruled and regulated by God. He had the positive knowledge that God would provide for the mother Mary. When he saw John "standing by" Mary, he at once recognized in that circumstance the will of God, indicating to him that the two should remain together. "Therefore" he spoke to them as he did. Accompanied with a look, perhaps also with nodding the head in the direction of John, his words made it clear to her that henceforth she should devote her motherly affections and confide her affairs to John. The woman who thenceforth was, with all others, simply a poor sinner saved by the blood of Jesus Christ, had the honorable distinction of being especially provided for by the Redeemer of the world.

Having thus shown his love to the mother, he also addressed John. "Then saith he to the disciple, Behold thy mother!" Even without that explicit request John would certainly have acted as a helpful friend to Mary. But the beloved disciple and faithful friend was not to depart from Calvary without a word of farewell, without a special token of confidence. The duty imposed on him amounted to an honor: The dearest relative of Jesus was to become the dearest possession of the Lord's best friend on earth; as his own mother John was to respect and love Mary. That was a declaration to the effect that John was more than a disciple, more than a mere friend to Jesus: the Lord esteemed and loved him as a brother. Let us not overlook the implied compliment to Salome the mother of John: with her the unmarried disciple made his home and, naturally, she would have in Mary an additional member of

her household. The Lord was surely convinced of Salome's
willingness to receive his mother and to consider her presence a favor and honor. Finally, let the fact be emphasized
that it was not John who was given into Mary's care, but
that the mother of Jesus was to depend on John. Nothing
in the text supports the idea that John, whom Jesus simply
addressed as a friend and brother, stood there as the representative of the future church, and that he with all
believers was committed into the protection of the interceding Holy Mother!

By assigning Mary to John, Jesus virtually expressed
the wish that his mother should leave Nazareth, should
part from her own family and relatives. Why that? Did
the Lord merely provide for her material welfare by substituting John in his own place as a supporter of the woman?
But during the years of his public ministry the Lord was
scarcely ever at home and, because he himself was poor,
he did not what we would call providing for or supporting
his mother. Again, although Mary was not rich, she would
not suffer want in the midst of the four brethren of Jesus,
or in the house of her sister the wife of Cleophas. And
even if all these relatives had been unable to support her,
the numerous believers, particularly the women who had
ministered unto the Lord, would surely transfer their loving
ministration to the needy mother of the adored Master.
No, the question of daily bread did not prompt that arrangement. Nor was it a desire to put her into the midst of
believers where her faith could be strengthened. Was not
her sister a true believer, a dear companion to her? And
though the four sons were yet unbelieving, did not the Lord
foresee their conversion after the resurrection? And why
should the faith of Mary need such extreme care! She had
endured severer tests than the sneers and insults with
which unbelieving neighbors might receive her in the next

few days. Even the tumults and persecutions of the near
future could not shake the faith of a woman who had been
so wondrously guided by God all her life. Just remember,
it is a "mother" whom Jesus gives to his best friend. What
engages the heart of a mother by day and by night when
her dearest child is taken from her? Waking and sleeping
she thinks of the departed one; every word is recalled, every
detail becomes important. Who, then, in all the land was
better enabled to discuss the subject with her than the
most intimate friend of Jesus, who had been constantly with
him in the past three years, who had so profoundly read
the nature of the Lord? After the clouds of this Friday
have passed away, when finally the glory of the Ascension
illustrates the whole earthly career of the Redeemer, then
the thousand renewed inquiries can be discussed with and
answered by John to Mary's joy and satisfaction. Thus we
discover in this incident a promise of a pleasant future.
Light at evening, peace and quiet contentment in her de-
clining years, a feast of golden memories, await this mother
after the storms of earlier life. Truly, a fate in which we
rejoice for the sake of her who so willingly was the hand-
maid of the Lord. Truly, a testament worthy of the thoughtful physician of the human heart. Incidentally we get an
idea of what the courteous, considerate, and obedient conduct of the young Jesus toward his mother must have been
when he was yet subject in the home of Nazareth.

"And from that hour that disciple took her unto his
own home." Not immediately did they leave Calvary,
though they retired from the cross. Later we find John still
on the hill, also the women and acquaintance standing "afar
off." We do not think that John took Mary home and left
her there alone, he returning to Calvary. The mother may
have waited at least until Jesus had died, and may be supposed standing among those other friends. But on that

same day, obedient to the Lord's will, she went with John "into his own home." Like Peter, John could say that he had forsaken all to follow Jesus. However, that does not exclude his being remembered in his father's last will. It seems that John had inherited a house located in Jerusalem, to which he now took Mary. But they remained in the capital only a short time, for about two weeks after the

John 21, 1, 2 resurrection we find John in his old parental home on the shore of the sea of Tiberias. There Mary seems to have spent her remaining years. For the legend is untenable according to which she lived eleven years in Jerusalem, or that she went with John to Ephesus where she died and was buried. It was many years after this Friday that John took up his work in Asia, and as she was then too old to accompany him, we may conclude that he did not go thence until after Mary's death.

Why do we hear nothing of a word spoken to the mother's sister or to Mary Magadelene? The Lord surely appreciated their visit too. No doubt, whatever there was in that incident that could strengthen and encourage the faith, was said for the benefit also of those women. They had not come to engage in a conversation; and since they noticed how short and few were the words granted to Mary and John, the two unselfish friends retired without waiting for a special greeting from the agonized Lord. Entirely free from all human ties the Lord now stepped into the hour that was darkest in more than one sense of the word.

62. NOONDAY DARKNESS

Matt. 27, 45-47   Mark 15, 33-35
Luke 23, 44-45

"And it was about the sixth hour, and there was a darkness over all the earth until the ninth hour. And the sun was darkened. And about the ninth hour Jesus cried with a loud voice, saying Eli, Eli, lama sabachthani? which is, being interpreted, My God, my God, why hast thou forsaken me? And some of them that stood by, when they heard it, said, Behold, this man calleth for Elias."

———

Three hours had elapsed since the Lord was nailed to the cross, and each passing moment had brought fiercer pains. The following three hours, from noon to three o'clock, marked the climax of bodily tortures. When nailed to the tree, the Lord uttered his tender prayer; after that he consoled the dying thief; then he greeted Mary and John; but the succeeding three hours he hung in silence. Not until he had stepped into the deepest depths of agony, did he speak; or, rather, he cried out, he shrieked. And that agonized outcry was so strange, so fearful, that the death-struggle in no wise can have caused it. The bodily tortures were augmented by a conflict the like of which Jesus had never before experienced and in which he dreaded his defeat. While the world without was darkened, the rich world of his inner life was also overcast with shadows. These two phenomena, then, claim our attention: the

(123)

peculiar darkness in nature; and the extraordinary anxiety of Jesus.

"And it was about the sixth hour, and there was a darkness over all the earth until the ninth hour. And the sun was darkened." About twelve o'clock at noon, when the sun stands highest and brightest in the sky, an unusual gloom swiftly settled over Jerusalem. The darkness was not local, as if a mighty shadow had enwrapped the crosses alone, but it covered "all the earth." This expression does not specify the holy city, or the country of Judea, or the Roman empire, but signifies that to the observer the darkness appeared as general as if all the lands were overspread with the veil of night. No doubt, afterwards reports came in from different sections of the country where the darkness also had been noticed, so that the Evangelist was justified in writing, "all the earth." There was not merely a dim twilight, but a thick "darkness" of which nothing had been observed before noon. At its height the darkness was so dense that "the sun was darkened"; which may mean, simply that the sun had lost all lustre and hung in the sky as a dull red ball; or that the sun was not visible at all. This obscuration lasted three hours in full force, being densest perhaps about three o'clock, after which it rapidly cleared up and the sun shone again. As unnatural as it was that Jesus the Light of the World was to lose his lustre in the black gloom of a horrible death, so unusual was the darkening of the sun at high noon.

How must we explain that phenomenon? Was the eclipse of the sun cause or effect of the darkness on earth? Several ancient writers relate a total eclipse of the sun about that time; but, either it did not take place during the hours specified by the gospel, or it was not visible in Palestine; or if it was, it cannot have happened on the Friday in question. An astronomical eclipse of the sun cannot have caused the darkness because the Lord died on the pass-over, at the time of the full moon, and eclipses of the sun occur only at the time of the new moon. The darkness must have had its origin on our globe, spreading like a veil and effectually obscuring the sun. The gloom cannot have been the result of a very cloud day, perhaps of a frowning thunderstorm; for the preceding night had been clear and cold. In fact, so intense had been the cold, that even in the city, in the protected yard of the palace, fires had to be kindled to keep warm. Furthermore, if exceptionally black storm clouds had filled the skies, the Evangelists would have clearly said so; particularly, because they knew with the prophet that "the Lord hath his way in the whirlwind Nah. 1, 3 and in the storm, and the clouds are the dust of his feet." Evidently, the darkness is described as something extra-ordinary, a phenomenon which the recorders failed to under-stand and which they did not venture to explain from nat-ural causes. Meteoric dust may have filled the air, but who can prove it? Something like an earthquake followed shortly afterwards; was the darkness connected with that? Volcanic ashes may travel hundreds of miles in such volume as to dim daylight. The failure ever to discover the real cause of that darkness does not imply, of course, that the sacred record must be discredited; for we have reports of similar phenomena nearer our age and in our own country, which have never been satisfactorily explained. For in-stance, the "Dark Day in New England," May nineteenth, 1780, when a dense darkness covered the land from ten o'clock until noon, while in some regions the obscuration lasted nearly fifteen hours, causing dismay to the brute creation and bringing alarm to thousands of people, who regarded it as a token of God's wrath or even as the end of the world. We need not indulge in fanciful speculations as to supernatural causes specially set to work by God; nor do we believe that the black hosts and forces of hell itself darkened Calvary. But the God of the universe, by sending that darkness when and where it appeared, and though employing the laws and elements of nature only, certainly gave that sign as a special message to mankind.

God used the language of nature to indicate his attitude to the crime committed by men. The Lord of nature died on the cross, and all nature now sympathized with him. This suffering Lord was from eternity with God, and "all things were made by him; and without him was not anything made that was made." Him God had "appointed heir of all things, by whom also he made the worlds." When the cornerstone of the world was laid "the morning stars sang together" for joy. When that same Lord of nature came as a child to save the human race, God made the heavens his messenger to guide the people of the East: "Lo, the star, which they saw in the east, went before them." When the Savior dwelled as a man among men, "he rebuked the winds and the sea, and they obeyed him." This wide nature was also involved in the work of redemption, "for we know that the whole creation groaneth and travaileth in pain together until now." Through this Savior, now suffering, later "all things are become new," and "we, according to his promise, look for new heavens and a new earth." This nature is said to rejoice in the wonderful work and success of God on earth: "Sing, O ye heavens; for the Lord hath done it: shout, ye lower parts of the earth: break forth into singing, ye mountains, O forest, and every tree therein: for the Lord hath redeemed Jacob, and glorified himself in Israel." That same nature is represented as mourning when man goes wrong: "Be astonished, O ye heavens, at this, and be horribly afraid, be ye very desolate, saith the Lord. For my people have committed two evils; they have forsaken me the fountain of

John 1, 3

Heb. 1, 2

Matt. 2, 9

Matt. 8, 26

Rom. 8, 22

2 Cor. 5, 17

2 Pet. 3, 13

Isa. 44, 23

Jer. 2, 12, 13

living waters and hewed them out cisterns, broken cisterns, that can hold no water." The sun ceased to shine, as if neither heaven no earth could endure to behold the crime committed on Calvary with all its grief and shame. But that noonday darkness also amounted to a threatening prophecy against Jerusalem. The rulers had repeatedly asked this Christ for "a sign from heaven" and here their request was granted. When Egypt was punished by God, Moses received the following command: "Stretch out thine hand toward heaven, that there may be darkness over the land of Egypt, even darkness which may be felt. And Moses stretched forth his hand toward heaven; and there was a thick darkness in all the hand of Egypt three days: they saw not one another, neither rose any from his place for three days: but all the children of Israel had light in their dwellings." Now on Calvary a greater one than Moses stretched forth his hands toward heaven, and darkness befell the land, and there was no light in the homes of Israel, for this nation was now doomed. The interceding prayer of the Lord alone prevented the immediate punishment, which was sure to follow: "For thus hath the Lord said, The whole land shall be desolate; yet will I not make a full end. For this shall the earth mourn, and the heavens above be black: because I have spoken it, I have purposed it, and will not repent, neither will I turn back from it." And more: since Jew and Gentile were accomplices in that crime on Calvary, and since Jesus bore the sins of the whole world; therefore not only the doom of Jerusalem but also the final judgment of all nations was prefigured by that darkness. The holy God had been offended, his wrath was kindled against the murderers, and all who helped to shed the innocent blood of the Son must fear his sure punishment as announced by himself: "The indignation of the Lord is upon all nations, and his fury upon all their armies: he hath utterly destroyed

Ex. 10, 21-23

Jer. 4, 27, 28

Isa. 34, 2-4

them, he hath delivered them to the slaughter. Their slain also shall be cast out, and their stink shall came up out of their carcasses, and the mountains shall be melted with their blood. And all the hosts of heaven shall be rolled together as a scroll: and all their host shall fall down, as the leaf falleth off from the vine, and as a falling fig from the fig tree." Such darkness at the day of judgment was foretold by the Savior himself: "In those days, after that tribulation, the sun shall be darkened, and the moon shall not give her light." The natural darkness was God's frown upon the sins of all who ever reject the Anointed. Even as Jesus was crucified in full view of all the people, and even as Pilate's superscription was to publish the Lord's death to all nations, so in that darkness "all the earth" was notified of God's displeasure.

What may have been the immediate effect of that darkness on the people witnessing it? In Jerusalem the gay dinner parties were, no doubt, thoroughly disturbed; for natural phenomena have generally something weird and overawing in them. Perhaps all the citizens had an idea that, in some manner, that gloom was connected with the crucifixion of the Nazarene. The rulers may have momentarily lost their triumphant smiles. On Calvary the number of spectators must have materially decreased, most of the people preferring the security of their homes. Some were detained on the hill in the pursuit of their duty. These were the Roman guards and, probably, the deputies of the rulers. We find it difficult to believe that the rulers, who afterwards took the precaution of watching and sealing the tomb, should have returned to Jerusalem without leaving behind them some of their trusted men to witness the execution to the end. The assembled spectators may at first have been moved by a superstitious fear, or by a feeling of guilt, by a misgiving in their hearts, that, after all, this

Mark 13, 24

Jesus might be the Messiah, that a miraculous interference might be expected at any moment. Since nothing of that kind happened, their revived courage and conceit may have interpreted the darkness as a sign against Jesus: As the fiery eye of the sun, so also the eye of God turns from the blasphemer on the cross, the cloud of divine wrath lowers upon him. The outcry of the Lord was apt to confirm their perverted thoughts, and their renewed mockery was the results of such opinions.

It is certain that the darkness was in no wise cheering to the crucified Lord; if nothing else, it was at least a picture of the darkness reigning within him. During the sixth hour on the cross, the torture of his body, together with the anguish of his soul, reached its culmination. At last the silence was broken by a pitiful outcry: "And about the ninth hour Jesus cried with a loud voice, saying, Eli, Eli, lama sabachthani? which is, being interpreted, My God, my God, why hast thou forsaken me?" And about the time when the evening sacrifice was offered in the temple, the most mysterious part in the world's sacrifice was also enacted on the cross. When the darkness without was deepest, the dejection in the heart of Jesus was also greatest. The words were not spoken with a mere sigh or groan scarcely audible; they were rather "cried with a loud voice," with an effort, as if the exhausted sufferer gathered all his remaining strength for the one purpose of crying out. The words are given in the language in which they were spoken: it was an additional humiliation, a part of his Passion, that the confession was made so as to be understood and misconstrued by his bitterest enemies. Many a cry has ascended from the depths of earthly sorrow to the throne of God, but never one so ardent, so strange, so mysterious, as the one from the cross on Calvary.

Ps. 22, 1

The words correspond exactly to those spoken by David in one of his psalms: "My God, my God, why hast thou forsaken me?" Are we to believe that this saying, in the course of time, had become a familiar and almost meaningless phrase used by the Jews in hours of distress? The Lord was never in the habit of thoughtlessly repeating the sentences of others, least of all on the cross. Was it a prayer or a prayerful application of a Bible passage to his own case? Undoubtedly, he did make the word of God his meat during those three hours when his meditations, instead of going out to other people, dealt with himself and his relation to God. But if the Lord silently prayed a psalm or other portions of Holy Writ, why should he among all passages select for crying out that suspicious prayer which the enemies could readily twist to his disadvantage? Or if he prayed any passages aloud, why should not the Evangelists mention that fact, why should they record only that single outcry so welcome to the foes, so perplexing to the friends of Jesus? Since it was no prayer, was it an involuntary cry of despair, then? The Lord was not delirious, but hung there fully conscious of the approaching end as well as of the purpose for which he had come into that hour. He had spoken of this baptism of blood in terms which revealed his knowledge of the greatness of his task. The nearer he had come to the cross, the clearer stood before him all the details of his sorrows. In Gethsemane he rose from his prayers with the firm resolution of enduring all that might come. Was he so fickle in his convictions, so frail in his courage, that all good resolutions were forgotten and that, at finding the pains severe beyond his expectation, he wailed like a helpless child? That means putting Jesus on the same level with Peter who boasted of his readiness to go into prison and death, but who, at the critical moment, failed and changed his mind. Perhaps, then, if an opportunity of being freed from the cross had been offered, the prophet of Nazareth would have welcomed it! Such theories are at the expense of the Master who thereby is practically placed far below Peter and many other believers who later gladly endured a thousand tortures without despairing of Christ or of God's mercy. That vehement outcry is neither more nor less than a heart-rending lamentation, a direct address to God, in which the sufferer complains of something which has really taken place: he is forsaken by God; an actual separation interferes with the wonted communion between him and the Father.

Forsaken by God! This is strange to hear of him who said, "I and the Father are One; whosoever hath seen me hath seen the Father." Has he discarded the idea of being the Son of God? Does he now admit that he deceived himself and his followers? Then Caiaphas may draw near and listen: was he not right when he said, "This man blasphemeth"? Then the rulers were pious men who justly doubted whether God "will have him." Then Pilate trusted in the only abiding wisdom in the world, when he indifferently asked, "What is Truth?" Then Judas made a mistake with his rash suicide, for he might come now and learn that he was a benefactor of his nation, that he betrayed no innocent blood but helped to rid the country of a dangerous impostor! There is a tremendous amount of humiliating sorrow in the mere fact that Jesus had to open his disconsolate heart in the presence of his foes. How greatly they must have triumphed! And what an enigma must it have been to the dejected friends present on Calvary to hear a lamentation like that!

Let us inquire what it was that induced Jesus to make the statement of his being forsaken by God. Did he only imagine to be forsaken when in reality God was as near to him as ever? Did the ineffable pains which by that time

pierced his tender body give him the impression that God
had entirely abandoned him into the will of evil men? Did
therefore a feeling of despondency overpower him; did he
momentarily think that all his work was in vain; did he
lose confidence or faith in his own mission? As to his pains
and abandonment: had he not foretold that he should be
delivered unto the Gentiles, signifying thereby what death
he should suffer? Who will believe that Jesus was not able
to meet his death as bravely as any hero or martyr? And
as to his momentary doubt: how weak in faith would it
reveal him to us! Why must pain and misery necessarily
lead away from God? How often are his visitations the
means of drawing the heart closer to him! Never can we
imagine Jesus so superficial as to teach faith and endurance
to others while he fails just in that respect at the first severe
trial. Nor can we think of him as having been so selfish
that he rejoiced in God only in days of prosperity, at the first
adversity losing all hope, complaining of being left alone by
God! Or were the profound sorrows of his heart the circumstance which made Jesus think that he was forsaken?
How bitter was that ingratitude and unbelief which led the
people to reject and crucify him; how deep was the grief
caused him by the unrelenting mockery of priests and
people; must he not gain the discouraging conviction that
his work will be appreciated by only a few, that he cannot
hope to save many with all his sorrows? Such thoughts,
however, would just point out his being conscious of his
high mission and of the fact that, after all, some precious
souls would be his reward. It is inexplicable how, with
such thoughts of the future, he could call himself forsaken
of God. Again, the fear of death has been suggested. Since
death is the wages of sin, we may justly speak of the
"sting" of death. If this separation of body and soul is
something unnatural in man, how much more unnatural

must it have been in Jesus the perfect man whose entire organization was the expression of highest life. And not only his human side, but also his divine powers had to succumb to death: may he not have been afraid of such transformation? But Jesus had frequently predicted that he must die, and that through death he was going to the Father. With such knowledge he had no reason to complain of being forsaken, he had rather cause to rejoice at the approaching reunion with God. When death actually came to him, there was no fear in him at all, a grand feeling of peace prevailed. In order to obtain the correct view we must bear in mind why Jesus was hanging on the cross. He had taken upon himself the sins of the world, he had come to offer himself as an atoning sacrifice for all. On the one hand, he performed a work on the cross, which called forth the admiration and approbation of the highest heavens. Yet again, the holy God, to whom all sin is an abomination, must withdraw from that Jesus who came burdened with the sins of ages and generations; God could be no longer with him, and where God is not, there hell is. If that part were lacking in Christ's Passion, there would be no atoning sacrifice. For then only the shedding of blood, a few hours of torture, the natural death of a good man, would remain. And then we would have nothing left but the crude idea that pain, blood, and death in themselves can appease an angry God. The sacrifice offered in the temple every day, with the only exception that, instead of a lamb, a man was slaughtered. The eternal value of the Savior's sacrifice, however, consists in the fact that he, in the place of sinners, endured that separation from God which, as the rightful punishment and curse, every sinner himself ought to feel. Even if Christ's being forsaken by God lasted only a few hours, it was nevertheless the real and the greatest part of his Passion, the one which forced the only complaint from him because he could no longer endure the abandonment.

Not an impatient murmur, not a despondent doubt, but a pious inquiry did Jesus send to the throne. "My God, my God," he said, instead of using the familiar "father." As the distance between God and himself grew greater, the sufferer no longer ventured to address the Most High with a term expressive of intimate communion and oneness of nature. He felt that awe which overpowers every sinner in the presence of the Holy One. Here, it seems, we approach the mystery of mysteries, the real turning point of the Passion, where it must be decided whether Jesus Christ was to succeed in establishing our salvation, or whether he should fail. For if it was possible at all that the Son of God took upon himself our flesh, our trials, our temptations; then this last and greatest temptation must also have been a real one: whether he would declare himself against this mode and extent of punishment, or whether he was willing to be submissive to the last. Jesus came forth victorious. Even the withdrawing God, who would not speak to the Son when some assurance was needed most, was still eminently "his" God. This is clear from the two-fold ardent "My God, my God." Jesus has no desire of separating himself from God, has not lost faith in him, has not ceased to love him despite all afflictions. He claims God as his own in the word "my," as if calling after the withdrawing God not to depart too long, not to forget him entirely. He submits an humble question to the God to whom he wants to cling under all circumstances: "Why hast thou forsaken me?" Why! The Lord has searched his life and found no trace of guilt, no just cause in himself why he should be cast off by God. How wonderful a testimony concerning his own conduct, at the moment when he was hanging under the fearful judgment of Jehovah! No act, no word, no thought

of his was wrong; for if he had found but the slightest
transgression, he would have seen cause enough for being
forsaken by the God who hates all unrighteousness. The
Lord has searched the Scriptures without discovering an
answer to his "why." The Old Testament with all its
numerous information concerning the suffering Messiah
failed to describe the pangs of abandonment endured by
Jesus at that time. This particular feature of the Passion
was one hidden from publicity, as it were, until it befell
Christ. It was too high for human mind and language,
wherefore God withheld it even from the prophets. But did
not Jesus remember that he bore the curse of the world, that
he suffered in the place and for the sake of sinners? This
knowledge never forsook him. However, up to these hours
he had pursued his work of mediation with the consent and
the approval of God, in uninterrupted communion with the
Father. Now God ceased speaking to him, seemed to have
become his enemy; why was that necessary? This is what
Jesus wanted to know. It need not surprise us that here
Jesus was confronted with an enigma in the plans of God.
There were other things which the Son did not know, but
the Father only, as Jesus himself said: "But of that day and   Mark. 13, 32
that hour knoweth no man, no, not the angels which are in
heaven, neither the Son, but the Father." Thus we find
the forsaken Jesus in the act of learning that pleasing
obedience for which God has given him a name above every
name: "He humbled himself, and became obedient unto   Phil. 2, 8, 9
death, even the death of the cross. Wherefore God also hath
highly exalted him." Obedient unto death in its most repulsive form; not only to the moment of ascending the cross,
but to the last, in all temptations that might, in those hours,
try his obedience: "Though he were a Son, yet learned he   Heb. 5, 8
obedience by the things which he suffered." In such obedience Jesus declared his willingness to endure the greatest

tortures, even the separation from God, if he was but told
the reason why it must be so. And his God did tell him
by returning in kindness to him who was obedient unto
death.

During the hours of darkness deep silence had reigned
not only on the crosses, but also among the spectators. Their
lips may have been sealed by a superstitious fear that something unforeseen might happen at any moment. But as
no divine interference was noticed and the people began
to be accustomed to the darkness, they regained their levity,
and large numbers of people returned from the city. The
Lord's outcry took away their last fears. God had forsaken
him! "And some of them that stood by, when they heard it,
said, Behold, this man calleth for Elias." Who were these
revilers? The Roman soldiers were not acquainted with
the Jewish hopes concerning Elias. Illiterate Jews standing
near would not so quickly select theological subjects for
their ridicule. We surmise that "some" rulers or their
deputies had been present all the time and now were
speaking. Taking up the words "Eli, Eli," they explained
them as a cry for "Elias." Did they misunderstand Jesus?
That cannot be, for they "stood by," not far off; and the
Lord cried "with a loud voice"; and "they heard it" plainly.
It was a malicious twisting of the words. It may appear
strange that they did not use the entire sentence as it was
uttered, in order to mock the Lord. What greater satisfaction could they have than the knowledge that Jesus admitted his being forsaken by God! What a relief for them
to learn that they had committed no crime against God
and that the darkness, instead of threatening the people,
was directed against the blasphemer on the cross! Observ-
ing their mockery closely, we perceive that they indeed
used the entire sentence, but in their own effective way.
They had well understood that ardent address, "My God,

my God"; they did not relish the idea of this man speaking of or to "his" God. Whatever effect those solemn words may have had on the people must be jested away. Forsaken? That must be taken for granted! What can God do but forsake one like that Jesus? It was not God at all whom he called, but simply Elias. Failing to find mercy or help with God himself, he has tried his luck in another direction: perhaps Elias may be willing to come and assist him. The Jewish expectation was, and still is, that the prophet Elias should usher in the kingdom of God, that he should come as a precursor and herald of the Messiah. This belief was shared by the rulers, as we learn from the question of the disciples: "Why then say the scribes that Elias must first come?" That story was based on a prophecy of Malachi: "Behold, I will send you Elijah the prophet before the coming of the great and dreadful day of the Lord." What kind of Messiah must this Jesus be that he is compelled to cry for assistance; instead of Elias crowning him or announcing him to the nation, he is piteously called to console the crucified Messiah! He who claimed to be the great helper implores his servant for help. What further demonstrations are needed to prove that this Jesus cannot be the Messiah, much less the Son of God? Indeed, most effectively was the Messiah thus held up to ridicule.

Matt. 17, 10

Mal. 4, 5

Derisive laughter took the place of angelic hallelujahs as the captain of our salvation stepped forth victorious from the greatest battle; insulting shouts formed the farewell greeting to him who now draws near the open gates of death.

63. THE LAST REQUEST

Matt. 27, 48, 49   **Mark 15, 36**
John 19, 28, 29

"After this, Jesus knowing that all things
were now accomplished, that the Scripture might
be fulfilled, saith, I thirst. Now there was set
a vessel full of vinegar: and they filled a sponge
with vinegar, and put it upon hyssop, and put it
to his mouth. The rest said, Let be, let us see
whether Elias will come and save him. And
straightway one of them ran and filled a sponge
full of vinegar, and put it on a reed, and gave
him to drink, saying, Let alone; let us see whether
Elias will come to take him down."

———

With the disappearing darkness the night of agony in
the Savior's heart also passed away. The bright sun was
shining again above and within him. The profound peace
now pervading the sufferer is noticeable in the precious word
before us. "After this, Jesus knowing that all things were
now accomplished, that the Scripture might be fulfilled,
saith, I thirst." A while ago he was in ignorance of that
particular feature of his Passion, he was forced to send up
an inquiring Why. But "after this" dreary hour, the
familiar expression of Jesus "knowing" all things indicates
that God had answered his question and had given him light.
When going to the cross the Savior "knew" all that should
befall him, and when the parting hour from cross and
life arrived, he again "knew" all about what he had suffered.

(138)

What did he, in that respect, know? To answer this question we must inquire as to the purpose for which he uttered the complaint "I thirst."

Some hold that the Lord complained of thirst with the intention of fulfilling one Scripture passage hitherto neglected. Whether or not he actually suffered thirst, he spoke the word in order "that the Scripture might be fulfilled" in that specific detail. The passage is thought to be the following: "They gave me also gall for my meat; and in my thirst they gave me vinegar to drink"; or also this one: "My strength is dried up like a potsherd; and my tongue cleaveth to my jaws." While Caiaphas and the whole Sanhedrin, Pilate and his soldiers, the mocking multitudes and the enemies in general, fulfilled the Scriptures unconsciously, without intending or knowing their action to be part of a definite divine plan; Jesus always acted and spoke not only with a heart willing to perform God's service, but also knowing just which Scripture he had fulfilled, and which passage was next to be fulfilled by him. God spoke to Jesus not only directly in him through intimate communion, but also indirectly through the Old Testament; and Jesus, ever alert and obedient, conducted himself in a manner that no detail of the program outlined to him was overlooked. There is certainly much truth in this view. But however attractive it may be, and no matter how much it glorifies the Lord, our text furnishes no basis for it. We are told that Jesus knew "that all things were now accomplished": was he mistaken in his knowledge? Did he suddenly remember that one passage was yet to be fulfilled, and did he hasten to do so? And, in addition, the passages adduced are only analogous, not prophetic. In that of the twenty-second psalm nothing is said about the suffering Messiah asking for relief in his weakened condition; and that of the sixty-ninth psalm, whilst it also

Ps. 69, 22

Ps. 22, 15

fails to state that the sufferer asked for the vinegar, speaks
of gall, which was not given to the thirsting Jesus.   The
Lord complained of thirst because he knew that all things
were fulfilled; had he not been certain of the fact, he would
not, or not yet, have uttered that complaint.

The "knowing" of Jesus, therefore, included a two-fold
condition: that all things were accomplished; and that all
things had been accomplished in the most perfect manner,
just as the Scriptures had predicted and desired.   But how
could Jesus think that "all things" were ended, when there
was yet so much before him?   Did he think of his work
on earth in general?   His death and his resurrection were
an important part of that work and had yet to be done.
Did he think of his pains and sorrows?   They were by no
means past, for he was just complaining of intense thirst,
and the vinegar was not given him without some bitter
mockery.   No doubt, the Lord thought of the work of salvation in which he was engaged.   Though "all things" per-
taining to the full salvation of mankind were not completed
until he had actually died, and risen, and ascended to the
right hand of God; yet "all things" connected with the
atoning sacrifice, with the suffering Redeemer, were finished.
Death itself was no torture to him, but rather the welcome
return to the Father.   The remaining pains of the body
and the final mockery had lost their bitterness since the
peace of God and the light of heaven re-entered his soul.
The great High priest of our souls has accomplished his
eternal sacrifice, he is ready to leave the altar.   Those things
that are yet to be done are but the consequences, the glorious
fruits of the glorious work accomplished.   And how did
that sacrificial work glorify the Savior!   He had done it so
"that the Scripture might be fulfilled" in every respect.
All things had come and gone according to the prophecies
of the Scriptures.   God had done his part by directing men

and events to submit to his plans; and Christ on his part had acted so that not a single trait, or sorrow, or duty of the suffering Messiah, as foretold in Holy Writ, had been avoided or neglected. If the Lord had to do the same work over, he could not improve on it. In that knowledge the Savior had a cause for holy self-congratulation, a source of satisfaction in a work done well in his own judgment as in the judgment of God who spoke through the prophets. As the Lord Creator, when the world was just created, "saw everything that he had made, and, behold, it was very good"; Gen. 1, 31 so the Lord Redeemer, having just redeemed the world, saw everything that he had made, and, behold, it was very good. That knowledge of Jesus was of exceptional grandeur because he possessed it under such adverse circumstances. All Jerusalem believed that he was lost, his work destroyed, his name blotted from the pages of history. At the same time, in the presence of his mocking foes, he knew that the opposite was true, that not he but Israel was weighed in the balances, and was found wanting. For we must not forget to look at the reverse side of that expression, "the Scripture was fulfilled." It shows how positively the Savior regarded the Old Testament as the Word of God, and how diligently he had obeyed its precepts; in the measure in which he had honored that Word, the Jews were guilty of transgressing the same. It declares that Jesus had not invented a new plan, had not followed his own ideas, when he came to save the world, but in all respects carried out the will of God; and as much as he had glorified the Father, so much had the Jews despised and insulted their God. If the Scriptures were fulfilled, then the mission of Israel is also fulfilled. They may still hold the Word of God in their hands; but when they read of their expected Messiah, they have no longer any foundation for their hope. If the Scriptures concerning the suffering Messiah are fulfilled, then the

iniquities, the crimes causing his sorrows, are also "fulfilled"; and if the Jews still read the Word of God, they
can appropriate only the threats and curses contained in it
against those who rejected the Messiah.

The knowledge that his work was ended and that the
Scriptures were fulfilled, was very pointed and specific.
All things were "now," literally, "already" accomplished.
Sooner than the Lord had expected, the end drew near. It
was very unusual that crucified persons died after six hours,
while it was not infrequent that they suffered for days, and
starving to death. The Lord knew that he was not to
linger days, or but several hours longer, but that death was
to relieve him after a few short minutes. His "already,"
apparently a surprise to the Sufferer himself, gives us an
insight into the anxiety of that time when he was forsaken
by God. So fearful were those moments, so endless did
they seem to him, that he dreaded further unknown and
prolonged tortures. That "already" illustrates the quick
and comprehensive reply of God to the inquiring "Why"
of his Son. The inexplicable and intolerable abandonment was the last and lowest degree of his abandonment;
the unexpected though necessary test to prove his submis-
sion a real obedience; the acme of pain, penetrating his
entire human nature, and the remotest recesses of his divine
nature, rendering his sufferings a genuine sacrifice in every
respect. With that unforeseen ordeal successfully passed
divine justice was satisfied; the work was finished, the victory won.

As soon as Jesus knew, and just because he knew, that
his task was finished, that he had performed his duty faithfully, he said, "I thirst." There was true heroism in the fact
that he had waited so long with this complaint. Burning,
insatiable thirst, was one of the most dreadful tortures

tormenting crucified persons. It was so agonizing that even the barbaric judges and executioners recognized the need of taking vinegar along to quench the thirst of their victims from time to time. It is not surprising, then, that Jesus complained of thirst. The last refreshment coming over his lips was the wine at the passover meal the previous evening. After that meal he had spoken his long farewell address to the disciples, had spoken much on the way to Gethsamene, had prayed in the garden, was led before Annas and Caiaphas and Pilate, was granted no rest, was maltreated often and severely. He had refused the stupefying drink before the crucifixion, and the soldiers had aggravated the feeling of thirst by holding up the cup without giving him to drink. During all these hours the Lord was left without the least refreshing draught, yet he paid little attention to his physical pains. He took no time, as it were, to think of the needs of his body during the ardent task of interceding for the human race. Now, after the victory was assured, he said, "I thirst." The cry, "My God, my God, why hast thou forsaken me," marked the climax of his soul's anguish which he had silently borne until its intense force broke forth into an outcry; and this present request marked the culmination of his physical pains which hitherto he had also borne without a complaint. This fifth word differs decidedly from the fourth in that it was no cry of despair; it was not spoken exceptionally loud, he simply "saith," I thirst. It was more a quiet request rather than a vehement complaint. Without speaking to any persons directly, giving all bystanders a chance to serve him, he submitted his request trusting that somebody would be willing to wait on him. And if those spectators had but known what Jesus in that moment had done for mankind, whether they would not all have hastened to assure him of their love and gratitude?

As it was, we discover also a fine heroism in the fact that he condescended to ask a favor of those people. How contemptuously had these soldiers treated him in Pilate's hall and on Calvary; how bitter was the hatred of the Jews to pursue him with heartless mockery to the brink of death! How easily could they refuse him even that small favor, or use his request for further mockery. With a magnanimous confidence did he make known his wish appealing, as it were, to the good traits left in his enemies, convinced that someone would be ready to serve him: a kind of prophecy that in the future, no matter how godless the masses are, persons may be expected to be found willing to listen to his word, ready to be at his command.

That last request has a still deeper significance. Why should Jesus ask for a refreshment at all since he knew that death could be expected momentarily? If he had so desired, he could have suppressed his thirst a few minutes longer. Did he aim to furnish an example of ingratitude: for his wonderful love and exertion the world has nothing but vinegar to offer him? The Lord, who would not forget the cup of water given in his name, certainly also appreciated the drink of vinegar proffered here. Or did he wish to revive his powers, to strengthen the forces of life, in order to impress the enemies so much the more with his quick, unexpected departure? A few drops of vinegar are not effective enough to prolong the life of one so near dissolution as the Lord was. Or was the refreshing drink to keep him from falling into unconsciousness? That was unnecessary, as the Lord hung there "knowing" all things; his mind was clear in every respect. Or did he indicate no bodily thirst at all, rather signifying a spiritual thirst: that his soul thirsted for the living God, that his loving heart thirsted for the souls of men? No doubt, a fervent yearning like that was always in him, but here he did not speak of it. That the bystanders correctly understood his word as referring to natural thirst is clear from the circumstance that the Lord actually accepted the vinegar, while he would have refused it had he meant a spiritual thirst. The last request rather proves that the pains of his body were real, and that he felt them as such. When we speak of the more important sorrows of his soul, we must not overlook the intense sufferings of his body. His divine nature was not confined in a thin, unreal, ethereal form resembling that of mortal man, but he lived in a real body of flesh and blood. And Jesus with all his fine self-possession did not want to be an unfeeling stoic who proudly despised the claims of human nature. That request serves as our example; in sickness and affliction we are entitled to use the means ordained by God to alleviate pains and refresh our failing body. Thus the object for asking to drink was simply to overcome the annoying thirst so as not to disturb the last few moments of his communion with God. But just because that mere human desire was not suppressed, the incident tells us so much. How easily could the maltreatment and mockeries have the effect of embittering Jesus, filling his heart with disgust and with the resolution to suffer all tortures with sealed lips rather than asking a favor of his foes. But he did not die as a misanthrope or as a pessimist who despised man and the world in general. He did not depart with silent contempt in his heart. Much more difficult than showing favors to the enemy is the asking and accepting of favors from the enemy. Thus the request reveals the sum total of kindness dwelling in Jesus. He has forgiven them the offenses and crimes against his person; they also shall have a parting word of good will. It is the crowning act, the final testament of that yearning love which, though wounded, unappreciated, and ill rewarded, yet "beareth all things, believeth all things, hopeth all things, endureth all things."

The Lord did not ask in vain, his feeble words were heard. "Now there was set a vessel full of vinegar: and they filled a sponge with vinegar, and put it upon hyssop, and put it to his mouth. The rest said, Let be, let us see whether Elias will come to save him." The guards had made the customary preparations occasionally to give drink to the three crucified men. An earthen "vessel" was set near the cross, ready for use. It was not the same vessel from which the soldiers drank, but one especially placed there for the crucified ones. It contained "vinegar," or sour wine, as the beverage best adapted to quench the thirst. That vinegar was not the "wine mingled with myrrh" offered to Jesus at the beginning and refused by him. It was of the same quality as the soldiers' wine. The guards were wont to take their meals along, for the watch at the cross might be a protracted one; and their regular fare included a quantity of sour wine, the kind they had mockingly offered to Jesus during the derision without giving it to him. The vessel was "full" of vinegar. If one vessel was assigned to each cross, that near the Lord's was naturally still untouched, and the quantity left indicates the greatness of the thirst and the length of time for which the soldiers had prepared themselves. A plurality of vessels may be assumed, because later one of the men "ran" to fill a sponge somewhere else. Or if but one vessel was provided for the three crosses, it had been refilled. It is but natural to assume that the two malefactors had repeatedly been given to drink, and then the vessel could no longer be "full" without its contents having been replenished. In this case again we would have a sign of the extent of the Lord's heroic abstinence. To the vessel belonged a sponge and a short rod, a reed of "hyssop." On the mountains about Jerusalem hyssop shrubs were plentiful, furnishing stems a foot or a foot and a half long; though at first thin and flexible, those stems hardened with age and were then strong enough to support a wet sponge. No great length of the rod was required since Jesus hung only a few feet above the ground.

The only way in which a crucified person was enabled to drink was by having held a saturated sponge to his lips. This they attempted to do but apparently were interrupted. "And they filled a sponge with vinegar, and put it upon hyssop, and put it to his mouth. The rest said, Let be, let us see whether Elias will come to save him." Who were "they" so willing to help, and who "the rest" objecting to it? Nobody among the Jews was willing to defile himself by handling any of the tools used in the crucifixion, even if one or the other had been ready to comply with the Lord's request: And no volunteer would have been permitted to render the service, for the Roman soldiers were the appointed executioners on whom that duty devolved. The soldiers simply did what they were bound to do, when they saturated the sponge and put it upon the reed. Though at first all four may have gone to the vessel, they were not all needed in that simple operation of handling rod and sponge. Probably only two stepped at last up to the cross, one holding the sponge to the Lord's lips. But they were demanded to desist with a quick "Let be" of the others. We observe that the soldiers were not told to stop as soon as they took hold of reed and sponge, nor when they stepped towards the crosses. If the drink had been intended for one of the malefactors, there would have been no objection raised. But when it was seen that the sponge was put to the Lord's mouth, then the others interfered. This may mean that "the rest" had not heard the Savior's request, as it had been uttered with a feeble voice, and that therefore the spectators did not until then know who was to get the vinegar; or, again, they may have taken for granted that the soldiers would refuse to wait on the Nazarene. However, the expression "the rest" signifies that no "multitudes" stood very near; "the rest" was somehow connected with the four soldiers: the rest stood in close proximity to the guards and to the crosses. Then "the rest," like the soldiers themselves, must have heard and understood the words of Jesus. And as the soldiers must be expected to perform faithfully the duties for which they were stationed there, the spectators cannot have been surprised to see them step up to Jesus. Then we discover a deep malice in that delayed objection, an intentional tantalizing of the suffering Lord: Just as the sponge came to his mouth and as he was about to taste the welcome drink, his cruel persecutors spoiled and denied him even that poor favor with their "Let be." Jesus received little or nothing at all of the vinegar. This heartless interruption was justified with the words, "Let us see whether Elias will come and save him." In this mockery we readily recognize "the rest" as the same Jewish persons who shortly before had sneered, "He calleth for Elias." That jest still occupied their minds, and now they were able to put the sharpest sting into it. If the soldiers had not understood the allusion, they were now informed. They should wait in order to give Elias a chance to manifest his interest in the Nazarene. It is implied that Elias was a reality and probably did hear the call for him; but they insist on a proof showing whether he actually "will" come to his aid. If he does come, he himself will give this man to drink or perhaps save him at once from all his troubles;

if he does not come, why should the soldiers exert themselves for one who deserves no favors at all? And the
soldiers? Either they consented at once and turned away,
or they stood undecided, still listening to the arguments of
the inhuman Jews; in either case Jesus had not yet received
the craved drink.

Nevertheless, his request was to be granted in an unexpected manner. "And straightway one of them ran and
filled a sponge full of vinegar, and put it on a reed, and
gave him to drink, saying, Let alone; let us see whether
Elias will come to take him down." This man was "one of
them," one of the soldiers. That he "straightway," instantly
"ran" when he saw his comrades hesitate, shows his firm
determination to accomplish his object. He "ran" some
distance to fill a sponge: his comrades had not thrown theirs
away when the Jews spoke to them, and he could not snatch
it from their hands. Perhaps near one of the other crosses
he found a sponge, and then "ran" to find a reed; he "filled"
it, either from the common vessel that was yet "full," or
from his private portion if the crosses had no separate
vessels. What motives actuated that soldier in his service of
kindness? Did he pity the Lord who by this time had made
some impression on him? It may have been his sense of
duty; or he did not want to be dictated to by the Jews;
but why, then, did he give another excuse when they tried
to hinder him? He was quick about his work; before the
others realized it, he "gave him to drink," not merely putting
the sponge to his mouth, but actually seeing that Jesus did
get the vinegar. That the bystanders sought to dissuade
him, is clear from his reply, "Let alone," "let me have my
way," assigning this reason for his act: "Let us see whether
Elias will come to take him down." He argued that by pro-
longing and strengthening the life of Jesus, Elias had a

better chance to show his power, for he will not take down a dead man. Elias is able to manifest his interest in other ways than by merely giving him to drink; at any rate, even if they want to wait for Elias, there is no reason why the vinegar should not now be given to the sufferer. Was the man in earnest with his arguments? How can a Roman be expected to believe so suddenly in Elias and his office? Did the soldier speak in an angry mood? Then he would simply have pointed to his duty which tolerated no interference from the superstition of the Jews. Or were his words intended as a mockery of Jesus? If he was of the same mind with his comrades, he could have joined them, waiting for Elias without first running about to secure reed and sponge. Did he think that Jesus might momentarily pass away? But why then should he trouble himself in vain for a dying man who a minute later suffered no more from thirst, or how could he believe that a little vinegar would spare Jesus for the indefinite arrival of Elias! We perceive, rather, that the man sought to hide his kindlier feelings under the pretense of joining the mockery of the enemies; he acted as if he believed in the coming of Elias, as if he tried to preserve the sufferer until then. The cruelty of refusing a few refreshing drops to a man in the throes of death, was too much even for that hardened soldier, and he endeavored to be helpful in his own way. Whether the Lord, always so gratefully acknowledging the least favor, rewarded this last kind service? Whether that momentary burst of natural goodness developed into a nobler virtue? Whether in his later life this soldier sometimes thought of the dying Jesus, and perhaps learned the truth that the expiring sigh of the Savior was also for his benefit?

A Gentile has rendered the last service to the dying

Lord. Behold a prophecy that henceforth the pagan has some advantage to his credit before the erstwhile chosen people who offer but the gall of mockery. The Gentiles from the East brought gold, frankincense and myrrh to the new-born king; and a gentile soldier from the West brought a few drops of vinegar to the crucified Savior of the World. The Passion of the Lamb has already moved one of the benighted hearts. Now Jesus may die in peace; he takes the assurance along that his work of blood and tears shall not be in vain.

64. IT IS FINISHED

Matt. 27, 50   Luke 23, 46
Mark 15, 37   John 19, 30

"When Jesus therefore had received the
vinegar, he said, It is finished. And when Jesus
had cried again with a loud voice, he said, Father,
into thy hands I commend my spirit: and having
said thus, he bowed his head, and gave up the
ghost."

The solemn moment when death was to swallow up
Him who was and gave life, had arrived. Three Evangelists state that Jesus departed after having uttered a loud
cry, a great voice. Ordinarily, a crucified person at the
point of death could speak only in whispers, for the strength
of the body was completely exhausted by the many prolonged tortures. That the loud cry was quite unusual, is
attested by the centurion upon whom it made a profound im-
Mark 15, 39 pression: "When the centurion, which stood over against
him, saw that he had cried out, and gave up the ghost, he
said, Truly this man was the son of God." The forceful
cry, then, would indicate that the Lord's vitality was not reduced to its lowest minimum; but how does that agree with
the fact that immediately thereafter, he died of weakness
and exhaustion due to the crucifixion? We may assume
that in the cry all his remaining strength was gathered and
now left him at once. Through all these hours the Lord had
exerted his will-power to an eminent degree, for the purpose of enduring everything in perfect consciousness, with
submissive patience, and in strict obedience. Now all was
ended, he knew that the Father wanted him to return
home; therefore he relaxed his will-power, he was ready to

(152)

go, and with this yielding of the will the remaining strength of the body also relaxed, or, rather, was consumed in the cry. This implies a twofold truth: that, if Jesus had so willed, he could have lived on the cross for hours to come, in which statement there is nothing strange if we bear in mind the effect of will-power in other cases of sickness; and, again, that the Lord did not merely suffer death, but actually gave his consent to die, permitting death to come near. Even as he deliberately yielded his spirit into the hand of God with the thought of taking it again, so he deliberately yielded his body into the power of death with the intention of reclaiming it. Exactly such perfect control over his body and life, such sovereign authority of disposal, was avowed by him as a special decree of the Father: "I lay down my life, that John 10, 17, 18 I might take it again. No man taketh it from me, but I lay it down of myself. I have power to lay it down, and I have power to take it again. This commandment have I received from my Father." This applies not only to his free will ascending the cross, but equally to his descending from the accursed tree.

Twice the crucified Lord cried or spoke exceptionally loud. The first instance was when with a loud voice he inquired why God had forsaken him; after that he cried "again." Does this "again" refer to the sixth word or to the seventh? Or was it a separate outcry? There is no occasion and no reason for a cry independent from the last two words. After he had commanded his spirit to God "he breathed out" his spirit, and in such condition no outcry can be expected. And why should there have been a cry between the words, a cry of pain or despair, when he knew that all was finished? Immediately after receiving the vinegar he announced that all was finished, which leaves no space for a special outcry before the sixth word. That loud voice necessarily belongs to one of the words, but to which one? Luke may be claimed as stating, "And Jesus cried with a loud voice, saying, Father, into thy hands I commend my spirit"; but several considerations induce us to reject that translation. At the very point of death, when the eyes begin to close and the head droops, a man does not utter an entire sentence, a whole prayer, with a great voice; at that moment the peace of God and the calm of death have quieted the troubled heart and relegated to the rear all earthly considerations. Again, why should he specially inform the spectators with a loud cry that he went to the Father? He had told them often enough, and Easter would demonstrate in a much more effective manner than words could do that such was the case. This prayer concerned Jesus exclusively, it was his own private affair. In the plan of salvation the believer asks or needs no extra emphasis on the assurance that the Son of God, after accomplishing our salvation, returned to the Father. It would be strange indeed, if the last word had been spoken in a loud voice, and the short, victorious "It is finished" in soft or, at least, ordinary tones. That sixth word contains the wondrous fact which was to be impressed forever on the mind of men: that all was finished despite the discouraging surroundings on Calvary, despite all opposition of the unbelievers, despite the doubts of frightened sinners. Heaven and earth must hear the voice of victory. But perhaps both the last words were spoken unusually loud? We cannot circumvent the arguments given before and, besides, such continuous shouting not only appears out of place in that dying scene, but detracts from the emphasis which ought to distinguish the "It is finished." Therefore we return to the translation adopted by the English version: "When Jesus had cried with a loud voice, he said, Father, into thy hands I commend my spirit," and refer the "had cried" with Matthew's "when

he had cried again with a loud voice" to the sixth word.
"When Jesus therefore had received the vinegar, he—cried
again with a loud voice and—said, It is finished." Though
John uses the plain "said," he does not thereby contradict
the "loud voice," for he also mentions that Jesus had received the vinegar; the speaking was now easier and at
once louder than when the "I thirst" was said with parched
lips. After the drink the Lord was able to lift up a great
voice.

 "It is finished." What did this short utterance, which
in the original consist of but one word, intend to convey to
the hearer? Of course, it was no cry of disappointment
1. and despair, as if Jesus realized now the vanity of his hopes,
the futility of his efforts, the failure of his life. A dis-
illusioned dreamer would have reached this conviction
earlier in the hour of trial, and then he would not shout his
defeat into the world, and at last would not so peacefully
2. commune with God. Nor was it a sigh of relief or a forced
resignation to his inevitable fate. For in that case he would
have deceived himself, because then not all was finished: the
fate of his soul was not decided; and Jesus was no infidel
to consider the committing of his soul as a matter of small
3. import. It was the joyful announcement of his victory.
Which part of his victory gave him so much joy that he had
to publish it with a loud voice? That now all the pains and
sorrows of the crucifixion were ended, was indeed a cause
for joy; but if his followers are exhorted to "count it all James 1, 2
joy when ye fall into divers temptation," he would have been
very superficial to think so little of his trials as to exult in
his release exclusively. Did he rejoice that now the poverty, the disgrace, the hardships and humiliations of his
entire life were a thing of the past? But the days of his
flesh were also filled with precious experiences and noble

blessings which forbade any contempt for his earthly existence. When he thought of his years on earth he did it with the gratifying knowledge of having done his full duty, and that was a better cause for rejoicing than his mere departure.   Or was he so glad because his sufferings were ended so unexpectedly soon, because his return home to the Father came earlier than he thought and death was his gain in this and many another sense? So selfish all at once, he who always had the interests of others at heart? Did he not, at least, pity his friends who still remained in this evil world? The loudly and joyfully spoken word of triumph expressed above all his satisfaction that something had been accomplished for the world. The work of atonement was finished, the salvation of souls established. Now he together with his friends could be of good cheer, for he had truly overcome the world.

"It is finished."   A while ago already Jesus was "knowing that all things were now accomplished." The knowledge of his heart was now published to friend and foe. There is no difference between "all things" that were accomplished, and the "It" that was finished. The Lord had surveyed, as it were, the whole field of prophecy, comparing the Word of God with his accomplished task; and all the different things suffered and done by him constituted the great "It," the wonderful Atonement in which he now rejoiced for the sake of redeemed sinners. The Lord did not describe that which he had finished, but simply said, "It." Thereby he indicated that the serious inquirer cannot fail to explain that "It" correctly; there is but one thing finished and that one is the only work for the sake of which he had gone to the cross: the salvation of mankind. It was no inopportune modesty that kept Jesus from describing his glorious work; the plain "finished" was rather an invita-

tion to study what that one word implied. The foes may
compare that word with what they saw and heard in those
hours, and decide in their hearts whether they really
"finished" the career of a blasphemer. The friends of
Jesus may take the word to search the depth of mercy, love,
and life, included in it. Besides its own eternal and surpassing value, the work of atonement carried many other
things with it that also were finished. It attests the truth-
fulness of Jesus. It was no mere afterthought when he
knew that the Scriptures were fulfilled; he had repeated
those prophecies and made them his own. Thus in regard
to his entire Passion: "Then he took unto him the twelve,
and said unto them, Behold, we go up to Jerusalem, and all Luke 18,
31-33
things that are written by the prophets concerning the Son
of Man shall be accomplished. For he shall be delivered
unto the Gentiles, and shall be mocked, and spitefully entreated, and spitted on: and they shall scourge him, and
put him to death." Exactly as he said, so it is finished, and
his friends may find a rich consolation in that fact. He also
appropriated the prophecy concerning the betrayer: "I
speak not of you all: I know whom I have chosen: but that John 19, 18
the Scripture may be fulfilled, he that eateth with me hath
lifted up his heel against me." This also was literally finished, together with the many crimes committed against
him by the accomplices of the betrayer. How can the friends
lose hope when they remember that he said: "Now I tell
you before it come, that, when it is come to pass, ye may John 19, 19
believe that I am he." When he was arrested he said to
Peter and to his captors that the powers of darkness had to
have their way as to the enemies and Jesus himself, nobody
else to be included, that "the Scriptures of the prophets Matt. 26,
54-56
might be fulfilled." And literally so was it finished: the
captors failed to apprehend the disciples, and Peter's good

resolutions to die with him failed, Jesus was crucified alone; the fear of the rulers that an uprising might occur and Jesus be liberated, was in vain, for Jesus had predicted a different end; the efforts of Pilate to set him free after scourging him or by presenting him together with Barabbas, proved futile. All events came and went and were now finished, as Jesus had foretold. Finished was the entire task of his life for which he had come into the world and to which

John 4, 34

he had devoted all his energies: "My meat is to do the will of him that sent me, and to finish his work." The moment has come when the work is completed in every detail to the full satisfaction of God himself, as the Son anticipated the

John 17, 4, 5

evening before: "I have glorified thee on the earth: I have finished the work which thou gavest me to do. And now, O Father, glorify thou me."

"It is finished." Not only was the work ended, but it was successfully ended, just as it ought to be done in order to fulfill the purpose for which it was undertaken. Death often leaves some things undone and others only half finished. Nothing was missing or incomplete in the work of the Savior, it had been well planned and well carried out. By removing the controlling brain and hand, death frequently threatens a well begun enterprise with swift failure, or suddenly destroys the foundation on which some great work rests. The work of Calvary was finished for all ages to come. It cannot be destroyed, it cannot be improved, it cannot be exhausted, it cannot acquire a different value in future progress. The Redemption of a sinful world is forever complete and unique in itself; it is simply and in all respects "finished."

"It is finished." That is true, although the exalted Jesus continues to be the High priest of the souls, who intercedes in our behalf at the throne of God. Whatever he dis-

tributes of pardon, of blessings, of eternal life, is taken
from the unfathomable ocean, from the unceasingly flowing
fountain opened on Calvary. It is finished what mankind
sought but never found of themselves, what no philanthro-
pist or philosopher could supply, for which there is no substitute in the wide world: peace to the quiet heart, a balm
to heal every wound, a salvation to satisfy every soul. "It
is finished," though not comprehended. Forever will this
word remain the brightest star to shine upon our night. Its
pleasant light consoles and guides us and makes us stand in
awe at the immense distance from which the light comes;
but the star itself with its treasures of another world can
never be searched by the wisdom of this earth. It is the
store-house of divine things and mysteries which even "the
angels desire to look into."

1 Pet. 1, 12

Since Jesus had finished his task, there was no necessity why he should suffer any longer. He had not come
into the world with the time of his stay specified to the
minute, that so many years and days and hours he was
obliged to remain in humiliation. He rather came with a
work set before him, and when that work was completed
he was free to go. Now he returns from the journey in this
foreign land here below to his proper world and sphere on
high. He knocks at the gate of his celestial home with the
last of his seven words: "He said, Father, into thy hands
I commend my spirit." Let us not pass unheeded the circumstance that this and no other word was the last, and
that he spoke it neither too soon nor too late. When a
genuine believer suddenly sees himself in the presence of
death, when he is convinced that recovery is impossible,
this his life is counted only by the hour, then his first
thought is of his soul and of his God; he will not put it off,
for he knows not how soon he has to appear before God, or

whether he will remain conscious to the end to say his prayers. The history of the martyrs relates many instances of believers who, as soon as they were arrested and led forth, gave expression to their confidence of going to their glorified Lord; that knowledge was their joy during the imprisonment and in the hour of torture. How much greater was Jesus even in that respect! During those six hours he had thought of his enemies, of repentant sinners, of his friends, of the peculiar sorrows of his soul, of the pains of his body, of the Scriptures, of his work, and not until now did he think of his state after death. That shows that he came to the cross with ideas different from mere thinking of his going home; it shows that he knew he would remain conscious to the end; it shows that, first of all, he thought of the work assigned to him. And when at last he spoke of his going home, it was not too late; death did not interrupt his last sentence, did not cloud his mind; he had time to utter a complete, clear sentence full of meaning; and what he said, was not a plea for mercy, a prayer to make his peace with God: it was the word of one having authority to return to God: "Father, into thy hands I commend my spirit."

This word is full of Biblical language and thought. David in the adversities of his flight from Absalom sought refuge with the Most High: "Into thine hand I commit my spirit." The Preacher knew that when the golden bowl of life is broken "the spirit shall return unto God who gave it." Did the Lord, in saying his last work, think of those two passages? If he did, then we have here the most striking illustration of the Lord's vast knowledge of the Scriptures. What manner of man is this, whom no Bible Society furnished a copy of the Old Testament, who perhaps never owned a single book, who nevertheless was so well versed in Holy Writ that not only at the high noon of

Ps. 31, 5

Eccl. 12, 7

his ministry he could instantly quote, explain and apply
the most fitting passage under any circumstance; but who
also, when hanging weary and exhausted over the brink of
death, with his life swiftly ebbing away, still retained and
used that knowledge, that almost involuntarily the words
and thoughts of the Bible occurred to him! Nothing else
reveals better the fact that he lived, and moved, and had his
being in God, that he uttered a fundamental truth of his
nature when he said, "Man shall live by every word that Matt. 4, 4
proceedeth out of the mouth of God." Yet, glorious as that
knowledge is, it lags far behind the real glory displayed in
that parting word. If he did think of the passages mentioned, he did not simply repeat and appropriate them, but
vastly transcended them in his own authority, thereby
proving himself in the sublimest sense the Master and Lord
of the Scriptures. This is evident from the omissions Jesus
made. The Preacher, before speaking of the spirit's return
to God, says in the first half of the verse: "Then shall the
dust return to the earth as it was." That important and
general truth, which applies to all men without exception,
was not applicable in the Lord's case. He would not and
did not say those words, because he knew that his body
should not become the prey of dust, that it was to be raised
on the third day in a glorified form to be reoccupied by him.
David, after committing his spirit to God, continues in the
same verse: "Thou hast redeemed me, O Lord God of
truth." This blessed consolation, so welcome, so vital to
every believer in the hour of death, was not appropriated by
Jesus. He was in no need of redemption, he stood in no
opposition to the God of truth, for he is The Truth himself.
That the parting Jesus spoke as not even the holiest among
the mortals dare speak, is also clear from the new and exalted meaning which he put into those passages. David

committed his spirit into the hand of God in order to preserve his earthly life in the midst of his enemies, and he rejoiced in God who had preserved him in a thousand dangers.
The Lord uttered no such prayer on the cross; relying on
his own resources he fought the battle, and not until he had
overcome all tribulations did he offer his spirit to God upon
whom he had not called once for help. How proud a declaration that he was in no such need of protection as the strongest man must seek! This all the more, since Jesus did not
give his spirit away to have it preserved for this earthly
life; he rather did so at the moment of stepping into the
other world, into the presence of that God who knows the
secrets of the heart. And again, while The Preacher knows
of a mere return of the spirit to God, and while David
simply asks the protection of God, Jesus uses a term for
which our "commit" or "commend" is far too weak. Literally, he "deposited" his spirit with God, he entrusted it as a
treasure to him with the intention of claiming it again.
His spirit shall not be dissolved and lost in God as the
vapor is in the air, but it shall have a separate existence.
As little as his body was mingled with the dust, so little was
his spirit absorbed by the Spirit of God. We notice that
here in the highest sense Jesus spake as the Son of God to
his Father. And God has restored the precious deposit to
1 Pet. 3, 18, 19 the Son, who was "quickened by the Spirit: by which also
he went and preached unto the spirits in prison."

"Father, into thy hands I commend my spirit." Not
to the hidden God, not to the Holy Judge of the World, but
to his own "Father" did he speak. This going to the Father
John 14, 28 he had announced before: "I go to the Father." The intimate relation between Father and Son was re-established
John 17, 5 now to be exalted into the state of that glory "which I had
with thee before the world was." The first word on the

cross and the last commence with the endearing term "Father"; he left the tree with that divine knowledge with which he ascended it. And more. The first word ever heard of Jesus was when as a boy in the temple he said: "Wist ye not that I must be about my Father's business?" _{Luke 2, 49} And the last word of the Son of man speaks again of and to the "Father." From his earliest days to his dying moments he was faithfully, obediently about his Father's business. His first word and his last join in beautiful harmony and, like a glorious rainbow, connect the beginning and the end of his life, the manger and the cross.

"And having said thus, he bowed his head, and gave up the ghost." Immediately after that last word, the head, hitherto held erect, drooped and fell upon the breast, as if wearily seeking repose or as if beckoning to King Death to draw near to the King of life as a ministering servant. "He gave up the ghost." Under ordinary circumstances "the soul departs" from the body, "the breath goeth forth" in _{Gen. 35, 18} death. Even such men as "laid down" or "have hazarded _{Acts 15, 26} their lives for the name of our Lord Jesus Christ" could not thereby hasten or retard the advent of death. "There is no _{Eccl. 8, 8} man that hath power over the spirit to retain the spirit; neither hath he power in the day of death." With Jesus it was different. He laid down his life with his consent; the spirit was not taken away from him, he "gave up" the ghost voluntarily at the chosen time.

"He gave up the ghost." So soon! It was an extremely rare occurrence that the victim of the cross died within six hours, if it had ever happened at all. Twenty-four and thirty-six hours were the much more general duration. That the early death of Jesus was a great surprise we learn from the centurion and much more from Pilate. When Joseph of Arimathea asked for the body, the governor

Luke 15, 44

would not believe even so prominent a man as Joseph that Jesus had died so soon: "And Pilate marvelled if he were already dead: and calling unto him the centurion, he asked him whether he had been any while dead." Was there a special cause for that premature death? It is not imperative to assume a supernatural interference which shortened the sufferings of the Lord. God did not spare him from being forsaken, from tasting a prolonged anguish of the soul, why should he hasten the end merely to spare him a few more hours of pain? Or did Jesus die of a "broken heart," did the untold sorrows of his soul overwhelm his powers of life? But we would rather have expected that to happen during his cry, "Why hast thou forsaken me"; for afterwards he was quiet and peaceful. Did he die of heart failure; did a blood vessel burst in his heart or head? All such theories are unnecessary, because the natural course of the crucifixion suffices to explain the early end. With his pure life and sinless body Jesus had been a perfectly healthy and strong man. But what had he endured! They had buffeted and beaten him in the priest's palace: Pilate's soldiers had scourged him so that he was unable to carry the cross, how terrible must have been that scourging! He had undergone an exhausting anguish in Gethsemane, had spent a restless night, had been cruelly mocked on the cross, had suffered from thirst, had felt agonies and sorrows of which neither sinner nor saint has a true conception: is it surprising that his body was quickly worn out and that he died sooner than the two malefactors?

The noble heart of Jesus has gone to its rest. The shadows of death have lowered upon the central cross. The High priest has entered the Holy of Holies; the veil before the mercy seat is parted in heaven, and, behold, also on earth.

THE BURIAL

65. THE SIGNS AFTER THE LORD'S DEATH

Matt. 27, 51-53

Mark 15, 38

Luke 23, 45

"And, behold, the veil of the temple was rent in twain in the midst, from the top to the bottom; and the earth did quake, and the rocks rent; and the graves were opened; and many bodies of the saints which slept arose, and came out of the graves after his resurrection, and went into the holy city, and appeared unto many."

When the name Jesus was spoken the very first time on earth, an angelic "behold" called attention to the mysterious and wonderful coming of him who "shall be great, and shall be called the Son of the Highest." When the same Jesus departed from this life, when the rulers believed that they had rendered his name a byword and his memory a curse forever, another "behold" announced that a Great one had died. This "behold" refers not only to the rending of the veil, but introduces the whole series of exceedingly unusual incidents. If we mistake not, three distinct phenomena are recorded: a sign in the world of religion: the rending of the veil; a sign in the kingdom of nature: the earthquake; a sign in the realm of spirits: the resurrection of the saints. The Prophet has hours ago ended his sayings; the Priest has a while ago accomplished his sacrifice; but now the King who rules in the Kingdom of nature, grace, and glory, made

(165)

his entry into the other world. Right at this point it is advisable that the reader decide in his heart what he expects to find in this mysterious record: an integral and literally true part of the Word of God, or something else. If something else, then what? Perhaps an enthusiastic meditation, a parable, an allegory of the Evangelists! But any of these must have a real fact as a basis; what was that fact? And strange, that the authors of the sacred records, who hitherto carefully avoided all allegories and similar pastime, relating only mere facts, should all at once and at the most inopportune time turn fanciful! The gospels were written many years after that Friday. In that length of time the apostles had gone through many sad experiences in their preaching tours, meeting everywhere with unbelief and mockery. Would a sensible man, when writing the source and sum of his teachings, include assertions not strictly true, specially when such statements rendered the account more difficult to believer and unbeliever alike? Or still worse, an invention, a myth is here given. Does one suppose that the Evangelists were so unscrupulous as to deal in direct lies? No; may they not have honestly believed the stories gradually growing up among the Christian people until they accepted and inserted them in good faith? How superficial, how little conscientious were then those writers to accept, without criticism, reports which they could easily verify or disprove. They had been in Jerusalem on that Friday themselves, or had associated with men who were there on that day; even at the time of writing, persons could be found who had been eyewitnesses of the Lord's death, and these Evangelists neglected to inform themselves properly! It is certainly a desperate act to accuse those sober, pious, matter-of-fact men of ignorance and negligence so detrimental to their own gospel and its readers. But the Evangelists may not be the guilty parties at all? Long after their time a translator or copyist—the scapegoat of modern criticism—may have added the account by him believed to be true. But the passage in no respect betrays marks of interpolation. Judging from the language of the passage, which is in the exalted tone of a solemn hymn, the writer must have been an intelligent and truly pious man who had thoroughly entered into the spirit of the gospel. And that same man, after displaying so much understanding, at once reveals a surprising lack of discrimination by putting this account into the wrong place! For it has been observed that an invention of such character would have found a much more fitting and convincing position in the story of the Lord's resurrection. On Easter morn there was a great earthquake, the stone was rolled from the tomb, the Lord arose: how logically the rising of the saints could have been related there! An interpolator would have surely chosen that connection. On our part, we will not let any flimsy tendencies spoil the beauty and profit abounding in this passage which we find a reliable and profound as any portion of Holy Writ. We have in this account one of the most precious gems of the Bible, and all who appreciate its value look with holier emotion and deeper interest upon him who just expired on the cross.

The sign in the world of religion is related in the following words: "And, behold, the veil of the temple was rent in twain in the midst, from the top to the bottom." There were two veils in the temple. One covered the door leading from the court into the holy place. If this veil, which could be seen by every worshipper, was the one rent, we would understand how the news of the occurrence spread immediately; but we would not comprehend why its tearing should be connected with the death of Jesus so as to see an ill omen in it. That veil was frequently lifted and passed by the priests, and the unfortunate incident could be easily explained or excused. That which gave the temple its dignity and significance, the heart of the whole sanctuary, was the Holy of Holies; and the veil separating this secluded spot from the less holy room in front of it, was preeminently "the" veil of the temple, and the rending of that veil was indeed an evil portent of coming calamity. This inner veil, now rent, used to hide the space where in ancient times stood the ark of the covenant overshadowed by two worshipping cherubim. The holiest room was entirely vacant in the days of Jesus, but still was thought to harbor the presence of God in a peculiar manner. Nobody, not even a priest, was permitted to set foot on that sacred floor, excepting the high priest once a year, on the great Day of Atonement. A more frequent access was already forbidden to Aaron, the first high priest: "And the Lord said unto Moses, Speak unto Aaron thy brother, that he come not at all times into the holy place within the veil before the mercy seat, which is upon the ark; that he die not: for I will appear in the cloud upon the mercy seat." In the same chapter the solemnities preceding and following the singular visit in the Holy of Holies are described. It was only with sacred awe that the people could think and speak of that mysterious veil which was wrought according to directions given by God himself: "And thou shalt make a veil of blue, and purple, and scarlet, and fine twined linen of cunning work: with cherubim shall it be made: and the veil shall divide unto you between the holy place and the most holy." Josephus also gives a description of that precious piece of workmanship: "This house was divided into two parts of which the inner part was lower than the space of the outer, and had golden doors of the altitude of fifty-five cubits by sixteen in breadth. Now before these doors there was a veil of equal size with the doors. It was a Babylonian curtain, embroidered with blue, and fine linen, and scarlet, and pur-

Lev. 16, 2

Exod. 26, 31, 33

B. I. 5, 5, 4

ple, of wonderful texture. The mixture of colors was not without its mystical meaning, but was a sort of image of the universe. The scarlet signified fire; the fine byssus, the earth; the blue, air; and purple, the sea; in two of the four, their colors were considered the point of resemblance; but in the byssus and the purple, their origin was the point, the one being produced by the earth, the other by the sea. The embroidery pictured all that was mystical in the heavens with the exceptions of the twelve signs of the zodiac."

This sacred inner veil "was rent in twain in the midst, from the top to the bottom." The rent was made "in the midst," not from one side to the other, but commencing at "the top" extended clear to the "bottom," as if an invisible hand, reaching down from on high, had done the work. It was not a small fissure somewhere in the fabric, but a complete rending "in twain" in the middle, as if by design, making two equal parts. Through the gap between the torn halves, the interior of the forbidden place was now exposed to full view. What was the immediate cause of that strange rupture? It has been surmised that the veil was very old, and its own weight tore the rotten texture. Though it is too extreme to suppose that, because the rich treasury of the temple permitted such extravagance, the costly curtain was replaced by a new one every year; yet we may be sure that nothing shabby and time-worn was tolerated in that sanctuary. Periodically that veil was renewed and was therefore always in excellent condition. Or had the subsequently related earthquake something to do with it? The strongest seismic shock will split and overthrow the most solid building sooner than tear a loosely hung and yielding veil. But was the temple injured? It has indeed been supposed that the large and heavy lintel spanning the door broke and thus caused the veil to be torn. But if such a calamity had befallen the sanctuary, would not the gospels relate it as even more significant than the destruction of the veil? We must not look for natural causes alone. God's hand was in that act in a direct manner. The high priest had rent his garment when he condemned Jesus for blasphemy; now God rent the veil as a testimony that he was deeply insulted and sinned against by the authorities of the temple.

With his "behold" Matthew does not simply mark the incident as noteworthy and amazing, but also as taking place instantly after the Lord's death. Luke even puts it immediately before the last word of Jesus. This shows that the death of the Lord and the rending of the veil occurred simultaneously, or so close together that it was hard to decide which was first. But that "behold" was not for the spectators on Calvary, who did not then know what at that moment happened in the temple. How was it ascertained that both incidents coincided at the same moment? Did some people hasten towards the city to announce the Lord's death, and others coming from the temple, met them with the news from the sanctuary? But did the common people, or even the priests, know already that the veil was torn? The Lord died at the hour when the evening sacrifice in the temple was being offered. We may not only assume that his duty brought one or the other priest into the holy place, but that the one selected for that day to burn the incense was just engaged in that act which he was permitted to perform only once in his life and which he therefore considered the highest honor; and the ceremony was not a very short one. This priest then stood on the same spot where Zacharias had seen Gabriel, who announced to him the birth of John and the advent of the Messiah. That event was in every respect a joyful and highly honorable revelation; and, moreover, old Zacharias walked "in all the commandments and ordinances of the Lord blameless";

Luke 1, 6, 12

yet despite his good conscience, "when Zacharias saw him, he was troubled, and fear fell upon him." The priest on that Friday, whether or not he favored the Lord's crucifixion, could not so composedly attend to the sacrifice. The events of the night and this day had caused a tremendous excitement in the temple; the darkness cannot have been without some depressing effects upon men. The shock rending rocks must have been felt by him in the temple, and when he saw the parted veil, this most extraordinary sign, fright must have chilled him, may have driven him from the temple at once. The effect of that fright must have been noted by the people who waited for his benediction, and upon inquiry he stated what had happened. Why should he not? The priests may have wished to keep the incident from the people, but could they? The veil had to be quickly repaired, in which case some skilled workmen had to be summoned; or it had to be replaced by a new veil at once, and that meant also heavy work for a number of men. And as to Jesus, nobody in the temple at that moment knew that he had expired and that on this account secrecy ought to be observed. Who was thinking of all that in the excitement of the moment? We discover no reason why the incident should have been hushed until a talkative priest or one of the converted priests informed the followers of Christ, so that only weeks afterwards the two incidents were compared and, with the time computed, were found to have occurred at exactly the same moment. Quite simultaneously, or almost so, the news of the Lord's death and of the torn veil spread; there is nothing to oppose this view.

What must have been the consternation of the rulers when they were apprised of these facts! Jewish tradition knows of some strange incidents happening forty years before the destruction of Jerusalem, that is to say, about the time of the Lord's death. The light on the golden candlestick in the temple was mysteriously extinguished, and the heavy temple gate, of which Josephus says that twenty men could shut it but with difficulty, was seen opening by itself in the hours of night. We do not know whether that transpired at the time of the Lord's death, but the parted veil was ill omen enough. The rulers could not, as in the case of the darkness, misinterpret the meaning of the sign, for it was a glaring profanation of the holiest house, by unusual means, at a significant time. They may have realized that Jesus had uttered no vain threat when he said: "Fearful sights and great signs shall there be from heaven." His word to the Sanhedrin began to be fulfilled: "From now on ye shall see the Son of man coming in the clouds of heaven."

Luke 21, 11

What was the divine message conveyed to the rulers in the sign? First of all it was a threat against the sanctuary itself. If the most holy place is so profaned by God himself, how little must he think of the other parts of the temple. It was an Amen from heaven attesting the truth of Christ's prophecy: "Behold, your house is left unto you desolate." Then that sign was a notification to the high priest that his services were no longer required. The glory of God had forsaken the doomed temple, a hiding veil was henceforth an absurdity. The holy place where the blood of the atonement used to be sprinkled before the Lord, for the sins of the nation, had been vacated by the merciful God, henceforth no pardon need be sought or can be found there. But if this supreme office of the high priest is abolished, all his other duties lose their import. And if the high priest is nothing, then the entire Jewish priesthood with its sacrifices and services has become superfluous. One and all of their ceremonies, prerogatives, and promises, are abolished. Again, since the fundamental and central idea of Jewish worship and religion, the sacrificial idea, is declared

Matt. 23, 38

to have no object and no right to exist any longer, then that religion itself, the entire dispensation of the Old Testament, is superceded. The people who still cling to the old form do so without God's sanction. Here we have, as it were, the official conclusion of the Old Testament. "It is finished." When the high priest rent his garment, he practically tore the ancient covenant that Israel wanted to be the Messiah's people, the chosen nation of God; and he did it in the name of all the Jews. Here, in the rending of the veil, God on his part tore the ancient covenant that he wanted to be, in a peculiar sense, their God. Whereas that happened at the very moment of Christ's death, this death assigned the reason for God's act. The rent veil conveyed the declaration that henceforth the cross is the true altar of God, and the sacrifice of that new altar is that which renders all the sacrifices of the temple without meaning. The place of the human and impious high priest is taken by the holy and divine High priest, by him who said: "I am the way, the truth, the life: no man cometh John 14, 6 unto the Father, but by me." The official recognition and affirmation of that word is given in the temple; the New Testament, privately instituted the evening before, is here publicly inaugurated. Thus through that parted veil the Old goes out and the New comes in.

That portentous change in the religious world was not without its attending solemnities in the kingdom of nature. When the Old Testament was crowned with the giving of the Law, "Mount Sinai was altogether on a smoke, because the Lord descended upon it in fire: and the smoke thereof Exod. 19, 18 ascended as the smoke of a furnace, and the whole mount quaked greatly." And when the inviting gates of the New Testament were thrown open to the world, Mount Calvary also trembled with the powerful interest which nature took in the event. This second sign is related as follows:

"And the earth did quake, and the rocks rent; and the graves were opened." An earthquake took place, which need not have been of a general extent, shaking the entire Asia Minor; it may have been confined to Judea or to Jerusalem and the region round about. Earthquakes cannot have been uncommon in Palestine judging from the exceedingly numerous passages in the prophets and the psalms, which speak of the trembling earth and mountains. Perhaps also volcanic action was not entirely unknown in the land of the ancient Israelites, at least it is now-a-days a widely accepted theory that the Dead Sea, the destruction of Sodom and Gomorrah, was the result of a volcanic catastrophe. The significance consisted in the fact that the shock came at the moment of the Lord's death. The rulers and most of the Jewish people thereby knew that God was present on Calvary: "He looketh on the earth, and it trembleth." God, who had departed from the temple, made his presence known on this hill. And if he "looked," his eye must have rested on the cross. In ancient times the shaking of the earth had been indeed a promise to Israel that the faithful God was near his people: "The earth shook, the heavens also dropped at the presence of God: even Sinai itself was moved at the presence of God, the God of Israel." When he led Israel forth from Egypt "the mountains skipped like rams, and the little hills like lambs." He encouraged his people with the promise, "I will shake the heavens, and the earth, and the sea, and the dry land." But since God has severed his affiliation with the temple and has transferred it to Calvary, to the cross, his promises of mighty protection also must apply to the Man on the cross and to his friends. Therefore we find that when the apostolic congregation "had prayed, the place was shaken where they were assembled together." God assured them of his help in the days of persecution. This divine presence and

Ps. 104, 32

Ps. 68, 8

Ps. 114, 4

Hag. 2, 6

Acts 4, 31

assistance was particularly manifest to two servants of
the crucified Lord: "At midnight Paul and Silas prayed, Acts 16, 25, 26
and sang praises unto God: and the prisoners heard them.
And suddenly there was a great earthquake, so that the
foundations of the prison were shaken: and immediately
all the doors were opened, and everyone's bands were
loosed." With such language in favor of the cross, it is
clear that the wrath and judgment of God, expressed in the
earthquake, must be intended for the enemies of that cross.
When the voice of the distressed saint was heard by God,
"the earth shook and trembled; the foundations also of the Ps. 18, 7
hills moved and were shaken, because he was wroth."
Threatening to destroy Babylon, God says: "I will shake the
heavens, and the earth shall remove out of her place, in the Isa. 13, 13
wrath of the Lord of hosts, and in the day of his fierce
anger." When he judges the land, "The earth shall reel to
and fro like a drunkard, and shall be removed like a cot- Isa. 24, 20
tage." That it will not be different during the reign of
Christ is indicated in the Revelation by the pouring out
of the vial by the seventh angel: "And there was a great
earthquake, such as was not since men were upon the earth, Rev. 16, 18
so mighty an earthquake, and so great." Therefore, God
announced in the earthquake that he would avenge the death
of his Son.

Not a slight tremor quivered through the earth, but a
forceful shock knocked against its foundations so that "the
rocks rent, and the graves were opened." Throughout the
land, wherever practicable, the Jews used natural or arti-
ficial excavations in the rocks for their graves. A specially
favored territory in that respect was the hilly and rocky
region about Jerusalem, and there particularly a part of
Mt. Zion, where the graves of the ancient Kings of Israel
were found. There was nothing mysterious or supernatural
in the circumstance that from the shock the large stones

leaning against the tombs were moved and thrown aside,
thereby the graves being opened; that may have happened
repeatedly in other countries during similar catastrophes.
The remarkable point was again that it happened at the
Lord's death: as if the earth rebelled at the thought of
receiving the crucified Jesus, some say. In view of the open
graves we say the very opposite: As if mother earth
hastened to make room and offered a prepared resting
place to her Master! The throwing aside of heavy tombstones was, in regard to force required, but a trifling instance in view of the rending of the rocks. The same word
is employed as in the tearing of the veil. To the power
of God it is as easy to rend the mighty rocks as it is to part
a veil. Was Calvary itself affected by the shock? A tradition tells us indeed that the hill was split in two, perhaps
as an analogy to what should happen to "the Mount of
Olives, which is before Jerusalem on the east, and the
Mount of Olives shall cleave in the midst thereof toward
the east and toward the west, and there shall be a great
valley; and half of the mountain shall remove toward the
north, and half of it toward the south." But the crosses
remained standing, neither friend nor foe present was
hurt; Calvary, though feeling the general quake, was spared.
For that shaking of the earth was not a threat to the spot
now sanctified by Christ, but to the Jews and the enemies
of the cross. And here they had a foretaste of the wrath
of him before whom the rocks melt; his day of reckoning
must be a dreadful day.

Zech. 14, 4

What was the lesson taught by that earthquake? Thus
far we have found three important lessons: God trans-
ferring his favor from the temple to the cross; God threatening the enemies of the cross; God's wrath so effective
as to reach even to the abodes of the dead. However, it is
insisted that the earthquake must also have a significance

concerning the earth. It is said to symbolize the great power of the cross, which is to move and disturb the world. No doubt, the cross has caused a vast commotion among mankind; but did it always and only work with elementary force like an earthquake and a storm? The most blessed work of the cross was and is done quietly, unseen, in the hearts of men. Also in the rending of the rocks more is seen than a mere wordy amplification, it is thought to signify the hardness of heart in Israel, as illustrated in such passage: "Thou hast stricken them, but they have not grieved; thou hast consumed them, but they have refused ^{Jer. 5, 3} to receive correction: they have made their faces harder than a rock; they have refused to return." But to overcome such obstinacy, the cross has been very slow hitherto; for the Jews still refuse to return. Or the power of the cross over hardened hearts of the worst type is illustrated, the conversion indicated of such as Zechariah describes: "They ^{Zech. 7, 12} made their hearts as an adamant stone, lest they should hear the law, and the words which the Lord of hosts hath sent in his spirit by the former prophets." But are wicked hearts the only hard problems encountered by the cross? False religions, idolatry, the strange gods and the "new gods that came newly up, whom your fathers feared not" ^{Deut. 32, 17, 31} are also likened to a rock: "For their rock is not as our Rock, even our enemies themselves being judges." And how did the cross shake and overthrow the altars of the idols everywhere! How successfully does it still overcome the sects and theories that resolve to dethrone the Son of God! We prefer to see in the earthquake the symbolized relation of the cross to the earth in general: as the rending of the veil marked a new era in the religious world, so the earthquake ushered in a new era in the history of our planet. How much did the influence of the cross affect the face of the earth! With the new religion a new civilization and culture travelled hand in hand; new enterprises, new arts, new conditions, new nations, new cities, new temples, have changed the life on earth, have even altered, to a wonderful extent, the appearance of mountains and vales, of forests and fields, of deserts and seas. The quaking earth gave a mighty welcome, a greeting to the gospel of the cross, in anticipation of a future great with glorious things.

By far the most remarkable sign at the Lord's death was the one affecting the abode of the dead, the realm of the spirits. "And many bodies of the saints which slept, arose, and came out of the graves after his resurrection, and went into the holy city, and appeared unto many." Does this rising and coming forth of the saints stand in close relation to the opening of the graves? We think not. Not everywhere in the country the graves were opened, but only in the vicinity of Jerusalem; whereas the rent veil was a sign to the whole nation and the earthquake threatened Jews and Romans as well. With the open graves no general information or lesson was to be given to believers and unbelievers alike. Not in all the opened graves about Jerusalem the bodies were revived, but only the bodies of the saints. All the bodies may have been shaken or shifted in their position by the force of the shock, but that the reviving was not due to the shock, is evident from the rising of saints alone, while the others remained dead. Thus not all the people of Jerusalem, not even all unbelievers, rather no unbelievers at all, but only a part of the believers were to be instructed by that resurrection. Now if God for some specific purpose wanted to raise a number of saints, he did not have to open the graves first, he could lead his people forth despite the stones. Therefore we conclude that the opening of the graves was merely a threatening sign to the infidels showing that God would punish their crimes even in death. Only after the Lord's resurrection it may have become a sign

to them of the power of that Jesus who opens his grave
and the graves of all.

That the reviving of the bodies was entirely independent from the opening of the graves is at once clear if
we seek to answer the question: when did the saints arise
and when did they come out of the graves? Some hold
that the rising and coming forth did not occur until after
the Lord's resurrection. Against this not only the position
of the words protests, but especially the fact that the rising
is given as a wonderful sign at the moment of the Lord's
death. Yet they cannot have arisen and gone to the city
at once, for the text distinctly says that they went "after
his resurrection." No doubt, when the Lord bowed his head
in death the saints were revived: where did they keep
themselves until Easter morn? The queer theory has been
advanced that they remained in the tombs spending their
time in prayer and meditation, awaiting the signal for them
to come forth. All Jerusalem knew of the open graves:
would they not, after the first fright, go out to see them, to
close them again? As there was still time for Joseph to go
to Pilate to ask for the body, to buy spices, and to bury
Jesus before six o'clock, so the Jews had time to attend to
the open graves, especially as each family would care for
its own tomb. If not finished on the same day, it could be
done on the sabbath following. The friends of Jesus, after
witnessing his burial, "rested the sabbath day according to
the commandment." This quiet rest is the opposite to work
and commotion: may this unrest not have been caused by
work at the open graves? It is certainly a striking coincidence that on the same day the rulers asked Pilate to
watch and seal the Lord's tomb; perhaps the request was
suggested by the open graves they had seen. Now if any
persons visited the graves, though out of mere curiosity,
they did not see the living saints? Or did the saints, at the

sight of the intruders, cautiously feign still to be dead?
And if the people rolled the stones back into their places,
did they make a distinction between the sinners whose
graves were closed, and the saints whose graves they left
open? But if they closed them all, the saints were buried
alive, and the object of the opening of the graves for their
escape was frustrated! The desperate solution is offered,
that they at once left the tombs and stayed somewhere in
the neighborhood, perhaps hiding themselves. Instinctively
we feel how absurd this suggestion is. It is a picture little
edifying to see these saints, to whom God had done wondrous things, go vagabonding in the mountains or hiding
themselves we know not for what reason? This premature,
though secret, leaving of the graves is directly against the
doctrine of the Bible stating that Jesus was the first to

Acts 26, 22, 23
rise from the grave. Paul preached to Agrippa "none other
things than those which the prophets and Moses did say
should come: that Christ should suffer, and that he should
be the first that should rise from the dead." In his great

1 Cor. 15, 20
chapter on the resurrection the apostle writes: "Now is
Christ risen from the dead, and become the first fruits of
them that slept." The Colossians he informs that Christ is

Col. 1, 18
"the first-born from the dead; that in all things he might
have the preeminence." Our text also precludes any coming
forth from the graves, secret or otherwise, before Easter:
they "came out of the graves after his resurrection." The
most appropriate explanation is certainly this, that at the
moment of the Lord's death those saints were revived and
reunited with their bodies; or, rather, they were given the
glorified, refined body which is adapted to the conditions of
the other world and yet distinct enough to preserve their

Matt. 17, 3, 4
identity; even as Moses and Elias were recognized by the
disciples on the mountain of transfiguration. When Jesus
went to the spirits in prison, those saints were his retinue,

his trophies, a living testimony to the entire realm of spirits that Jesus had overpowered death not only for his own sake, but for the benefit of all who believe in him. Those men were specially privileged to accompany Jesus not only in the other world, attending his triumphal entry among the spirits, but also in his resurrection, or immediately after his own rising from the grave, to act as special messengers to the friends of the Lord.

The men so distinguished are called "saints which slept," and of them there were "many." Were they deceased friends of Jesus? It has been remarked that during those three years not so many of the Lord's friends can have died; he had only few believers in Jerusalem. Among those sleeping saints we may count people like Simeon and Anna, the shepherds of Bethlehem, and all who at that time had waited "for the consolation of Israel." And we need not confine ourselves to those who had died since Jesus came to earth. Throughout the centuries there had been pious men, saintly people, to whom death was but a "sleep," who had gone to their rest with the hope of being restored by the Messiah. Such as "slept in the Lord" were here highly honored. Of them "many" came to the city. We are at liberty to assume that many more were revived to accompany the returning Lord than afterwards actually appeared on earth. Only as many as were needed were selected to fulfill a special errand in the city. How "many"? We are told that they came to "many" friends. But in Jerusalem the number of believers was small. Six weeks later "the Acts 1, 15 number of names together were about a hundred and twenty." But among them were some who at the time of the resurrection were not at Jerusalem or did not yet believe in Jesus, like his brethren. Many also of those hundred and twenty may have been converted after the resurrection and on account of it. These, together with the disciples and others, we must subtract at once from that number, so that perhaps far less than a hundred friends come into consideration. And of these not "all" were favored with a visit, but only "many," a certain limited number.

The saints "went into the holy city." Jerusalem was "the holy city" not only in the opinion of the common people; prophets like Isaiah and Nehemiah had used that proud designation. But if that ancient name was correctly applied to the city of God and his house, why should it still be given to that place of crime and abomination forsaken by God and doomed to destruction? The gospels want the people of the New Testament still to regard Jerusalem as holy, for great things have been done there. Jesus wishes us to remember that "salvation is of the Jews"; that we should not rejoice in their downfall, but rather pray for them. Similarly the wondrous works of God done in the "holy city" are to claim our attention rather than the deplorable misdeeds causing its destruction. This word "holy city" is a beautiful flower in the garden of the Lord's Passion: He is not vindictive and his followers are not fanatical; they do not hate but pity the unfortunate Jews; they gladly acknowledge their merit in the preparatory work of religion; and they bear in mind that the crucified Savior died for them too. And was not Jerusalem truly become a "holy city" to all Christians, through their glorious Master, who walked and taught in its temple, who prayed and wept in the garden near by, who died on the hill before its walls, and rose from his tomb not far away?

In the city the saints "appeared unto many." Not merely in a dream or in a vision did they "appear." It was a bodily visit in that body which they had received for their existence in the other world, and which can be made perceptible to the eyes of men as, approximately, in the case of Moses and Elias. Who were those "many" to whom

Marginalia:

Is. 48, 2

Is. 52, 1

Neh. 11, 1

John 4, 22

they went? Throughout this chapter we have assumed that they were believers, friends of Jesus; and this for the following reason. If the earthquake with the open graves was a threatening sign to the enemies of Christ, he would not send his saints to console those people. Perhaps to frighten them? That would be very undignified work for the saints. Besides, the Jews had enough to frighten and warn them on that Friday as on Easter. "If they hear not Moses and the prophets, neither will they be persuaded, though one rose from the dead." From the friends visited _{Luke 16, 31} we must necessarily except the disciples and those women to whom the Lord showed himself after his resurrection. If the glorious Master himself spoke to them, the message of the servants becomes superfluous. Thus we also understand why after this in the entire New Testament not a word is said about this incident. The apostles and the leading Christians of their circle had seen the Lord, but nothing else, and therefore could relate nothing. Those to whom the saints went, were no writers, were no leaders, but quiet people leading a secluded life; and their experience was nothing for publicity, it was a private affair. Believers whom the risen Lord himself had not met, were visited by his messengers the saints. Now we can also surmise their message. Many had evinced extraordinary faith during these days, had hoped and trusted in the Lord's victory to the last, had perhaps suffered intensely from the mocking insults of their infidel neighbors and friends; now an extraordinary sign is to reward these faithful ones. What, if sickness or old age had prevented them from bidding him farewell on Calvary? What, if the duties of their homes, duties to visitors entertained during the feast, or the command of an unbelieving husband or father had kept them from seeing the crucified Lord? What, if they then in their lonely hours wept for grief, thinking of Him whom the

soul did love? These "little ones" in the Kingdom were not
forgotten, the Lord sent them a greeting, a glad Easter
message for their wounded hearts. And if they were op-
pressed by hardships of this life, the presence of the messenger itself spoke of a life to come, assuring them that
not only the Lord arose, but that others shall follow him.
And if the messenger did speak at all, what glories could
he relate of the other world from which he came, words
which the hearers kept sacredly treasured in their hearts,
as they were "unspeakable words, which it is not lawful for
a man to utter." Let us not slight the circumstance that
not only angels, but also resurrected men testified of the
risen Lord. Though the angelic hosts rejoiced in the victory
of the Son, yet the blessed benefit of the resurrection is best
appreciated and praised by mortals, who sink into the dust
and know that they shall live again.

2 Cor. 12, 4

What became of those saints after their service was
done? Did God divest them of their bodies and did he bid
them to return to the grave while the spirit returned to the
company of them that still slept? Though their resurrection
was but for the glorification of Christ, yet it is not credible
that God should have discarded them after so gracious a
distinction. They did not stay on earth longer than necessary, but with their spiritual bodies were taken into the
other world there to be like Moses and Elias, as a special
testimony of Him who took the sting from death and
wrested victory from hell.

We return from the open graves of the saints to the
cross on Calvary. A ray of Easter light has touched the
head bowed down in death. And a ray of that light seems
to have found its way also into the hearts of those who still
stood about the cross in awe.

66.   THE WITNESSES OF THE LORD'S DEATH

Matt. 27, 54-56   **Mark 15, 39-41**
Luke 23, 47-49

"And when the centurion, which stood over
against him, saw that he so cried out, and gave up
the ghost, he glorified God, saying, Certainly this
was a righteous man. Truly this man was the Son
of God. Now when the centurion, and they that
were with him, watching Jesus, saw the earthquake, and those things that were done, they
feared greatly, saying, Truly this was the Son of
God. And all the people that came together to see
that sight, beholding the things which were done,
smote their breasts, and returned.

"And all his acquaintance, and also many
women were there beholding these things afar off,
among whom was Mary Magdalene, and Mary the
mother of James the less and of Joses, and Salome,
the mother of Zebedee's children; who also, when
he was in Galilee, followed him, which followed
Jesus from Galilee, ministering unto him; and
many other women which came up with him unto
Jerusalem."
                        ———

The death of Jesus has affected the world of religion,
the history of our planet, the conditions even of the great
Beyond: how did it then impress man in whose interest
those realms were established and without whom they would
have no value, no meaning? Henceforth we meet a variety
of people who can answer that question. Near the cross

we find three classes: the centurion and his men; the Jewish spectators; and the acquaintance of Jesus. Of course, the sign of the parted veil was not known to them at that time, and the resurrection of the saints was also still hidden from them.

Did the centurion testify once or twice? Possibly not until the earthquake came did his deep emotion find expression in words; but it is more natural that he said one thing when he heard the cry, and another when the signs were perceived. "And when the centurion, which stood over against him, saw that he so cried out, and gave up the ghost, he glorified God, saying, Certainly this was a righteous man. Truly this man was the Son of God." Though occasionally an officer of much higher rank superintended a crucifixion, a centurion ordinarily had charge of such executions. This man stood "over against him," directly in front of the central cross, in full view of Jesus. This is generally explained as a proof that he was dutiful and conscientious, he choosing the best position to watch the three crosses and to see everything that transpired about him. We see something else in the fact that he stood over against him. Think a moment: in order to overlook the three crosses, he had to stand at a little distance; then between him and the cross the soldiers were passing to and fro, perhaps also some of the revilers; and then he could not see everything. And why should he so incessantly watch the crucified men? Was he afraid that they would free themselves or fall down? The soldiers had fastened them securely and were ready to act if any mishaps should occur. Watching the crosses rather meant watching the people; but how could he do so if he turned his back to them? For these spectators were not assembled behind, but in front of the crosses. Or did he continuously turn about? The most advantageous position for him to select was a little to one side from where he saw the crosses, the soldiers, and the people at the same time. There we rightly suppose him to have stood during the six hours. All at once he came and stood "over against" the central cross, not watching the two malefactors, but "him." Something unusual had attracted him; and since he expressed his astonishment at the cry, something similar must have brought him near. That can but have been that loud cry when Jesus asked why God had forsaken him. The centurion made no remark about that first and weirdest cry piercing the darkness; is it possible that it did not impress him? His surprise, his interest, his emotion, is just revealed in his coming and standing "over against him," looking intently at Jesus. As it grew lighter, he studied the features of the Lord, he "saw" that second cry, that is to say, he had his eyes fixed on the Lord's face. Therefore we see here not only a conscientious officer at the post of duty, but a man deeply interested in Jesus and moved by what he say and heard. We find him at the moment when the thoughts of his heart had ripened into convictions ready to break forth in words. The man, whom tradition names Longinus, was very much in earnest, and his words must be taken seriously. Let us collect all the good things that may be adduced in his favor, for it will enable us better to understand his words. He refused to take his share of the Lord's clothes, which shows that he was not avaricious and vulgar. He took no part in the mockery of the soldiers or of the rulers, and this silence tells of finer feelings, of a sense of propriety in him. He evinced interest in Jesus, he was no thoughtless listener to the accusations of the Jews, and this testifies of his sense of justice, of independent thinking. He said some words concerning the Lord, words which indicate that he was religious. When the soldier pierced the Lord's side, he must have done so with the consent of the centurion, and this would mean that he was dutiful as well as merciful. Pilate demanded his report and thereupon gave the body of Jesus to Joseph, which implies that the centurion was an officer trusted by his superiors. Thus he stands before us as an officer of many qualities; as a soldier who, despite military service, had not lost interest in higher things; as a man in whom confidence could be reposed.

And we also put confidence in him. When he "saw that he so cried out, and gave up the ghost, he glorified God, saying, Certainly this was a righteous man." The cry impressing him here was the "great voice" with which Jesus said, "It is finished." Two circumstances set the centurion to thinking: the force of the cry; and the time of the cry, so near death. The centurion had witnessed many crucifixions and knew that it was not natural for one who hung on the cross six hours to cry so loud; the victim was by that time utterly exhausted. Did that surprising cry remind him of his pagan gods which were said to possess a voice surpassing the human, and which acquired a fearful strength when the gods were in agony? But the cry did not convince him that Jesus was the Son of God, but simply that he was "a righteous man." Later it is said of him and his soldiers that they saw "those things that were done." The careful noting of all things was especially true of this man who had all these hours observed the Jews and the crucified ones. And what had he learned since morning! An execution like that one was an entirely new experience to him. How strange a sufferer was this Jesus, who hung there so patiently! The centurion had heard his prayer for pardon, his word to the repentant malefactor, the farewell to Mary and John. He had seen the rulers take a profound interest in the Nazarene, for they had come out to mock him. Vaster multitudes than usual were there in the morning and again in the afternoon, and the numberless people had joined in mercilessly mocking the sufferer. And Jesus did not revile again, had no curses for the soldiers, the rulers, the people; did not complain of pain, did for so long a time say nothing of his burning thirst! Such bravery as Jesus evinced in the hours of sorrow had not been seen by the centurion in all his experiences, and as a brave Roman he was capable enough to appreciate the same, though at a loss how to explain it. This heroism may have been the first trait in Jesus to appeal to the heart of the centurion. And the words of Jesus had an additional effect. A man guilty of such crimes as Jesus was accused of, does not pray to God, does not plead for his foes, does not speak of paradise, does not wonder why God should forsake him, does not commend his spirit to God. As the loud cry was immediately followed by the last word, the centurion must have heard it also. All these considerations gradually convinced him that Jesus was no criminal; he made the confession of the one malefactor his own: this man had done nothing amiss.

"Certainly this was a righteous man." Did he use the word righteous in the Roman or in the Jewish sense? If he put a Roman meaning into it, he declared that Jesus was a loyal citizen, one who had obeyed the laws of the land, a virtuous man who could not possibly have committed a foul crime. Did he thereby criticise Pilate who had sentenced an innocent man? A subordinate officer does not accuse his superior of injustice, especially not publicly. May he not have known that Pilate had condemned this Jesus unwillingly, had himself declared him guiltless, had written that revengeful superscription? Even if he meant to say nothing but that Jesus died innocently, his testimony is very impor-

tant. The commander of the executioners admits the humiliating truth that his unpleasant duty forced him to kill a
guiltless man. But the word "righteous" seems to indicate
that he used it in the Jewish sense, and consequently he
wanted to say much more. Righteous! That was the word
so oft repeated by the Jews in the streets, in their business,
in their services. How frequently may the centurion have
heard it when his duty brought him to the temple or into
other gatherings of the Jews. To be a righteous man before
God and before their fellowmen, that was the highest ideal
of the earnest as well as the superficial Jews; that was the
glory of the nativist against the Gentiles; and that was the
boast of the upper classes against the ignorant common
people. Whether the heart and secret life was ever so corrupt, if only the people praised their outward actions and
called them righteous, that constituted the aim and effort of
the whited sepulchres the scribes and Pharisees, as Jesus
himself testified: "Even so ye also outwardly appear
righteous, but within ye are full of hypocrisy and iniquity."
The centurion, therefore, ranked Jesus with the very best
and prominent people among the Jews. And this Jesus was
not only apparently righteous, but "certainly," he was it
"in reality," And more. Of crimes against the temple, of
blasphemy against the living God, the rulers had accused
Jesus there on Calvary. If the centurion believed those
charges, he could not say that Jesus was righteous. Evidently all those mockeries and insults had made no impression
on him, he had seen and heard much more in favor of Jesus.
What was that? The words of Jesus together with his patience constituted his evidence. No blasphemer of God dies
as Jesus died. But God looks with pleasure upon a righteous man, and therefore the centurion could understand
how in the last word Jesus commended his spirit to God.

Matt. 23, 28

The centurion probably did not say his words for the benefit of the Jews, at least he did not speak directly to them.
Nevertheless, all who heard him speak must have felt the
sting in his words. His judgment of the Jews was sharp
and cutting. He actually declared that the charges of the
rulers were untrue, that the treatment of this man, innocent before men and before God, was unjust. That was an
effective way of putting the Jews to shame, who had not a
good word to say for Jesus, who rejoiced in having crucified
him, whom they called the greatest malefactor in the country. Here the people had a telling portrait of themselves
and of their rulers: outwardly righteous, but at heart corrupt and full of spite. While Jesus was outwardly disgraced, within he was innocent and righteous before God.

The Lord's cry became still more impressive to the centurion, because it was so quickly followed by death. He
saw that Jesus "cried out, and gave up the ghost." If it
was remarkable that one hanging six hours on the cross
could speak with such force, it became doubly significant
that death, always so tardy in relieving the crucified sufferers, came so swiftly and, as it were, at the command of
Jesus who had commended his spirit to God. This circumstance gave the centurion the conviction that the Lord was
more than a righteous man. "Truly this man was the Son
of God." His "truly" indicates that for some time he has
been thinking of the matter, has been weighing the arguments for and against, and has finally reached a conclusion:
the Lord's claim to be the Son of God was no vain boast, no
untruth. Did he speak from the standpoint of Roman
superstition, believing that Jesus was a kind of demigod,
one of the fabled heroes of ancient mythology? This is
impossible, for he had just declared Jesus righteous in reference to the God whom the Jews worshipped. Naturally, he

could not have a clear insight into the blessed mystery of the Son of God, but in good faith he asserted that Jesus was the Son of the Jewish God. He could not possibly think of anything else, in view of the arguments that necessarily must have occupied his mind. Even if he did not know that the Jews had accused Jesus before Pilate of calling himself the Son of God, he learned it from the mockery of the rulers on Calvary. They had reviled him as the Messiah of Israel and as the Son of God. Now it is important to note that the centurion did not reach the conclusion that Jesus truly was the Messiah. The idea of a coming Messiah was quite foreign to his way of thinking, especially since the Jews of that time connected coarse political hopes, so offensive to the Romans, with that expectation. The centurion had declared Jesus guiltless also of political aspirations. when he called him a "righteous" man. But he did understand and did share the belief in a great God of heaven, and he was now certain that this Jesus stood in a most peculiar and intimate relation to that God. To him the Jewish charges were contradicted by the words of Jesus. To the "Father" he prayed, to the "Father" he committed his spirit. Among the Gentiles nobody spoke to the deity as to a "Father"; not even the Jews dared to address their God with that endearing term. The conversation with the malefactor and the emphatic "my God" may also have moved the man. But particularly convincing must have been the last word. The Jews had doubted whether God "will have him." But was not the sudden death after the cry and the committal of the spirit an effective proof that God indeed "will have" him? And at the same moment the earthquake spoke its powerful language! Throughout the ancient world earthquakes were considered as manifestations of divine wrath; naturally, therefore, the centurion assumed that the angry God threat-

ened and punished the Jews for the death of Jesus. In view
of these mighty signs the centurion felt how inadequate it
was to call Jesus merely a righteous man. If he was
righteous before God, if God looked with favor upon him,
if God was his Father who took the spirit at his request, he
must be more: "Truly this man was the Son of God." The
centurion drew the logical consequences which are so frequently neglected in our age by people who call Jesus the
good and perfect man, without considering that he could
be neither good nor perfect if his claims of Sonship were
untrue. Jesus was decidedly less than a righteous man if
he was not decidedly more than a righteous man. All
earnest readers of the Passion must either condemn him as
the rulers did, or must exalt him with the centurion's word:
"Truly this man was the Son of God."

With his words the centurion "glorified God," an expression which is generally thought to contain but the opinion of the Evangelist. The man himself had no intention
of giving glory to God, of whom he knew little or nothing.
His statement is only to the Christian observer an unconscious glorification of God. We can indeed explain it as a
masterpiece of the glorious God who in the hour of Christ's
abasement and defeat began to give him the name above
every name that was to conquer the world. But why should
not the centurion intend to glorify God directly with his
praise of the Son? And why should he have known little or
nothing of God? Granting for the sake of argument that
his knowledge of God was very meager, was that a hindrance
to his glorifying him? The Bible furnishes at least two instances of Gentiles who gave glory to the God of Israel.
The Babylonian "captain of the guard took Jeremiah, and Jer. 40, 2, 3
said unto him, The Lord thy God hath pronounced this evil
upon this place. Now the Lord hath brought it, and done

according as he hath said: because ye have sinned against the Lord, and have not obeyed his voice, therefore this thing is come upon you." Here a man who certainly knew not much of Jehovah was so struck with the destruction of Jerusalem that he saw the hand of God in that calamity. Nebuchadnezzar, a typical Gentile, also glorified God after he had seen a miracle of his power: "Then Nebuchadnezzar spake, and said, Blessed be the God of Shadrach, Meshach, and Abednego, who hath sent his angel, and delivered his servants that trusted in him." He even issued a decree that all the people should honor the God of Israel. A much more impressive scene was witnessed by that Roman officer on Calvary; why should he not also stand in momentary awe of God who did such wondrous things on that day? But we are by no means ready to admit his religious ignorance. How thoughtfully had he watched all that transpired before his eyes; how carefully had he noted the charges of the rulers; how deeply had he studied the nature of the Lord. A man so attentive, so impartial, so exact in his judgment, cannot be said to have been ignorant in religion. He viewed the sufferings of Jesus from the highest standpoint, bringing them into relation with God himself. How much must he have learned in those hours alone! There is no reason to suppose that here for the first time in his life he thought of God. At the time of Jesus, Jewish congregations were found in all the larger cities of the Roman empire, and each congregation had some proselytes as members. The Savior himself testified of the fervor with which the Jews sought to make converts, saying to the scribes and Pharisees: "Ye compass sea and land to make one proselyte." Would these eager missionaries neglect the opportunity for work among the strangers in their own land? It is unnecessary to suppose that the centurion was a convert; but neither is it

Dan. 3, 28

Matt. 23, 15

necessary to call him ignorant. Wherever his duty brought
him, he came in contact with Jews and their religion, and a
man of his disposition had certainly learned much concerning God. Therefore we do not hesitate to accept his praise
as a direct glorification of God. He saw the hand of God
in the quick death of Jesus, and in his words expressed his
satisfaction that God had saved his Son from further pain.
Therein he differed widely from Pilate who had declared
the innocence of Jesus without taking a real interest in him
or in God. The centurion glorified the Son and glorified
the Father: a fine example for the Christians, who remember the Savior's words: "He that honoreth not the Son John 5, 23
honoreth not the Father which hath sent him."

That good confession was not without effect upon the
four soldiers. "Now when the centurion, and they that
were with him, watching Jesus, saw the earthquake, and
those things that were done, they feared greatly, saying,
Truly this was the Son of God." How many soldiers were
present? Some think that there were four to each cross,
or twelve in all. Strange, that we see and hear nothing at
all of the other men, as hitherto only the four assigned to
the cross of Jesus occupied our attention. Those eight must
have remained absolutely inactive throughout that entire
execution. For later, when the bones of the malefactors
were broken, each group of four did not, as we would expect, attend to that duty; only some came to do it; certainly
not twelve, for one would have hindered the other. Perhaps only two were required to break the bones, and "they
came" also to the cross of Jesus. If a larger detachment
had come out to prevent disturbances, it stood at a distance
and was not under the command of this centurion who had
his exclusive duty in watching the crosses. We confine ourselves to the four soldiers whom we observed throughout

these hours. They were now "with him," not only present as his subordinates, but gathered around the centurion. The cry of Jesus had also attracted them if they had not come already when one of their number gave the vinegar to Jesus. They "saw the earthquake, and those things that were done." Their seeing the earthquake refers to its effects. Not only did they feel the shock, but they beheld the open graves in the neighborhood, saw here and there a rock rent. These men also shared the general opinion of the ancients that earthquakes were threats of angry deities. But not alone the things connected with the earthquare did they see; they had noticed some other "things that were done." The cry and the sudden death of Jesus were also astonishing to them. Looking about, they perceived the Jews, shortly before so loud in their mockeries, standing mute and awe-stricken. And their own centurion spoke such startling words! That they should have so bitterly mocked a righteous man was a severe censure of their conduct; how much more, then, must the earnest confession frighten them that they had crucified the Son of God! "They feared greatly," and many reasons did they have to be afraid. How persistently had they insulted this Jesus, how cowardly had they treated the defenseless Sufferer, how cruelly had some of them acted when they desisted from giving him to drink. In their fear they repeated the centurion's word: "Truly this was the Son of God." Did they merely utter a compliment to the officer, as obedient soldiers acquiescing in his opinion, because they dared not contradict him? Who thinks of obedience and compliments when fright chills his body! Why, then, had they not also repeated his statement that Jesus was a righteous man? They may have greeted that opinion with a sarcastic smile, though they felt its sting. But when the uproar in nature, the death on the cross, and the awe of the people, worked together as if confirming the centurion's word that Jesus was the Son of God, their <u>levity yielded to great fear</u>. They repeated his word, not from conviction but because they did not know what else to say; their guilty conscience made them to fear and to speak in fear. Was there no exception? If we think of that one soldier who ran to bring the vinegar to Jesus, we may count him as one who did not repeat these words so superficially as his comrades. The centurion himself cannot have been entirely free from that fear, for he is included in them that "<u>feared greatly</u>." Though he had to obey the orders of his superiors, and though he had not reviled the Lord, he yet could accuse himself of neglecting to check the mockery of the soldiers, of failing to show any favor to Jesus, of waiting too long with his confession. If any such fears were in him, they helped to make his confession the more earnest and impressive. The centurion was the first witness who after the Lord's death took up the testimony which afterwards stirred the whole earth, saying that the crucified Jesus was the Son of God. Before taking leave of him we will, therefore, ask what became of the centurion after that Friday. Did he speak in a momentary emotion which quickly vanished again, or did he learn to believe "with his whole house," like his colleagues the centurion of Capernaum and Cornelius? Tradition relates that he became a Christian and was even made a bishop, and that at last he died <u>as a martyr</u> of the King of Calvary. His body was alleged to have been discovered by some crusaders, <u>A. D. 1098</u>, in the church of St. Peter at Antioch. Though we know but little of him, his testimony makes us think that he was not a man to stop short of the goal; and if he was converted, he certainly had the courage to seal his faith with a <u>martyr's death</u>. He would then be the first of that long procession of witnesses who went forth to preach Christ and Him crucified. Tradition also says that he belonged to the "German legion" at that time employed in Palestine; if that is true, he was a promising representative of those countries where afterwards the gospel of the cross scattered its blessings in rich abundance.

The great fear was not confined to the centurion and his soldiers. "And all the people that came together to see that sight, beholding the things which were done, smote their breasts, and returned." Over noon and during most of the darkness the people had remained at home, but as it grew lighter they returned, they "came together," collecting about the cross. Many thousands of visitors were in Jerusalem on that feast, and they desired some diversion. In a few moments large multitudes were again assembled, not from sympathy, but "to see that sight." A mere spectacle, an entertainment was the crucifixion to them. The discussion about the real character of Jesus had subsided, and nothing was left but a morbid curiosity to see the famous sufferer in his agony. These multitudes beheld "the things which were done"; the loud cry, the early death, the earthquake, the rent rocks and open tombs, the confession of the centurion and the consternation of the soldiers. These mighty events moved the superficial sightseers profoundly; they "smote their breasts" to signify their regret and sorrow. Thus Ephraim repented and said: "Surely after that I was turned, I repented; and after that I was instructed, I smote upon my thigh." In the parable the humble publican "would not lift up so much as his eyes unto heaven, but smote upon his breast." The fearful signs appealed directly to the hearts of the people, and at once they lost all desire to see "that sight" any longer; they "returned." How silently they went home! Loud and boisterous had

Jer. 31, 19

Luke 18, 13

been their coming out, heartless their mockeries, and frivolous their conversation; many of this throng may have
been of those who in the morning had cried, "crucify him."
Whether they now did realize their mistake? Their sorrow
cannot have been very deep, for we hear of no confession of
guilt, of no prayer asking God's pardon. On the other hand,
they did not mock the centurion for his belief that Jesus
was the Son of God. The incident gave them food for serious thought, and during the following days other events disquieted them. It is probable that one or the other among
those people retained his serious thoughts, was converted,
and joined the followers of him who had died in the midst
of such wondrous signs. To us the incident with the centurion and the people seems like a prophecy that sooner than
the children of the chosen nation the Gentiles hail the
crucified Lord as their King.

When the multitudes returned to Jerusalem, a number
of people still remained, the real mourning and deeply interested persons. "And all his acquaintance, and also many
women were there beholding these things afar off. In "his
acquaintance" men seem to be included as distinguished
from "also many women" who were present. By "all" his
acquaintance is not meant the complete circle of his relation
and friendship, as if not a single one was absent. All of his
acquaintance that happened to be at Jerusalem were assembled. This leaves the question open as to whether his
yet unbelieving brethren were of that company. With the
exception of John, none of the disciples had ventured out;
for their presence would have been noted, especially as the
disciples were more than mere acquaintance. If men were
there at all, they were outnumbered by the women of whom
"many" had come. These relatives, friends and most intimately acquainted people, stood "afar off." Did the sol-

diers, anxious to preserve the necessary order, forbid them
to come near? Had the guards given a special permission
to John and Mary, to her sister, and to Magdalene, to approach the cross for a short farewell? The soldiers did not
know the friends of Jesus and had no reason to make dis-
tinctions between different classes of spectators. Throughout the past hours we found many people near the crosses,
so that the friends of Jesus must have voluntarily chosen
their position at a distance. Their hearts were heavy enough
without being constantly wounded by the insults of the
mocking people. Their standing "afar off" had the purpose
of distinguishing them from the unbelieving throngs, and
to us it is an additional proof that the multitudes were largely hostile or indifferent to Jesus. Yet they were not too far
away; all were enabled to behold "these signs." In addition to the other signs, they saw the multitudes growing
silent, beating their breasts, and returning home. That
was a strong consolation to them, for they, better than
anybody else, could recognize the hand of God in those
events.

Two classes of women are mentioned: those who had
always followed Jesus, ministering unto him; and others
who had only joined the company on this last journey to
Jerusalem. Among the former, the first Christian deaconesses, three are specially pointed out. Mary Magdalene,
Mary the wife of Cleophas, and Salome. Magdalene and the
sister of the mother of Jesus had stood near the cross, then
retiring with the mother and John. Mary, the sister of the
Lord's mother, had two sons: James the less, or younger,
and Joses; that their names are mentioned here shows that
they were believers well known among the faithful, but
also that they were not present among the acquaintance
on Calvary, for nothing else is said concerning them. Sa-

lome was also a prominent woman, for she was the mother
of two of the leading apostles; one of them, John, was present, while we read nothing of James.   Salome certainly
looked upon the cross with special emotion, for but a few
days before she had approached the Lord with a peculiar
request: "Grant that these my two sons may sit, the one
on thy right hand, and the other on the left, in thy King- Matt. 20, 21
dom."   How well that the Lord had refused her foolish
petition!   He opened his royal reign with a baptism of
blood, and if in the new realm the two apostles were to be
prime ministers they had to hang on the crosses with him.
On Calvary she learned an earnest lesson of spiritual life
and duty.   Of these women it is said that they, "when he
was in Galilee, followed him."   This describes them as
earnest believers and regular followers.   On this last journey
from Jerusalem they "followed Jesus from Galilee," they
were in his company on the way to the feast.   They "ministered" unto him, not only during these days, but for several
years past.   Their contributions were surely considerable,
for Jesus was responsible for the support of twelve followers, and this expense also came from the gifts of his
friends.   That Jesus also "supported" his mother is not
probable, for with the four brethren at home Mary had no
need of depending on charity.   Among these ministering
deaconesses we miss two leading women: Joanna the wife of Luke 8, 3
Chuza, and Susanna.   The former was one of the early Luke 24, 10
visitors to the tomb on Easter, and her presence on Calvary would surely be mentioned.   For some reasons she,
as also Susanna, was prevented from coming at this hour.
The name of Mary the mother of Jesus, is also omitted in
this connection, for she, herself being poor, was not one of
the ministering friends.

    With them stood "many other women which came up

with him unto Jerusalem." These are distinguished from the ministering women, but they were also believers, else they would not have come "with him." We see in them a congregation of poor people, who would have gladly served the Master with substantial gifts, if they had been able. These women who in poverty and hardships had been often consoled by the Friend of the poor, had come to offer him what they had: a warm sympathy in the hour of distress. Is it not a beautiful picture to see those richer women stand side by side with the poorest of the land? All these mourners seem to have been Galileans. Where were the friends from Jerusalem? Why do we hear and see nothing of the people of Bethany, of Lazarus and Mary and Martha? Was it by the kind advice of friends that they stayed away? The resurrection of Lazarus had been the immediate cause arousing the rulers to final action; from that moment on they sought to destroy Jesus. Those three persons were well known in Jerusalem, and their safety may have been threatened. But who will believe that, after tasting so much of the Lord's friendship, they would hesitate to risk their lives for his sake? If they were not at home broken-hearted we may suppose them as standing among the "acquaintance."

No mere curiosity to see every particular retained those women after the multitudes had left. Since they had ministered to the Lord while he was alive, they now waited to serve him also after death. They had resolved to give him a decent burial, and their opportunity soon came. But was it a sadly prophetic incident that so many women were there while the men were conspicuous by their absence?

67. THE SIDE PIERCED
John 19, 31-37

"The Jews therefore, because it was the preparation, that the bodies should not remain upon the cross on the sabbath day, (for that sabbath day was a high day,) besought Pilate that their legs might be broken, and that they might be taken away. Then came the soldiers, and brake the legs on the first, and of the other which was crucified with him. But when they came to Jesus, and saw that he was dead already, they broke not has legs: but one of the soldiers with a spear pierced his side, and forthwith came there out blood and water. And he that saw it bare record, and his record is true; and he knoweth that he saith true; that ye might believe. For these things were done, that the Scripture should be fulfilled, A bone of his shall not be broken. And again another Scripture saith, They shall look on him whom they pierced."

While the friends on Calvary and the soldiers stood still in awe of the quick death of Jesus and the marvellous signs accompanying it, an order arrived from Jerusalem. In the city certain people had also thought of the crosses, but in a very different mood. "The Jews, therefore, because it was the preparation, that the bodies should not remain upon the cross on the sabbath day, (for that sabbath day was a high day,) besought Pilate that their legs

might be broken, and that they might be taken away."
Were the "Jews" securing this order those who smote their
breasts as they returned to the city? They must have
quickly abandoned their serious thoughts! Or did the
citizens in general make the request? But who among the
thousands would consider himself the guardian of the Law
and of the Sabbath? The people had their appointed
authorities who attended to such matters. Those "Jews"
were the rulers, the members of the Sanhedrin, who acted
and spoke in the name of the Jewish nation. Not Annas or
Caiaphas, nor any one or two judges decided this question,
but the entire council as such. It appears, then, that they
must have called an afternoon session, even as we found
them assembled on Tuesday afternoon when Judas visited
them. Frequent business meetings during the passover were
surely necessary, for these spiritual superintendents of the
feast had much to decide. Their main or sole discussion in
this Friday session concerned the removal of the three
crucified men. The rulers knew very well that crucified
persons might linger several days in their agony, and under
ordinary circumstances their revengeful spirits would have
been pleased to see Jesus suffer as long as possible. No
mercy, therefore, prompted the decision to have the bodies
removed before evening; they were forced to take that
action on account of public opinion. The Romans would, of
themselves, do nothing to accelerate death or to take the
bodies away; their custom was to leave them on the crosses
until the corpses decayed or were devoured by the birds of
prey. Pilate had no reason to deviate from the rule, since
the Jews had demanded this execution. Among the Greeks
and Romans it was indeed customary to remove the bodies
of crucified criminals on the eve of exceptional holidays;
but how could Pilate be expected to show so much respect
for a Jewish feast without they having petitioned him?

Must they not fear that Pilate would spite them by leaving the bodies exposed? At all events, the people would hold the rulers responsible for a public desecration of the sabbath; it was too great a risk to offend the masses in their religious ardor so shortly after regaining their good will, and especially as the new insult would not have been blamed on Pilate as in the case of the superscription.

Their arguments among themselves, and later submitted to Pilate, are outlined in the text: "Because it was the preparation"; not because they wished to end the misery of the unfortunate men, nor because they desired to interfere with Pilate's judgment, did they discuss and decide as they did. The preparation for a quiet sabbath observance included a twofold duty: to make ready all that was needed for the great celebration; and to remove all that was apt to detract from the sanctity of the day. The sabbath commenced at six o'clock, which left only a few hours to finish the preparations. Therefore their anxious concern was "that the bodies should not remain upon the cross on the sabbath day." On the sabbath day? Why did they not simply argue that the bodies should not hang exposed overnight or over the "next day," exactly as the law prescribed? Though crucifixion was not in vogue among the Israelites, yet they heaped additional disgrace upon executed criminals by hanging them on the accursed tree. Their law applied equally to persons merely "hanged" on the tree as to persons nailed to the tree: "If a man have committed a sin worthy of death, and he be put to death, and thou hang him on a tree: his body shall not remain all night upon the tree, but thou shalt in any wise bury him that day; (for he that is hanged is accursed of God;) that ^{Deut. 21, 22, 23} thy land be not defiled, which the Lord thy God giveth thee for an inheritance." From their making the sabbath day the cause of action, we surmise their regret that the next day was not a common day on which a transgression of the law could not have been so flagrant and on which they could have more easily blamed Pilate for leaving the bodies exposed. Again, the rulers were careful not to confront the governor as guardians and representatives of the ancient law; in that capacity they had suffered several defeats during the trial of Jesus before Pilate. They have him to understand that, if an ordinary day were to follow, they would not have molested him, but that for the sake of the people the sabbath day dare not be desecrated. The exposed bodies would defile the whole region about Jerusalem, including the temple, and the masses must not be insulted with such neglect, especially because "that sabbath day was a high day." It was high and great not because it was the first day of the passover; for this feast commenced on the day of crucifixion. But if throughout the year every sabbath was solemnly set aside for God, how much more solemn was the sabbath of the passover season, when the whole land came together at Jerusalem! It marked the very height of the religious and national life of the Jews. Therefore another consideration may also have induced the rulers to emphasize the sabbath: if the bodies are put away, the worshipping multitudes have no longer occasion to discuss the crucifixion; the affair will be partly forgotten and the day observed as if a Jesus had never existed among them.

The entire Sanhedrin need not be supposed as having waited upon the governor; a committee, a delegation was appointed to submit the request. To assure the removal of the bodies they "besought Pilate that their legs might be broken, and that they might be taken away." Notice, they "besought" him. Evidently they had learned a lesson since this forenoon when Pilate curtly refused to alter the superscription. Then they arrogantly "said" what as a matter of course they expected him to do; but now they politely beseech him, recognizing him as the authority to decide the removal. By no means must Pilate be insulted, for he might refuse to give permission. This humble attitude of the proud rulers explains why they emphasized the sabbath; not as the judges of the Jewish court, not as the guardians of the Law, not in their own name, did they demand the removal; they kindly requested it in the name and interest of the people, in order to be sure of success. As in the morning when they readily suggested how the inscription should be changed, so here they have agreed on the mode of removal: "That their legs might be broken." Among the Romans the shattering of the legs sometimes constituted a punishment in itself; but occasionally it was also a part of the crucifixion. With a heavy mallet or an iron club the legs were crushed on the cross which was not first taken down for that purpose. This painful proceeding did not cause instant death, but only accelerated it; the mangled bodies could still live an hour or more. If the object consisted in effecting an immediate death, the crushing of the legs was generally accompanied with a heavy blow upon the breast, which quickly extinguished the last spark of life. The Romans considered that operation as an act of mercy, for thereby the unfortunate sufferer was at once freed from prolonged misery. We notice, however, that the rulers said nothing concerning that final blow; theirs was no merciful intention to relieve the three men from further torture, but only a precaution to make sure of death at the beginning of the sabbath. The time of shattering the legs was left to the discretion of Pilate; only let it be done soon enough that the bodies are dead by six o'clock; the intervening additional pain did not concern them. And whereas Jesus must have been uppermost in their minds, we learn that they wanted him to suffer as long and as much as practicable in the remaining hours. The request seems to

have been made for the main purpose of disgracing the
Lord. Why should it have been necessary to ask for the
crushing of the legs, if the Romans were in the habit of
doing it always? They did not do it regularly, and would
certainly not have done it in the case of the King of the
Jews whom they gladly would have left hanging as long as
possible to ridicule the Jews. The breaking of the bones
was suggested by a secret desire of cutting off completely
the memory of the Nazarene; or, if some people will still
think of him, they must remember him as a common criminal who had suffered the most ignominious punishment.
After the bodies were dead, another permission was required: "that they might be taken away." As said before,
the Romans originally left the bodies to decay on the cross,
but in later ages permitted friends to claim and bury them.
Yet nobody was allowed to remove a corpse without special
leave of the proper authorities. The rulers were aware of
that restriction, wherefore they suggested vaguely that the
bodies "be taken away." If the Romans themselves will
bury the corpses, the rulers are satisfied; or, on the other
hand, let Pilate give them a permit, and they will see that
it is done. Later we learn that Pilate reserved the right
of disposing of the bodies to himself, at least in respect to
Jesus.

When was that request submitted to the procurators?
At or before noon, when the rulers left Calvary, it was too
early; it would have ended the tortures of the Nazarene too
soon. Or does the "therefore" in the text mean to say that
when and because they knew of the Lord's death, they went
to Pilate? Their request would then have been a defiant
answer to the emotion of the spectators, to the earthquake,
to the threatening God himself. While we believe that their
hearts were sufficiently hardened for such conduct, the
shortness of time and other circumstances contradict it.

To call a meeting, to deliberate and decide the question, to obtain Pilate's consent, and then to forward instructions to the soldiers on Calvary, required certainly the best part of an hour; and then Joseph would scarcely have had leisure to go to Pilate, after that to buy linen, and to complete the burial by six o'clock. If Jesus was dead when they came to Pilate, they must have informed him of that fact; and then we would not understand how Pilate, when Joseph visited him, could wonder and doubt whether Jesus had "already" died. Why should the rulers want the bones of the dead Jesus to be crushed? Evidently they supposed the three men still to be alive, for they did not speak of the two malefactors alone. Or did they hide their real intention of disgracing Jesus even in death, by suppressing the fact that he had expired? But who assured them that Pilate would not learn of the Lord's death as soon as they? And, finally, if the orders to break the bones had reached the soldiers so long after the Lord's death, there would be no sense in the statement saying that the soldier saw Jesus was "already" dead. Shortly after he expired, when the body was yet warm, he was pierced; and the rulers must have assembled at least half an hour, if not longer, before the Lord's death. This would put their deliberations into the time of densest darkness, and in their request we discover their explanation of that unusual phenomenon. Suspecting that the people would interpret the gloom as a sign in favor of the Son of God, the rulers hastened to prove that Jesus was nothing but a common criminal who must be treated as such even to the breaking of the bones. Again we are compelled to admire the wondrous contrast between the powers of earth and the powers of heaven. While God himself prepared to take away his Son, the rulers also considered his removal. These enemies are anxious to put him away as an abomination defiling the land; and, behold, they are too late! The

Father has taken him in a manner which reveals the homage of the Past and the Future, of heaven and earth, paid to the only begotten Son.

Pilate seems to have granted the request without hesitation. In view of the cold refusal when the change of the inscription was demanded, his present accomodating mood is somewhat surprising. What were his reasons for the ready consent? Generosity and an effort to please the rulers cannot be sought in the resentful heart of this proud Roman who still felt the smarting sore of the defeat of the morning. Is it possible that during the past hours his wife, who had warned him in vain, told him more about Jesus and his mysterious character? Such information cannot have been reassuring to him. Did perhaps the noonday darkness frighten this superstitious worldling, making him moody and restless? And was it, therefore, to his own interest to prove that Jesus was not the Son of God, was no supernatural being who would return to avenge his murder? Pilate was far too superficial and indifferent a character as to think long on religious subjects. Did he regard the observance of the sabbath and the breaking of the bones of so small import as to yield in such trifles without much ado? Roman policy enjoined on him due respect for the religious scruples and customs of the Jews; but he had the best excuse for leaving the bodies on the cross as long as he pleased. The rulers themselves had insisted on the crucifixion taking place on this day; did they not know that such an execution might extend over several days? Their request showed that they knew it very well. If Pilate now refused to hasten the end, then he was not the disturber of the sabbath, but the rulers must bear the blame for their insistence; the Roman law would sustain him for carrying out his sentence to the letter. That Pilate yielded so readily was due, to the effective plea and, partly, to his own desire to have this affair with Jesus closed definitely. Pilate knew that the masses must not be incited too much and to frequently; he was surely informed of the victory of the rulers on Calvary; and how his own mocking inscription had served to drive the people to the side of the priests. If in the morning he would have welcomed an opportunity to interfere with his legions, he did not now want further complications on account of Jesus. Let that incident be closed and forgotten, for he had no right to be proud of his conduct in that respect. Personal interests were the motives for his prompt permission.

The order, which may have been somewhat delayed by reason of the earthquake, reached the soldiers shortly after the Lord had expired, and was obeyed at once. For if the crucified men were to die from the effects of the blows and that before evening, it was time to assist the crosses in their deadly work. "Then came the soldiers, and broke the legs of the first, and of the other which was crucified with him." Were these soldiers specially sent out by the governor to break the bones? This has been supposed because they wondered that Jesus was "already" dead. But just this circumstance proves that they were no new arrivals; for men who had come with the order to crush the legs, would not long have looked and wondered whether one or the other was dead or hung in a stupor; they would have strictly attended to their duty whether the crucified ones were dead or not. We are dealing with "the" soldiers, with the same four men that were present since morning. The command of the centurion must be presumed; at his word the soldiers drew near to perform what was certainly a disagreeable task even to those hardened men. They commenced with the two malefactors, probably two soldiers at each cross breaking the legs of the two simultaneously. Why did they wait with Jesus to the last? Did a feeling of awe restrain them from inflicting those injuries on him whom they just had tremblingly called the Son of God? Did the centurion, who thought so highly of him, forbid them to mangle the body of the Lord? It is possible; though such motives need not be assumed to explain their action. Jesus was dead; they had heard his last cry, had seen his head drop upon the breast: as to him the breaking of the legs was absolutely superfluous; it could not cause him pain, nor could it accelerate his death. The two malefactors, however, still were comparatively strong; there was no sign of their demise; their remaining vitality warranted many lingering hours on the cross. If these men were to die from the effects of the newly inflicted wounds, their legs had to be shattered without delay. That was perfectly natural and practical. In this connection be it remarked that it is rather far-fetched to call the repentant malefactor the first martyr of the crucified Lord. Even as the little ones of Bethlehem had to die for the sake of the new-born King, so at the death of the Savior this malefactor died in his service! We fail to see the point of resemblance between innocent children, in every one of whom the minions of Herod suspected the new King, and the dying murderer who received the due reward of his deeds. He believed in Jesus, but did he die for His sake? Were his bones broken because he was a believer? His infidel comrade suffered the same fate.

The centurion and his soldiers had strict orders forbidding them to leave the crosses or to allow the removal of the bodies until unmistakably sure that death had actually ensued. They would not have done their duty by merely judging from a distance whether Jesus was dead or not; they were obliged to come close to the cross to look for the signs of death. "But when they came to Jesus, and saw that he was dead already, they broke not his legs: but one

of the soldiers with a spear pierced his side." Their seeing
that Jesus was "already" dead does not signify that they
were ignorant of it before, and now were surprised to find
him dead. It rather means that they were not mistaken
when they saw him die; their investigation disclosed the
fact that he indeed had ceased to breathe, that the heart
stood still. As a conscientious officer the centurion made or
ordered that close inspection. With the death of Jesus
established beyond a doubt, Pilate's command was not
transgressed when they omitted the now unnecessary breaking of the bones. However, the centurion was a careful
man; the early death was quite unusual and unaccountable
to him; if Pilate demands a report, his officer must be absolutely certain that no earthly possibility existed permitting the escape of Jesus from death on the cross. With that
object in view "one of the soldiers with a spear pierced his
side," apparently at the command of the centurion. It is
not stated which side the soldier wounded; but as the most
natural position was in front of the cross, he wielding his
spear or lance with the right hand, the Savior's left side
must have been opened, the region of the heart. The object
of the thrust was just to reach the heart; it assured death
beyond a question. Consequently, the wound was not a
mere scratch or a slight cut; the two-edged broad blade
plunged deep into the vitals of the Lord, causing an opening
deep enough that afterwards, despite the healing influence
of the resurrection, Thomas could be invited: "Reach John 20, 27
hither thy hand, and thrust it into my side." The wound
torn by that forceful stab was fatal; no one could live with
such a gap in his body; the Roman law permitted persons
thus wounded, even though they were not crucified, to be
buried. The centurion had done his full duty, Pilate can
be satisfied with his obedient officer. Were the two malefactors also pierced with the spear? Some exegetes assume

this, but, it seems, directily against the evidence of the gospel. Would John, as he does with his subsequent asseverations, describe the wound as something so remarkable if all three bodies had been cut in the same manner? The malefactors were not to be killed instantly; the crushing of the bones was but to assure their death by six o'clock. And it appears that they lasted for quite a while longer. For if the three men died within a few minutes, why did neither their friends, nor the Jews, nor the soldiers, make an effort to take the bodies down? The taking away before evening was also granted by Pilate, though he had not said who should remove the bodies. That the Lord was left undisturbed, proves that the malefactors lived quite a length of time after his death. For when Joseph asked Pilate for the body of Jesus, the governor marvelled that he was already dead, while the malefactors apparently were still living; the centurion had to be called from Calvary where he was yet watching the crosses of the two. Only Jesus had been wounded with the spear; this is what John intends to say.

The opening of the wound had a remarkable result: "And forthwith came there out blood and water." It is not stated how much blood and water came out; but there was a quantity sufficient to be perceived by the witness John who must have stood some distance away. Nor does the text employ a word signifying that the blood and water flowed or gushed from the open side for any length of time. Nor are we told whether the blood came separately, followed by the water; or whether it was neither pure blood nor pure water, but simply a fluid in color and substance resembling the two liquids. Was it a miraculous process? Or was the phenomenon owing to the sinless state of Christ's body, as if here his transformation into the glorified body took place? The Lord was not destined to succumb to decay and corruption, but otherwise he had to taste death with all its real and peculiar effects. The flow of blood and water was quite natural; but how? The spear may have pierced the pericardium so that the fluid contained therein flowed forth; a reddish lymph and a colorless serum; the strain due to the hours of crucifixion may have accumulated that fluid to an unusual degree. The simplest explanation is found when we bear in mind that the blood, after death, requires nearly an hour to clot and coagulate completely; but that deep wound was inflicted not later than about ten minutes after the Lord's death; and if the blade cut the pericardium, as was the aim of the thrust, there is nothing strange in that flow of blood and water from the body generally, and particularly from the region of the heart. A profound significance has been ascribed to that blood and water; it is said to typify the blood of the Lord's Supper and the water of baptism; or the baptism of blood and the baptism of water. However, John has not a single word to say as to the significance of that outflow: Why this silence? At the proper place we shall seek to explain that circumstance.

The incident of the pierced side was so remarkable to John that he emphasized it to his readers with the strongest asseverations: "And he that saw it bore record, and his record is true; and he knoweth that he saith true." This faithful witness is the beloved disciple himself; he speaks in the third person because he dislikes to mention his own name. He insists on the fact that he "saw it" with his own eyes. The valuable distinction of the apostles was that they did not repeat stories heard from others, but that they preached and wrote that "which we have heard, which we 1 John 1, 1 have seen with our eyes, which we have looked upon, and our hands have handled." Of those personal experiences he "bore record"; not only once or occasionally did he speak of what he had seen, but repeatedly and continuously he bore record of it, for it constituted the center of his preaching, of his entire gospel.   All the long years intervening between that Friday and the time of writing his gospel have not effaced from his memory the events of Calvary.   In his ripe old age, when writing the account of the Lord's Passion and death, he knows that "his record is true," is exact and complete and reliable.   He is aware that he records wonderful things throughout, but he also "knoweth that he saith true."   The scene of Calvary stands vividly before his mind, and he neither omits nor adds a single important trait.   What did he see, and what does he here record as absolutely true?   Simply the fact that blood and water flowed from the wound?   We do better also to include the circumstance that it was a spear that wounded the Lord, and that his bones were not broken.

What was John's object in attesting the truth of those things in a manner quite unusual with him?   He himself says, "That ye might believe."   But is it possible that the great apostle was compelled to assure the readers of his veracity in such strong terms?   How poor a preacher would he have been, if the people did not take for granted that he was absolutely truthful!   The esteemed man who was called a pillar of the Church, aye, the priest with the golden plate of holiness upon his forehead, was certainly not obliged to reassure his congregations that he did not lie or exaggerate. "That ye might believe": if we accept the statement of Irenaeus, John wrote his gospel at the request of his friends at Ephesus; but since they were believers, why should they be admonished to believe?   This word here does not simply mean accepting something as true, or beginning to believe. On Calvary John has been strengthened in his faith and he wants his readers also to be strengthened in faith by the incidents related.   Strengthened in what respect?   That

Jesus was the Christ, the Son of God! This, at least, is the almost unanimous reply of the commentators. But think a moment: from the rich store of his memory John selected a large number of the Lord's striking deeds and words for his gospel, concerning which he says: "These are written, that ye might believe that Jesus is the Christ, _{John 20, 31} the Son of God." Now if a reader has not yet been strengthened in that belief, how can the unbroken bones and the open side strengthen him? Not any better is it to say that the faith in the fulfilled Scriptures should be strengthened. John has told us that all things were accomplished according to the Scriptures; how many great and wonderful things are included in those fulfillments! If one does not yet implicitly believe the Word of God, the little circumstance that with the piercing of the side also a few passages are fulfilled, will not be apt to strengthen him in his belief. We insist, therefore, that John intended neither more nor less than what he actually wrote: "That ye also might believe," meaning the acme of faith, the highest art of believing, faith under all conditions and at all times. Learn to be believers in the highest sense of the word! Be pervaded and saturated with faith in all your actions and experiences. With such a believing heart, and eye, and ear, John stood on Calvary. Not mere curiosity, no carnal bravery, not even the friendship to the Lord only, had brought him to the hill, but his faith in Jesus Christ. By that faith all events were tested, and therein he discovered the wonders and miracles of God. Now let every believer go through this poor world, through his darkest hours of sorrow, through the midst of his enemies, with such wide-awake faith, and he will see the protecting, guiding, blessing hand of God everywhere. St. Paul, the apostolic specialist in matters of faith, could not have written a grander chapter on the power, the beauty, and the hope of faith, than John did in his brief word: "That ye might believe."

The faith with which John viewed the cross was here also richly rewarded: "For these things were done, that the Scripture should be fulfilled, A bone of him shall not be broken. And again another Scripture saith, They shall look on him whom they pierced." An apparently insignificant rule for the preparation of the passover lamb prescribed, "Neither shall ye break a bone thereof." The lamb was to be perfect and whole as the Creator made it, for the eating of that lamb was to be no common meal, but rather a holy sacrifice in the temple of the home. Likewise the perfect Lamb of God, dying for the benefit of mankind, and although numbered with the transgressors, was not to be mangled like the criminals at his side; he was a bloody but none the less holy sacrifice on the altar of the world. Therefore what God does to the righteous in different ways, he did to the righteous Jesus: "He keepeth all his bones: not one of them is broken." In Jesus not only the great truths of the prophecies are fulfilled, but also the minor details of the Jewish rite, to show that henceforth the old religion is a rite without meaning, for the true Lamb, "even Christ our passover is sacrificed for us." When the side was pierced, another passage, one of the mysterious sayings, received its light; namely the one in which Jehovah said: "And they shall look upon me whom they have pierced, and they shall mourn for him, as one mourneth for his only son, and shall be in bitterness for him, as one that is in bitterness for his firstborn." The scribes could never understand how the Spirit, the invisible God, was to be pierced. On Calvary the interpretation is given: they have pierced the Son and in the Son the Father himself. Although the Roman soldier wielded the spear, he would have had no occasion for piercing that side, if the Jews had not

Exod. 12, 46

Ps. 34, 20

1 Cor. 5, 7

Zech. 12, 10

brought Jesus to the cross. Therefore not the Gentiles, but the Jews have pierced him, and they "shall look" upon him. Many of them were and are yet hiding their faces from him; they refuse to look upon him whom they despise. But in the day of judgment they must open their eyes, whether they will or not: "Behold, he cometh with clouds; and every ^{Rev. 1, 7} eye shall see him, and they also which pierced him: and all kindred of the earth shall wail because of him." Meanwhile, as long as the gospel of the cross is preached to the world, many a one of the nation that pierced him, shall learn to mourn, to repent, to look upon him with faith and gratitude.

While John adduces two prophecies for the remarkable facts that the bones were not broken and the side was pierced, he speaks of no fulfillment concerning the blood and water. He seems to have had that circumstance in mind when in his Epistle he wrote: "This is he that came by water and blood, even Jesus Christ; not by water only, ^{1 John 5, 6} but by water and blood." But why does he indicate no significance right here? Did he see none in it? But his testimony that his record is true and apt to strengthen the faith belongs also to the blood and water. Or did he think that there were no prophecies on that point? But the same Zechariah, who speaks of the pierced side, also says that "by the blood of thy covenant I have sent forth thy prisoners out of the pit wherein is not water." This passage ^{Zech. 9, 11} refers to the words of Moses about "the blood of the ^{Exod. 24, 8} covenant, which the Lord hath made with you concerning all these words." Zechariah also predicts: "In that day there shall be a fountain opened to the house of David and ^{Zech. 13, 1} to the inhabitants of Jerusalem for sin and uncleanness." This plainly refers to the "water of purifying" wherewith ^{Num. 8, 7} the Levites were cleansed, and to the "water of separation" ^{Num. 19, 9} which was a purification for sin. These prophecies were surely fulfilled in the blood and water of the open wound;

did John, in his long life, fail to think of them? Who will accuse that thoughtful apostle of such ignorance and carelessness! His omission has a glorious meaning: that blood and water signifies the accomplished salvation of which all the prophets spoke; if he had wanted to mention any prophecies concerning it, he would have been obliged to quote practically the entire Old Testament. Throughout the past ages the sacrificial blood had spoken of pardon, and the water of purification testified of a spiritual cleansing. What the fathers in their religion did and believed and hoped, was now fully realized and accomplished in the blood and water shed by him who comes with life and salvation. That blood and water was the last gift of the suffering Savior, and that gift included all treasures secured through his holy sacrifice.

At this point there is something like a last farewell to him who walked on earth in the form of a servant. Hitherto his mighty acts, his wondrous words, his ineffable pains, his remarkable death, his glorious work, claimed our attention. He was the central active figure in the drama of the Passion. But now he is passive, is taken care of by his friends, and laid away. A picture of subdued and tender hues unfolds itself before our eyes. The aromatic fragrance of Joseph's garden wafts upon us, and the quiet of the open tomb hushes the loud word.

68. JOSEPH OF ARIMATHEA

Matt. 27, 57, 58   **Luke 23, 50-52**
Mark 15, 42-45   **John 19, 38**

"And after this, now when the even was come, because it was the preparation, that is, the day before the sabbath, behold, there came a rich man of Arimathea a city of the Jews, named Joseph, an honorable counsellor; and he was a good man, and a just: who also himself waited for the Kingdom of God: being a disciple of Jesus, but secretly for fear of the Jews. The same had not consented to the counsel and deed of them: He went in boldly unto Pilate, and craved the body of Jesus, and besought Pilate that he might take away the body of Jesus. And Pilate marvelled if he were already dead: and calling unto him the centurion, he asked him whether he had been any while dead. And when he knew it of the centurion, Pilate gave him leave, he gave the body to Joseph. Then Pilate commanded the body to be delivered."

———

The friends assembled on Calvary must have endured moments of great anxiety as they noticed the ebbing life in the shattered bodies of the malefactors. The sun lowered quickly in the sky, and every minute the command might come to deal the last blow to the dying culprits and to take the bodies down. As soon as the two malefactors had expired, all three victims were to be removed and buried in the same grave. On account of the hot climate of the country the burial almost immediately after death was imperative and, as we have seen, the law concerning executed criminals also required a speedy removal. None of the Jews would voluntarily touch the crosses or the corpses for fear of defiling themselves. Yet the rulers must be thought as having made preparations for the burial because Pilate had not definitely stated who should attend to it. However, the soldiers may have construed the order to kill the men by six o'clock as meaning that they should also take the bodies down and bury them. If then the guards had their own way, they would dig a grave on the spot to receive the three bodies, for such was Roman law and custom. In this case, however, they had to follow the directions of the Jews, who would want the bodies removed to the usual burial ground for criminals. This dreary cemetery was probably located in the valley of Hinnom the ancient region of abomination. No executed persons were permitted to be buried in the tombs of their fathers or in the common graveyard of the community. For them two separate tracts had been set aside amidst the ashes and debris of the desolate region: one for criminals that had been decapitated or strangled; and one for those that had been burned or stoned to death, as also for those who after death had been hanged on the accursed tree. With this last mentioned class Jesus and the malefactors would find their common pit, if no friends or relatives come to claim the bodies. We know not where the two malefactors found their last resting place. But there were numerous friends of Jesus present, eagerly waiting for the opportunity to bury his body; yet how helpless were they! Whom should they ask? The kind-hearted centurion took great interest in Jesus and would perhaps willingly have accommodated the friends, but he had no authority to give the body away. Should they go to the rulers? These had no definite permit from Pilate,

and if they had, they would have delighted in wounding
the adherents of Jesus by according him the most disgraceful burial. Or should they appeal to Pilate? Would the
proud Roman admit these plain and obscure country people
into his presence?

We can easily comprehend how helpless those friends
were and how meager their hopes of saving Jesus from a
grave with the godless. Nevertheless, there is something
in their irresolute waiting that, if we dare not call it displeasing, needs a valid excuse. Think of it: The adored
Master of Nazareth has, by this late hour, not a single one
ready to claim his body, not one among his immediate followers who has made the slightest preparation for his
burial! Where are the ten disciples? In Israel it was a
sacred duty to provide a decent burial for a loved one; the
son, the brother, the friend, would undergo severe hardships
to render the last tribute of love to the departed. After
John the Baptist was beheaded "his disciples came, and took
up the body, and buried it." Have we no right to expect Matth. 14, 12
of the disciples of Jesus more attachment and greater courage than they did manifest? Had they not yet overcome
the first shock of grief and fear? And if those ten forgot
the burial, why did not John think of it? He and the women
had stood on Calvary for several hours and saw the Lord
grow weaker from minute to minute; could not one of the
company go to the city to ask Pilate? The bodies were
generally surrendered upon request, and at least an effort
could have been made. They could also ask the assistance
of some influential citizens to plead for them before the
governor. But absolutely nothing was done. Did they
entertain some secret hopes that Jesus would descend from
the cross? Such hopes must then have vanished when he
died and his side was pierced; yet they did not stir. Were
those ministering women, otherwise so intelligent and re-

sourceful, suddenly so thoughtless as to neglect the most natural service, the burial? A satisfactory explanation offers itself if we remember that John stood there as a firm believer, as one who in every circumstance recognized the hand of God. Must we suppose that he remained mute in those hours? Would he not step up to the bereft mother and to the sorrowing friends imparting to them his own consolation, calling their attention to the fulfilled Scriptures? And if they stood there so composed and quiet because they knew that all events came and went in accordance with God's will, would they not also trust that his wisdom would provide a burial worthy of the Son? We find them in the act of believing against the evidence of their eyes, in the exercise of that faith which they afterwards preached to other people. Such reliance on divine providence does not exclude that they were now and then disturbed in heart with anxieties and fears.

Their suspense was soon relieved; God indeed made his presence felt in that emergency. "And after this, now when the even was come, because it was the preparation, that is, the day before the sabbath, behold, there came a rich man of Arimathea a city of the Jews, named Joseph." This "behold" points to the hopeless aspect of the scene before Joseph's coming, and to the unexpectedly glorious change caused by his appearance. It also calls attention to the time: at the right moment, neither too soon nor too late did he come; "after this," the side of the Lord having been pierced, the malefactors rapidly growing weaker; "when the even was come," the evening hours from three to six o'clock having partly passed away, the fleeting moments necessitating quick action if a burial was to be secured, then he came. The "behold" also speaks of Joseph: of him nobody had thought; when the friends did not know what to do, help came from a source least expected. This man "came" to Calvary, not by chance, but with a certain purpose which was far from a mere desire of satisfying his curiosity. The reason for his coming is stated in these words: "Because it was the preparation, that is, the day before the sabbath." The rulers had thought of removing Jesus before the sabbath, and this single ruler had also been thinking of it. He may have heard from the reports in the city that Jesus had died, he may have even heard of the ruler's demand that the bones should be broken. Yet even if he supposed Jesus still to be living, Joseph feared that toward six o'clock the Lord would be quickly killed and buried; if something was to be done, he must attend to it on this Friday which, though a feast day, was not so strictly kept as to forbid a burial. Why did he not go directly to Pilate? His coming to Calvary means that he believed the disciples and friends to have made some preparations, perhaps by securing the permission to take the body, and by selecting a place for the burial. He must have been greatly surprised to learn that absolutely nothing had been done and that the whole work rested now on him. Did the assembled friends entreat him to go to Pilate, and did they know him at all? He is called "the" Joseph of Arimathea, wherefore he seems to have been a widely known man in Jerusalem, and it is probable that some of the believers knew his name and titles; but were they aware that he was a secret disciple? If the Master had knowledge of his discipleship, we may assume that the confidential friend John had in some way been informed of that fact, while the women certainly were in astonishment to discover in Joseph an interested and influential friend of the Lord. The mutual interest soon made Joseph acquainted with the women on Calvary, but there is nothing to prove that they persuaded him to assist in the burial. He had come with the intention of taking part in the work. But why had this friend postponed his visit until so late

an hour? Where had he been all day? He was not with
the rulers in the morning session, nor during the trial before
Pilate; neither had he come in their company to mock the
Lord, nor had he met with them in the afternoon. Did he
cowardly hide himself when he learned of the sad fate of
Jesus? Why should we have so poor an opinion of this
man who now so bravely confesses his faith in the Lord!
This day had been a time of solitude and conflicting thoughts
to him. The moment of decision had arrived: either he
must renounce Jesus forever, throwing away all hopes in his
lost cause; or he must openly confess himself as a follower
of the Messiah. How severe a conflict, how fierce a tempest
must have raged in the soul of that man! This visit on
Calvary shows that at last he had won the victory over
himself, that he had reached a firm conclusion by which
to guide his steps.

So remarkable and praiseworthy a deed has Joseph
done that the Evangelists vie with each other in attesting
their respect to him and reporting his good traits. Joseph
was born in the village of Arimathea, also called Rama or
Ramathaim Zophim. It was the ancient birthplace of Sam-
uel, who also lived and died there. The town stood about
two hours north of Jerusalem, on the mountains of Ephraim,
and belonged to one of the three districts which King
Demetrius II. had taken from Samaria, adding them to
the province of Judea. Joseph seems to have spent his
advanced years in the capital, for there he owned real
estate, a garden, a kind of property which no one would
buy if he could not enjoy the same. Or if he had no per-
manent residence in Jerusalem, his official duties compelled
him to spend a large part of his time in the holy city.
Joseph was "a rich man," as we would naturally infer
from the circumstance that he owned a valuable piece of
ground so close to the largest city in the land. Far more

precious, however, than the earthly possessions were the treasures of his heart. The generous information furnished by the Evangelists not only serves to make us better acquainted with the man, but it throws much light upon his deed. He was "an honorable counsellor; and he was a good man, and a just: who also himself waited for the Kingdom of God: being a disciple of Jesus, but secretly for fear of the Jews. The same had not consented to the counsel and deed of them." The term "counsellor" cannot mean that he simply was a member of the village council in Arimathea, or that he belonged to a priestly conclave in Jerusalem. The judges of the Supreme Court had condemned Jesus, and since Joseph did not consent to their action, he must have had a seat and a vote in that highest council. This ruler in Israel was not a priest or a scribe, for in that case his proper title would have been given; he was therefore one of the elders, a representative of the people, who by reason of his merits had risen to the rank of supreme judge. The rich man had not used his money to buy himself into that office, nor did he exert his influence to enrich himself; for he was an "honorable" counsellor. Not all of the supreme judges deserved or received honorable distinction from the public; though the honors due to their high office had to be acknowledged outwardly, the people in their hearts despised many of their spiritual leaders for their well known avarice, dishonesty, and cruelty. Joseph was an exception. Even as the sacred circle of disciples was disgraced by a dishonorable Judas, so the corrupt council of the rulers was graced by the honorable Joseph. The community knew him as honest in his dealings and irreproachable in his reputation. His honorable conduct was not a mere varnish, for he was also "a good man" at heart, one who endeavored to do right in all respects, one who did not selfishly forget his suffering brethren. This

excellency was founded on his regard for religious duties:
he was a "just" and pious man; he observed conscientiously
the ordinances of the temple, the rules and regulations of his
religion, the precepts of the Word of God. If such a man
ventures the decisive step from the Old Testament into
the New Testament, the world may rest assured that he has
not trifled with the great questions involved. His piety
did not consist in barren theorems of a petrified orthodoxy;
it rooted in his longing heart and in the Word of God: he
"also waited for the kingdom of God." Like Zacharias
and Elisabeth, like Simeon and Anna, like many other pious
souls in Israel, he longed for the consolation and redemption
of Israel, for God's Kingdom to be established on earth.
Is that to say that those were the hopes of former days,
but that at the tragic death of Jesus he was sorely disappointed in his expectations? A man so utterly dis-
couraged would not be able to bring the greatest sacrifice
for the sake of a defeated Messiah! Even while bending
over the lifeless body of Jesus, Joseph still waited for the
Kingdom of God. Of how noble a nature must therefore his
hopes have been! He did not foster the worldly ambitions
of his fellow rulers who expected the Kingdom to increase
their political power and to strengthen their personal supremacy over the people. If he had ever shared the popular
opinion of a secular reign of Christ, of Israel's rule over
the nations of the earth, he had shaken off those super-
stitions quickly and completely in the presence of the cross.
But still he waited that through the dead Jesus the Kingdom
of God should come, although, if asked, he could not have
explained why and when and how it should make its
appearance.

A man so noble in character and conviction must necessarily have been opposed to the harsh and unjust measures
with which the rulers in the past years sought to destroy

Jesus and his work. Joseph was earnest enough to see and acknowledge the shortcomings of the chosen people, the wounds and defects in the national and religious life of the Jews; and he was sufficiently impartial to admit that a man like Jesus had a great mission and could accomplish much good among the masses. Such a man, if disagreeing with Jesus, would choose the cautious attitude of Gamaliel: "If Acts 5, 38, 39 this counsel or this work be of men, it will come to naught: but if it be of God, ye cannot overthrow it; lest haply ye be found even to fight against God." That would have been much. But Joseph did more: he became "a disciple of Jesus," recognizing in him the Anointed of God, accepting his doctrine, believing his words, hoping for his success, praying for his salvation. Like other upright hearts and yearning souls he also was irresistibly attracted by the Lord; but for a long time his faith was passive, he learned and believed "secretly for fear of the Jews." The fact that for a while his rank, his wealth, his social advantages, counted more with Joseph than his faith in Jesus, may detract from the good opinion we hold of the man. Before casting stones at him let us remember that it is much easier for people in Christian countries to make a public confession of Christ. Joseph's secret and inactive faith was perhaps more sincere and cost him more in money, time, and serious thought, than most of our avowed Christians are willing to devote to their religion. Instead of criticising him, let us look for mitigating circumstances that help to excuse his attitude. We remember that the fanaticism of the rulers knew no bounds. Quite early "the Jews had agreed already, that if any man did confess John 9, 22 that he was Christ, he should be put out of the synagogue." If Joseph had been detected, what a warning example they would have made of him just because he was a ruler! This man was not the only one who believed and feared: "Among

John 12, 42

the chief rulers also many believed on him; but because of the Pharisees they did not confess him, lest they should be put out of the synagogue." In such surroundings his courage could not easily be aroused into heroic action. We must also bear in mind that Joseph had little opportunity to see and hear Jesus himself, whose teachings and miracles were chiefly done in the provinces. The faith of the secret believer could only feed on reports, and how scant must they have been even if they did reach him through friends of the Lord. And how cautiously must he have received those accounts when they were spread by the enemies who perhaps distorted or exaggerated them. While there was little to strengthen his faith, he encountered many things that might rob him of it; for though the rulers probably did not invent direct lies against Jesus, yet their meetings were regularly furnished with hostile reports from spies watching the Master, and the discussions of the sessions must have abounded with insults and arguments to disparage the Savior. Finally, Joseph's fear of the rulers never amounted to a denial of his faith. Unstinted praise is bestowed on him in these words: "The same had not consented to the counsel and deed of them." Never was he the accomplice of the rulers when their schemes aimed to destroy the Lord. Though they did not suspect his faith, the others must have soon learned that they could not depend on the honorable counsellor when concocting spiteful plans; this neutral position alone required considerable courage of Joseph.

We must admit that, whatever his faith formerly lacked in boldness, it was made good on this Friday. He did not consent to the "counsel" of his colleagues: the pact with the betrayer, the disgracing arrest, the unjust trial, and the unwarranted sentence, were against his convictions. His dissent from the counsel shows that he did not come

directly from Arimathea to Calvary and just learned of
the events of the hour. He was in Jerusalem these days
and had complete knowledge of the transactions of the court.
Was he present at some of those meetings? Then his dissent
was a splendid bravery holding its own against the unscrupulous and determined Caiaphas. But probably he
stayed purposely away from certain sessions. He was not
known as an adherent of Jesus and therefore received the
summons to attend, for instance, the night trial. His
absence, then, must have been noted and interpreted as
dissent. His opposition to the rulers, if but by way of silence
or absence, would incur the resent of Caiaphas, and Joseph
with his conduct risked the forfeiture of the friendship of
the ruling priests and their followers. He also refused his
consent to their "deed." Despite his opposition Jesus had
been crucified. Now an ordinary prudent or diplomatic
man would have acquiesced in the accomplished fact; he
could not help the condemned Jesus any more, but merely
endangered himself by further resistance. Joseph put aside
all personal considerations and did not consent. Against the
"deed" of the rulers he set his own "deed" on Calvary.
What was his interest, his visit to Pilate, the burial, but
his public protest to the verdict of the Sanhedrin? By his
actions Joseph declared that he did not regard Jesus as a
blasphemer deserving death, that he did not want to be
numbered with the judges who condemned him. And vastly
more: he informed all the world that he was a believer, a
disciple of Jesus; voluntarily he published the secret so
long and carefully guarded in his bosom. It is safe to say
that a more surprising revelation or a greater insult could
not be offered to the rulers than was contained in Joseph's
daring act, which amounted to a public denunciation of the
judgment of the supreme court, to a complete renunciation

of their friendship. Caiaphas and his clique certainly never forgave that affront.

What was it that prompted this secret disciple to make known his faith under those adverse conditions? The heartless injustice of the supreme court may have opened his eyes. As a pious Jew he revered the laws and customs of the ancient religion; even as a secret adherent of Jesus he was convinced that much good was to be done with the old foundations and institutions as a basis; but when the trial of Jesus taught him that the very core was corrupt, that with such selfish leaders the slightest reform was impossible, he resolutely severed his connection with the godless priests. The cruel and unmerited death of Jesus must also have been revolting to his sense of justice, fanning the hidden faith into an open flame. The hand of God had taken hold of him, binding his heart in fervent love to the Lord, filling him with a profound desire to do something to attest his faith. And how gloriously did that faith shine forth! Never was Jesus poorer than when he died on the cross, and never was his cause nearer the brink of annihilation than during those hours on Calvary. The disciples had forsaken, forgotten the Master; the friends stood in helpless sorrow; none of those who had called Jesus the Son of God, who had profited by his divine power; were present to claim even his body! Then Joseph came, the man who hitherto had neither preached nor followed Christ, and he risked his station and future for the sake of the defamed Master, still believing in the Messiah, still waiting for the Kingdom of God. This is an impressive illustration of the truth that the life of the Church, the cause of the gospel, the safety of the Kingdom, in no wise depends on a select few, but that God raises his co-workers where and when he pleases. Tradition numbers Joseph with the seventy disciples and asserts that later he was the first mission-

ary to preach the gospel in England, of which country he
is the guardian saint. We do not care for the great things
he may have done in after years, but are satisfied to see the
erstwhile timid disciple step from the very caldron of enmity
into the light of the cross, giving us an example of moral
beauty, of courage and faith, which mankind must admire
as long as the gospel is read. Instead of being the frailest
among the believers, he proves himself one of the strongest
among the disciples of the Lord.

The text indicates that we do not overestimate his bravery; he himself realized the numerous difficulties of his
enterprise. "He went in boldly unto Pilate, and craved
the body of Jesus, and besought Pilate that he might take
away the body of Jesus." Joseph "went" without letting
the thought detain him that this service was of no practical
use to the dead body, or that this action tended only to
endanger himself. He went without delay as soon as he
grasped the situation on Calvary. There was no time to
be lost, for if the rulers learned of his intentions, they
would certainly seek to frustrate his plan. Again, the two
malefactors might expire at any moment, and then the soldiers would not wait with the burial. Or did Joseph together
with the friends entreat the centurion to postpone the removal if the malefactors should die before he returned?
The request of so prominent a man was surely not refused
by the centurion who himself took an interest in the Lord.
But Joseph could go in peace, the malefactors did not die so
soon. He went "boldly," the visit required courage. Evidently he had weighed the matter in his mind and was fully
cognizant of the obstacles in the way. Joseph must expect
to find the procurator ill-humored, if too many favors are
asked of him in one day. Joseph was a prominent man
whose request must not be treated lightly, but did he not also
belong to those rulers who defeated Pilate in the morning?

How can one of these men hope to be personally favored? Or will the governor be sufficiently impartial to distinguish between this man and the other rulers? Since he "craved" the body so ardently, he must adduce a valid reason for his plea, must inform Pilate of his secret discipleship, of his love to the Nazarene. What will the haughty Gentile say to all that? Much more serious were the consequences of his request when he thought of his fellow rulers. His action amounted to a repudiation of the Sanhedrin's verdict; he used his rank and influence against his colleagues; he exchanged the friendship and good will of the priests for the sake of the dead Jesus. Joseph must be prepared that the rulers put him out of the synagogue, that they deprive him of office and honor; undoubtedly they will never forgive him this insult. His popularity was also at stake particularly with the people controlled by the rulers. His influence will be gone as soon as they learn that he, a counsellor, affiliates himself with the lost cause of the Nazarene. His mere entering into Pilate's house was an unpardonable sin in the eyes of many Jews. Joseph went "in," not hesitating to defile himself in the residence of the Gentiles. We recall the fact that the rulers, when arraigning Jesus in Pilate's court, did not step into the Prætorium for fear of becoming unclean and excluding themselves from the celebration of the passover. But here one of those rulers goes into the unclean house, not unawares, not from urgent necessity, but voluntarily and with intentions hostile to the supreme court. How wanton a disregard of the Levitical precepts, how detrimental an example to the masses! What must Jerusalem think if one of the elders himself transgresses the laws of the elders? The unconcerned visit in the pagan's house proves the conversion of Joseph as genuine; he has completely separated himself from the dead formalism of the ancient religion, has resolutely and without reserve embraced the liberty as it is in Christ Jesus. No doubt he argued that, if Jesus could stand in Pilate's hall and hang on the accursed tree while still remaining the holy and beloved Son of God, one of his sincere followers would not be defiled by mere contact with heathen soil.

Joseph was readily admitted into Pilate's presence, but the visit was by no means a pleasant one. "And Pilate marvelled if he were already dead: and calling unto him the centurion, he asked him whether he had been any while dead." We are not told whether Pilate was astonished because a rich man, a prominent citizen and ruler, took such interest in Jesus; it is probable that he wondered, for at first he was very cautious as if fearing a trap. Especially strange was to him the early death of Jesus: "And Pilate marvelled if he were already dead." Already! This shows that Pilate was not informed of the death of Jesus; the centurion was still on Calvary because the two malefactors were yet living. Already! The governor knew how long the crucified ones generally lingered on the cross; why should Jesus die so exceptionally soon? Even with the bones crushed, the culprit might live several hours. If the bodies of the three men were mangled, why should one of them die so long before the others? Or if the soldiers had dealt the killing blow to Jesus, why not also to his two companions? Already! And yet by that time the Lord had been dead nearly one hour. His side had been pierced some minutes after he breathed his last; again some time elapsed before Joseph appeared on the hill, and with his stay near the cross, and until he stood in Pilate's presence, another half hour went by. If Joseph reported what he learned on Calvary, that Jesus died at the moment of the earthquake, the governor must have marvelled still more. There was something about it which he did not understand. He wondered "if" he were dead, whether it was actually

true. That "if" implied a suspicion whether Joseph's veracity or, at least, his judgment could be trusted. Pilate
would not believe until assured by the centurion. That was
quite a humiliation to the honorable counsellor. Had he not
come directly from the cross, had he not seen with his own
eyes that the Lord was dead? Yet the plain centurion was
accepted as a more responsible and trustworthy man than
this member of the Sanhedrin. How poor an opinion did
Pilate have of the Jewish rulers! "And calling unto him
the centurion, he asked him whether he had been any while
dead." Since the centurion was out on Calvary, a messenger had to summon him, and thus another half hour of
delay was caused. This time of waiting must have been
very unpleasant to Joseph. How little did Pilate care for
his anxiety, while the evening rapidly drew near. Verily,
the generous servants of Jesus, instead of meeting with
encouragement, find so many things in the way to kill their
enthusiasm, to dampen their ardor! Pilate questioned his
officer closely, demanding to know whether Jesus had been
"any while" dead. This may mean, that he referred to one
of Joseph's statements about the early death; he wanted to
discover whether the ruler had told him the truth. Or he
wanted to learn the exact time and the reasons why the
centurion thought Jesus was dead. This officer then must
have given the details of what he had seen, and what he
had done to ascertain death and to preclude any illusion.
Why was Pilate so painstaking in this matter? Did he keep
Joseph waiting with the intention of an offer, or of an
increased price, for the body? Pilate had better cause to
be careful and slow in granting the request. The rulers
were spiteful and hostile to him. If the governor was not
absolutely sure of the Lord's death, his foes might spread
false reports in the land, might even lodge complaint with
Tiberius, that he had taken a man from the cross but a few

hours after crucifixion when many doubted the actual death
of the Nazarene. It would have been very bitter to Joseph,
if Pilate suspected him as being an emissary of the Sanhedrin to trap the governor. Even without the burden of
such suspicion, it was humiliating enough for Joseph to
stand there as one of the rulers whom the procurator had
cause to distrust and despise. However, Pilate with his
caution was also an instrument in the hand of God. He
was forced to add his testimony that Jesus had really died,
in order to make the resurrection the more glorious.

God is a buckler to them that walk uprightly: "And
when he knew it of the centurion, Pilate gave him leave,
he gave the body to Joseph. Then Pilate commanded the
body to be delivered." The dutiful and conscientious officer
found his reward in the confidence of his superior, and
Joseph's courage won the precious prize of the Savior's
body. The procurator showed his good will to the petitioner
in that "he gave" it to him without pay, as a present. The
governor had the authority to dispose of the body, and covet-
ous procurators often extorted excessive sums from rich
people for the privilege of burying executed relatives or
friends. Now Pilate's avarice was notorious, and here he
dealt with a rich Jew, yet he surrendered the body free
of charge. He even "commanded the body to be delivered,"
giving the order to the centurion who returned to the
crosses. This command was more than a mere permission;
it signified either that the soldiers should do the heavy work
of taking the body down to give it to Joseph, or that he
and the friends should attend to it and to the burial under
the protection of the governor; the hostile Jews dare not
hinder or disturb the good work! What were the motives
of that sudden generosity? Perhaps Pilate wished to revenge himself on the rulers by saving Jesus from a disgraceful grave. He may also have been pleased with Joseph

who, unlike the other Sanhedrists, had entered the residence of the Gentile. He may have intended the present to make good his wrong against Jesus the favorite of God. Most of all, he was probably glad that the indisputable death of the mysterious Nazarene ended forever, as he thought, a disagreeable affair.

Joseph went his way. Was he conscious of the important part he filled in sacred history? It is to us as if in the golden evening sun God smiled upon him, asking, Seest thou not the wonders of my ways? Before the Savior entered this life, a Joseph, also a just man, was in great distress of mind whether he should care for the unborn babe; and when the Lord had departed from this earth, a just Joseph was in perplexity what to do with the body; and in both cases all ended well. A Joseph was appointed to watch over the manger of Bethlehem, and a Joseph came to provide a tomb near Jerusalem. When the infant Jesus was helpless and without friends, a Joseph lent his manly protection; and when the dead Jesus had none to bury the body, another Joseph prevented disgrace in death by offering his tomb.

69. NICODEMUS

Matt. 27, 59   Luke 23, 53
Mark 15, 46   John 19, 38-40

"And he bought fine linen. He came therefore
and took the body of Jesus down. And when
Joseph had taken the body, he wrapped it in the
clean linen cloth.

"And there came also Nicodemus, which at
first came to Jesus by night, and brought a mixture of myrrh and aloes, about a hundred pound
weight. Then took they the body of Jesus, and
wound it in linen clothes with the spices, as the
manner of the Jews is to bury."

———

Instead of retracing his steps to Calvary, Joseph went
from Pilate to the merchants. He was not a man satisfied
with half-hearted and scant service. Though haste was required, the burial was to be no hap-hazard removal of the
body; but to make it respectable, certain requisites were
needed, which he went to secure. "And he bought fine lin-
en." Though it was a feast day, the stores were open on
account of the preparation for the high Sabbath, especially
for the benefit of pilgrims who for some reasons had been
delayed in their journey, arrived late, and were compelled
to buy their provisions for the feast at the last hour. It was
quite unusual for residents personally to make purchases
for a funeral, servants and other members of the household
attended to such details. Joseph selected and bought a kind
of linen as if a friend, a brother, a son of his had died.

(239)

Since he "bought" the linen, he cannot have taken any along
to Calvary on his first visit there; which justifies our opinion that he came with the expectation of finding some preparations made. As a rich man he may have had sufficient
material for a burial at home; but probably his way from
Pilate to the hill led him past the stores, and his time was
limited; or he may have bought linen specially prepared for
the purpose, covered with gum on one side, and nobody kept
that kind regularly in the house. He secured nothing but
the linen, though a Jewish interment required also certain
ointments and spices; did he forget them? As a Jew, Joseph
cannot have inadvertantly neglected that part; perhaps the
large amount required was too heavy for him to carry, or
he had no time to get those spices because he had to hasten
to finish the burial before the sabbath forbade all work.
It seems that Joseph thought of only a temporary laying
away of the body, intending to care for particulars after
the Sabbath. But even if the burial was preliminary, the
due respect for the Master was not lacking, for he chose
"fine" linen, a costly material which rich people alone could
afford to use and which nevertheless was plain and very unlike the gorgeous and tasteless burial garments bought by
wealthy Jews.

Despite all haste, Joseph's errand to Pilate and to the
merchants must have consumed an hour or more, and when
he returned to Calvary, the centurion was already at his
post of duty. By that time either the two malefactors were
dead, or the governor's command to deliver the body meant
that it should be given to him whether the two had died
or not. At least, Joseph was in no wise detained: "He
came therefore and took the body of Jesus down." Joseph
himself attended to the work, for we read nothing of his
having brought servants along. But did not Pilate com-

mand to "deliver" the body to him? If that order was understood as including the removal from the cross, then Joseph declined the services of the soldiers, and for good reason. The Roman executioners generally cut down the cross, or tore it from the socket, while the body was still affixed to it, and the heavy fall necessarily contused and injured the corpse. The sacred body of the Lord was not to be handled so rudely; here was a tender friend who willingly made some extra exertions to show respect to the dead Master. Joseph himself took the body down: was that not much of the refined counsellor, no doubt well advanced in years, who perhaps had never done the slightest menial work, who had piously avoided all defilement? A whole week of uncleanness was before him as soon as he touched the corpse. Did not the friends assist him? They cannot have returned home as soon as they knew that Joseph went to Pilate, for how did they know that his mission was successful! They were still present, and their profound sorrow did not hinder them from assisting in the work. While it was not Joseph's disposition to invite others into defiling themselves so as to forego the privileges of the passover, the love of those friends did not permit them to remain inactive spectators, they rather assisted him as much as was in their power. If nevertheless their service is not mentioned, if it is said of Joseph alone that "he" took the body down, then this "he" stands in the gospel as a monument erected to him by unselfish and grateful friends who appreciated his kind work. Never again does the sacred account speak of this Joseph: let the eye of the reader ever rest upon him in his sweetest and bravest act of caring for the departed Lord.

"And when Joseph had taken the body, he wrapped it in the clean linen cloth." This taking of the corpse means

that Joseph took possession of it; did a discussion ensue
as to who should have it? Why should it be improbable that
some friends living in Jerusalem, also had a tomb and wanted the Master to be buried there? If such offers were not
accepted, it was not only a compliment to Joseph, but safety
demanded that the body be left in his care. For to him
the body was "delivered," and with the hostile rulers as
opponents it was wiser for the poor friends to leave the
body in the care of the prominent counsellor who did his
work under the protection of Pilate. Joseph "had taken"
the body, which also means that now he was bending over it,
tenderly doing what an affectionate friend would do under
the circumstances: the eyes of the departed were closed,
and his countenance was kissed. Among the Greeks and
Romans, and also with the Jews, it was customary to wash
the body, as was done in the case of Dorcas. This had to
be omitted on Calvary because there were neither vessels
nor warm water at hand; if anything like washing was done,
it consisted in cleaning the wounds, perhaps with a little
sour wine furnished by the soldiers; and this may have been
attended to by the women, for the duty of washing the
corpse generally devolved on women friends. Then followed the winding or enswathing of the body with linen
bands: Joseph "wrapped it in the clean linen cloth." It was
"clean" linen. Poor people were forced to use the inex-
pensive cheap goods, or linen that had served other purposes
already. Executed criminals and disreputable persons, if
an attempt to wrap their bodies was made at all, were
swathed with old soiled linen in which books, particularly
the scrolls of the Law, had been kept: the Law had been
transgressed by them, and by the Law they had to die. The
very opposite of what the Jews would have done to Jesus
was here given: new and unstained linen of fine quality,

Acts 9, 37

such as a rich and honorable man deserved for an appropriate burial, enwrapped the sacred body of the Lord.

Hitherto three men have unexpectedly and in their own way glorified the crucified Lord: the penitent malefactor implored the mercy of the Friend of Sinners; the centurion confessed the holy Son of God; Joseph of Arimathea honored the Messiah of Israel. Now appears the fourth, Nicodemus to whom the cross spoke of the divine Savior lifted up for the benefit of the world. "And there came also Nicodemus, which at first came to Jesus by night and bought a mixture of myrrh and aloes, about a hundred pound weight." Like Joseph, Nicodemus was a ruler of the Jews, a member of the Sanhedrin. He also was a Pharisee, one of that sect which despite its claims of perfection and holiness, had from the beginning persecuted the Lord and always remained hostile to his cause. While we do not know whether Joseph ever met the Lord personally, the visit of Nicodemus with the Master and the quite lengthy conversation between the two are recorded. It was nearly three years before the crucifixion when he "came to Jesus by night, and said unto him, Rabbi, we know that thou art a John 3, 2 teacher come from God: for no man can do these miracles that thou doest except God be with him." His coming by night was probably due to the fear of his fellow Pharisees, though his "we know" seems to indicate that he was acquainted with some of them who thought highly of the Lord. During these years fear had prevented him from confessing Jesus publicly, though in one of the meetings of the Sanhedrin he demanded justice for the Lord: "Doth our John 7, 51 law judge any man, before it hear him, and know what he doeth?" From this sense of fairness we may safely conclude that he never agreed with his pharisaical colleagues, never was identified with their espionage and persecution, and that at last he was one of those who, like Joseph, had not consented to the counsel and deed of the rulers when they condemned and crucified the Lord. Why is it that Joseph is described as a rich, honorable, good and just man, as a believer waiting for the Kingdom, and as a secret "disciple of Jesus," while nothing like that is said concerning Nicodemus? Was his coming to Calvary not fully as precious and courageous as that of Joseph? Is nothing said because this pious Pharisee was a little late? He may have had good reasons for his tardiness. Or must we suppose that during the past years his interest in Jesus was so small and his faith so weak as to make him undeserving of the title "disciple"? But then his heroic action on that Friday was still more marvellous, and the readers of the gospel would be anxious to hear a little more of the man. The answer it, that Nicodemus needs no formal introduction like Joseph of whom we never heard before; the statement that at first he came to Jesus by night is description enough. As a ruler and a Pharisee he was naturally rich, prominent, and highly esteemed by the people; and if such a man from the beginning called the carpenter's son a teacher come from God, he must have been deeply religious; and if this ruler and Pharisee laid aside his own righteousness to learn of Jesus the great truths of the Kingdom, he cannot have been superficial or hypocritical. The mention of the night visit in this connection is a hint that his conversation with the Lord marked a turning point in his life. He had never forgotten the instruction received from the Master, had always found ways and means to nourish his faith, and in the crucifixion he saw the full explanation of those mysterious words which

John 3, 14, 15 the Savior addressed to him: "As Moses lifted up the serpent in the wilderness, even so must the Son of man be lifted up: that whosoever believeth in him should not perish, but have eternal life." As a ruler and Pharisee, Nicodemus risked fully as much as Joseph, and he was certainly aware of the consequences his action might have. He was now also estranged from his colleagues and became the object of their contempt and hatred. The legend says that later he was baptized by Peter and John, that he was deposed from his office in the Sanhedrin, and exiled, and that during his banishment he found temporary refuge in the country home of the famous teacher Gamaliel.

The circumstance that Joseph bought nothing but the necessary linen while Nicodemus furnished the required spices, might lead us to believe that the two men had made arrangements to that effect. In this case, however, we would expect both of them to come to Calvary first to see what was needed, and to go to Pilate together. Joseph would not have commenced to wrap the body, if he had known that Nicodemus would bring spices. It was a complete surprise to both men to meet under such conditions. As judges of the same court they had often met and were surely well acquainted, but no intimate friendship united them, for then they would have consulted and acted together. Each learned here for the first time that the other was a believer, a disciple of Jesus. Both had been obliged to guard carefully the secret of their faith, for the Sanhedrin and Jerusalem were swarming with spies, and nobody knew whom to trust. Both had succeeded in eluding the vigilance of the hostile judges until this hour when they voluntarily opened their hearts to the world. Jesus had never compelled these two to follow him and to confess him openly; he left the hour of decision to the wisdom of God. Neither did the Lord publish the names of people who secretly came to him asking for his help, advice, and consolation. If the Master was so patient and lenient with them, we have no right to

censure these men for hiding their faith so long, but we
rather rejoice that at last they made a public confession and
joined their hands in noble friendship over the body of their
beloved Lord.

Nicodemus came with the avowed purpose of assisting
in the burial, for he "brought a mixture of myrrh and aloes,
about a hundred pound weight." Nothing is said of a
servant caryring the burden, though such help must be assumed, for Nicodemus, unused to manual labor, would
scarcely have been able to support such weight. What he
brought was not the liquid ointment, but the pulverized gum
of myrrh mixed in due proportion with the powder of the
fragrant aloe wood. Nicodemus had evidently just bought
the spices of the apothecary and brought them ready for
the purpose of embalming. How did he know that any
spices were needed? Is it possible that he was on Calvary
while Joseph went to Pilate, that he learned of the intentions of the honorable cousellor and that this encouraged
him to go and buy the spices? In that event he would have
remembered that Joseph was a rich and generous man who
might buy the mixture himself; why then should Nicodemus
bring a superfluous gift? It is better to assume that this
converted Pharisee also remained at home during the day,
thinking seriously of the fate of Jesus and of his duty to
confess him. He learned that Jesus had died and was to
be buried before the Sabbath, and he resolved to assist in
the burial. He knew that the disciples and many friends of
Jesus were in Jerusalem and he took it for granted that
they would take care of the body. But he also knew that
those friends were poor; if they were able to buy some lin-
en, the expensive spices were probably beyond their means.
They might need his assistance and advice in more than one
respect, and he was willing to do his share. There was

nothing stingy about the man, for he brought of the mixture "about a hundred pound weight," which cost him a considerable amount of money. Judging from the large quantity of the spices, Nicodemus must have expected a complete burial, while Joseph prepared only for a temporary
laying away of the body. How could these men differ so
widely in their views? Nicodemus presumed that at his late
arrival the body would be safe from a disgraceful grave,
and that all would be ready for the regular burial: Did he
not know the spite of the Sanhedrin and that Pilate's permission had to be obtained? Yes, but he thought he also
knew the disciples; he had no idea that these men would
neglect absolutely everything. His rich gift at so late an
hour proves that he had not been on Calvary before and was
ignorant of the real situation. Joseph, on the other hand,
had been present in time to notice the confusion, and since
he was so long detained by Pilate, he cautiously counted on
other unforeseen hindrances and therefore decided on a
temporary interment. The hundred pounds of spices which
Nicodemus brought were a token of his sincere love to the
Master; from fifty to eighty pounds would have been amply
sufficient, but as if a dearly beloved member of his family
had departed, he procured more than was generally required. Yet this affectionate abundance was far from lav-
ish extravagance such as wealthy Jews were wont to indulge in, as when, for instance, at the funeral of Herod the
Great five hundred servants carried spices! He well understood that a vulgar display would have been against the
modest character and wish of the refined Lord.

He came almost too late, for Joseph had already commenced the enwrapping of the body, and a few minutes later
it would have been laid to rest. It is a fine trait in Joseph's
unselfish nature that for the sake of his tardy colleague he

willingly unwrapped the body and permitted Nicodemus to share in the honor of burying the Lord. His love was not a narrow and jealous one. "Then took they the body of Jesus, and wound it in linen clothes with the spices, as the manner of the Jews is to bury." The two men brought a great sacrifice by thus rendering themselves unclean for a whole week:

Num. 19, 11 "He that toucheth the dead body of any man shall be unclean seven days." This last service to the Master was more attractive and important to them than all the hollow celebrations of the entire passover. The sacred body was now wound with long strips of linen, layers of spices being put between the strips. The two men were scarcely adepts at the work which they had probably never done before. The women, however, with the fine tact acquired in their intercourse with Jesus, did not offer to do it better. Though they were no longer reticent in the presence of these prominent men, whom they now esteemed as humble brethren, they did not disturb them, because they knew what satisfaction that last service gave to those believing rulers. In their hearts the women may have resolved to complete after the Sabbath what the lack of time forbade at present: the adding of little details in the correct and gentle manner as only pure and good women are able to do. Joseph and Nicodemus finished their task, putting most of the spices under the linen, while part of it was perhaps reserved to be strewn in the grave where the body was to lie, as was done at the burial of Asa: They "laid him in the bed which was filled

2 Chron. 16, 14 with sweet odors and divers kinds of spices prepared by the apothecaries' art." All this was done "as the manner of the Jews is to bury," quite distinct in character and object from the famous mode of embalming in vogue among the Egyptians. These endeavored to preserve the bodies in the form of mummies until the departed soul should return

to its erstwhile habitation of clay. Accordingly, manifold
and elaborate manipulations were necessary: the brain and
the intestines were removed, the skull and the abdomen
were filled with spices, the prepared body was for several
weeks, sometimes for seventy days, placed into natron and
saltpeter, then washed and wrapped with bandages of
byssus. That was an operation requiring the skill of pro-
fessional embalmers and causing expenses which only the
richest could afford to pay, whilst the common people had
to be satisfied with a sorry imitation that was worse than
useless. The Bible mentions Jacob and his son Joseph as
the only Israelites who, because they had lived in that
country, were embalmed in the complicated manner of
Egypt. The Jewish mode was quicker and less expensive,
nor was it designed to saved the body from decay. The
spices simply served as the expression of tender love to the
departed, even as nowadays the silent, yet eloquent, flowers
are placed upon a casket.

And now the two rulers cease from bending over the
lifeless form of the Master. Defying the hatred and the
intrigues which the Sanhedrin may have had in store for
them, they have publicly attested their love to Jesus, have
courageously confessed their faith in Him whom their fellow judges had condemned. There is no class of people in
the world except it harbors some friends of the crucified
Lord. For "the wind bloweth where it listeth, and thou John 3, 8
hearest the sound thereof, but canst not tell whence it
cometh, and whither it goeth: so is every one that is born
of the Spirit." Did Nicodemus remember those words while
he helped to bring his Savior to the quiet resting place in
the rock?

70. THE TOMB IN THE GARDEN

Matt. 27, 60, 61   **Luke 23, 53-56**
Mark 15, 46, 47   **John 19, 41, 42**

"Now in the place where he was crucified
there was a garden; and in the garden a new
sepulchre, wherein was never man yet laid. And
Joseph laid him in his own new tomb, which he
had hewn out in the rock: There laid they Jesus
therefore because of the Jews' preparation day;
for the sepulchre was nigh at hand, and the sabbath drew on. And he rolled a great stone to the
door of the sepulchre, and departed.

And the women also, which came with him
from Galilee, followed after, and beheld the
sepulchre, and how his body was laid. And there
was Mary Magdalene, and the other Mary the
mother of Joses, sitting over against the sepulchre,
and beheld where he was laid. And they returned,
and prepared spices and ointments; and rested the
sabbath day according to the commandment."

———

The preparations for the funeral were soon finished.
No coffin was required, as the Jews carried their dead away
on an open bier, and this could be quickly improvised
from branches of a tree near by, or even the ropes with
which the body had been tied to the cross could be used.
The more important question was where to bury him; but
thanks to Joseph's generosity an excellent spot was provided. "Now in the place where he was crucified there was
a garden; and in the garden a new sepulchre, wherein was

never man yet laid. And Joseph laid him in his own new
tomb, which he had hewn out in the rock." Interment was
practised in Israel from the earliest times. Adam and Eve
are said to have learned it from seeing a raven burying its
young in the sand. Cremation, which was in vogue among
the Moabites and Edomites, was among the Jews only an
additional disgrace to the bodies of criminals, as the burning of Achan and his family shows: "And all Israel stoned Josh. 7, 25
him with stones, and burned them with fire, after they had
stoned them with stones." Or in time of war, when a
regular burial was not practicable, the bodies were burned
to save them from further disgrace by the foes: "All the
valiant men arose, and went all night, and took the body
of Saul and the bodies of his sons from the wall of Beth- 1 Sam. 31, 12
shan, and came to Jabesh, and burnt them there." Under
ordinary conditions interment was the rule with no exception, even as Abraham already, at Sarah's death, purchased
Machpelah from the sons of Heth: "Give me a possession Gen. 23, 4
of a burying place with you, that I may bury my dead out
of my sight." The graves were considered unclean and
therefore had to be outside the city, at least fifty cubits
from the walls, according to Rabbinical precepts. Only
kings, prophets, and perhaps also high priests were allowed
to be buried within the city; but Ezekiel already protested
against the close proximity of royal tombs to the temple,
and demanded that they "put away the carcasses of their
kings, far from me." The vicinity of Jerusalem abounded Ezek. 43, 7, 9
with tombs, but the one reciving the Lord was distinguished
from most of them. It was a sepulchre "in the garden,"
in an enclosure not neglected, but beautified and sacredly
set aside for the last long rest. Kings and wealthy families
loved to select gardens as fit surroundings for their graves;
King Amon "was buried in his sepulchre in the garden of 2 Kings 21, 26
Uzza." In the "garden" of Gethsemane the Passion began,

and in Joseph's "garden" it was ended. In the garden of
Eden the divine death-sentence was uttered over fallen
mankind, and in a garden the ancient curse was removed
by the repose of him who took away the sting of death.
The sins of all bygone ages drove the Lord into death; and
the members of the Sanhedrin, as willing servants and representatives of all transgressions, brought the Master into
this tomb. This is the view St. Paul took of this burial
when he said: "They that dwell at Jerusalem, and their
rulers, when they had fulfilled all that was written of him,
Acts 13, 27, 29 they took him down from the tree, and laid him in a
sepulchre." In Joseph's garden the guilt of all mankind,
originating in a garden, was buried. It that garden rest
Is. 65, 3
Is. 66, 17 was secured also for the Gentiles who restlessly "sacrificed
in the gardens" and vainly hoped to "purify themselves in
the gardens." This garden was "in the place where he was
crucified," in the same region, in the immediate neighborhood, so that some think Calvary was selected for the crucifixion in order to spite Joseph by defiling his property. But
Joseph does not look like a man who undertook the burial
merely to revenge himself on the rulers. The proximity of
the two spots is rather another masterpiece of divine control over human events. Numerous instances in the Bible
illustrate how God often works by contrasts; we cite but a
few concerning the Lord: Humble Bethlehem where he was
born was near the famous Jerusalem where he died; the
dark Gethsemane where he knelt in agony was very near
the sunny top of Olivet from where he ascended to heaven;
the public temple where the rulers had listened enraptured
to the Boy who wanted to be about his father's business,
was close to the palace where the Son of God was secretly
condemned for blasphemy; and Calvary with its bitter
humiliation adjoined the garden where the brighest Easter
glory was to burst forth.

The tomb itself is described as one which Joseph himself according to his plans "had hewn out in the rock." It was not a mausoleum erected of stone blocks, but an excavation dug into the solid limestone rock. This mode of building tombs was originally suggested to the Phenicians by the many natural caves of their country, which with a few finishing touches could be easily turned into chambers for the dead. The Jews adopted that type of tomb very early, especially prominent men like the treasurer Shebna: "Thou hast hewed thee out a sepulchre here, as he that heweth him out a sepulchre on high, and that graveth an inhabitation for himself in a rock." Though some Jewish Is. 22, 16 tombs were not level with the ground and were reached by small stairways leading up or down to them, Joseph's tomb seems to have been cut horizontally into the rock, enabling a person to walk straight into the chamber. The grave consisted either of a single room, or of several low, oblong, unadorned apartments; in either case the sides and the rear wall contained a number of narrow niches or holes sufficiently deep to receive a body. Such family tombs were the rule. The tomb which Joseph offered was "new," not one lately finished, but a grave "wherein was never man yet laid." The "never" seems to indicate that the tomb had ? *contrary!* stood unoccupied for a long time: Joseph had been highly favored, not a single member of his family having died before him. In a "new" tomb Jesus slept, for his state of exaltation had commenced and no defiling circumstances dared disgrace his rest. A new tomb: He who was in the world, but not of the world, who walked on earth without being soiled by the dust of sin, was to lie in the earth without coming in contact with the corruption of mortals. A new tomb: for by his death he made the grave an entirely "new" place; to him and his followers it is no more a yawning abyss of darkness, but an entrance into light and life. This tomb was emphatically Joseph's "own." This does not only mean that he was the proprietor, for we would surmise his ownership from the mere fact that he could not have ventured to enter the garden of a stranger and to use a grave not at his absolute disposal. To bury a stranger in a family tomb was considered a desecration of the sacred place; how could Joseph decide to put the body of the condemned Nazarene into this grave if it had not belonged to him! But it was his "own" also in the special sense that he himself wanted to rest there. He had prepared it with the thought that he would be the first of his family to need a last resting place, and then he wanted to sleep near the holy city. How noble a sacrifice was it to offer this precious grave to the Lord! The selection of a prominent tomb was a special distinction conferred upon a departed king whom a loving people wished to honor: "And Hezekiah slept with his fathers, and they buried him in the chiefest of sepulchres of the sons of David: and all Judah and the 2 Chron. 32, 33 inhabitants of Jerusalem did him honor at his death." A royal burial was given to the beloved Lord! And more: Joseph was not ashamed later to lie at the side of the crucified Nazarene. Like the penitent thief, Joseph expected the Lord to come in his Kingdom, but he surely had no thought of the resurrection of the body, he did not know that after a few days the Lord should leave this grave. By burying Jesus in his own tomb, Joseph adopted him as a member of his family, willing to sleep in the same grave with him whom the rulers had condemned as a blasphemer. We hear nothing of Joseph's family, but it must have been a noble household since he assumed that all would be content with his very unusual arrangement. Or must we suppose that Joseph stood alone in the world, and that the tomb was peculiarly his "own" because it consisted of one chamber all for himself? Even in that case his deed remains a

sweet sacrifice, for then he abandoned for the sake of Jesus
his long cherished hopes of sleeping in his favorite spot and
was compelled to seek another resting place.

"There laid they Jesus therefore because of the Jew's
preparation day; for the sepulchre was nigh at hand, and
the sabbath drew on." Two reasons seem to have decided
the choice of the place; the nearness of the garden; and the
lack of time to take the body to a more distant spot. The
sabbath "dawned" upon Jerusalem; the light of the setting
sun was considered the daybreak of the sabbath which now
was so close as to leave but a few minutes for the work.
Was this burial then made only temporarily with the intention of removing the body to another place after the sabbath? Did the Galilean friends perhaps entertain the plan
of transporting the body to their own country? When on
Easter the women came to anoint the Lord, they showed no
inclination to take the body with them, and the disciples sat
at home inactive and sorrowful. Evidently all considered
this tomb the final abode of the departed Master. The
question of putting the Lord somewhere else may have been
discussed immediately before the burial. There was, for
instance, the grave vacated by Lazarus, which may have
been offered. Other friends in Jerusalem may have owned
graves with vacant chambers; or Nicodemus also was surely willing to give his tomb. But all definitely decided in
favor of Joseph's garden, and it was probably he who urged
the lack of time as the best reason for doing so. If he had
grudgingly granted the privilege of his tomb, he could have
refused to unwrap the body when Nicodemus came so late,
he could have sent some of the waiting friends to secure a
grave as soon as he had the permit to take the body down.
He did nothing to evade the final selection of his own tomb,
but with the work of enwrapping finished, he naturally
called attention to the fact that the body, made heavy with

the weight of spices, could not be borne quickly any
distance; the sabbath would overtake them and the rulers
might stop them on the way. The generosity of the offer
was modestly disguised by the plea of the approaching sabbath which necessitated the choice of the grave "nigh" at
hand. There was true nobility in such conduct! The
friends were made to feel that they did not intrude but
conferred a favor on him by acceding to his request. It
was providential that the Lord was placed into this new
and distinguished tomb, for thereby an ancient prophecy
Is. 53, 9   was strikingly fulfilled: "He made his grave with the
wicked, and with the rich in his death." Numbered with
the transgressors, he was to be buried with them in a disgracing pit, as the rulers intended; but God had provided
an honorable burial in the garden of the rich Joseph. In
a garden the Lord had always loved to rest and to pray
after a day's wark; and after the heat of this Friday, after
the toil of his whole life, he rested in the garden of the
honorable counsellor. "And he rolled a great stone to the
door of the sepulchre, and departed." The worst enemy of
the graves were the ravenous beasts, especially the jackal,
wherefore the entrance was secured with a large and heavy
circular stone, the "roller," which sometimes ran in grooves,
permitting the stone to be swung into position with ease.
This stone must not be confounded with the tombstones
erected in memory of the dead, for it served only as a door
and bore no inscriptions. Having done his full duty, Joseph
"departed" as if he had rendered a trifling service not
worth mentioning. He did not linger to receive expressions of heart-felt gratitude from his friends, but immediately went his way. Yet to us it seems as if we could dis-
cern the eyes of the thankful women turned long upon the
noble man as he slowly disappeared from them, and from
us, in the shadows of the sabbath night.

Though darkness fell rapidly upon the earth, the garden was not at once forsaken. "And the women also, which came with him from Galilee, followed after, and beheld the sepulchre, and how his body was laid." The faithful women who through long hours had watched the cross, waited until Joseph and Nicodemus carried the body to the grave, whereupon they formed the small funeral procession of sincere mourners. We are surprised to see only "women from Galilee"; where were now "his acquaintance," and where the ministering women like Salome, who besides Mary and Magdalene had stood near the cross? Why did only women from Galilee and not also some from Jerusalem follow to the grave? Later we read that "they returned, and prepared spices and ointments." They did not bring those materials along from Galilee, and the citizens of Jerusalem were not always prepared for a funeral, as little as the modern families make full provisions for such emergencies. First they had to buy the spices, and the purchase could not be made after the sabbath set in, for by six o'clock the stores were closed, which was also the case on the following evening. Those women, then, must have left Calvary as soon as they saw that the body was well cared for by the rich friend; they returned to the city to purchase spices. Therefore in the women at the grave we recognize chiefly those poorest people from Galilee, who had followed the Lord to Jerusalem, and who perhaps had not the means for even a small gift of spices, whose only contribution was their pleasing fidelity and profound sorrow. They "beheld the sepulchre"; it was an object of interest to them and no detail escaped their scrutiny. They went up to the entrance and saw "how his body was laid"; even as nowadays it is a satisfaction to the mourners to cast a parting look upon the lowered casket and to notice that nothing is lacking in the last tribute of love. The women were such close observers not from curiosity, nor for their own information, but largely for the benefit of anxious souls at home where particulars were eagerly awaited. The absence of the disciples must have been painful to these women; yet they could also understand that grief and fear kept the men away, and that everyone of them was yearning for news from the Master. When the disciples at last come forth, the women can tell them not only of sadness and gloom, but they are able to point out glimpses of honor, little incidents that revealed the hand of God in the burial of Jesus Christ.

At last the women departed, with the exception of two. "And there was Mary Magdalene, and the other Mary the mother of Joses, sitting over against the sepulchre, and beheld where he was laid." How they made themselves at home in the garden of the rich owner! The others of the company had freely come and gone, and these two felt at liberty to stay as long as they desired. The distance between the two chief rulers and the humble Galileans had been bridged over by the common love of Jesus, over whose body a tender friendship was formed by widely different classes, a union prophetic of the blessed ties that ever afterwards should bind together all Christian hearts. After the grave was closed the two women "beheld where he was laid," their eyes were riveted on the large stone concealing their dearest possession on earth. They were "sitting" over against the sepulchre, having it in full view. Their restful attitude was not chosen because they were tired from standing several hours on Calvary; when heavy grief weighs upon the heart one prefers to sit. No conversation between them is recorded; each sat in silence engaged with her own thoughts. How much may have passed through their minds! Mary Magdalene could remember the years of her ailment, and the gracious day when the Lord's power gave her health; her life and being she owed since then to him. And the other Mary was able to recall many a touching incident in the home life at Nazareth, to think of the proud moment when she gave her consent to the two sons Joses and James to become disciples of Jesus. How many gentle traits of his beautiful life may have been revived in their memories! Heartrending though their sorrow must have been, we hear none of the wailing customary with Jewish women under such circumstances. A charming picture to behold these two friends sitting hand in hand, with their eyes fastened on the tomb, with their thoughts in a dreamlike Past, quite forgetful of the world now overspread with shadows of the night. And they sit until the stars twinkle in the firmament, and the round moon begins to shed a peaceful light, admonishing them to go home.

Far beyond the moment of the dawning sabbath they had sat, until the advanced hour forced them to retire. "And they returned, and prepared spices and ointments; and rested the sabbath day according to the commandment." That must have been a dreary return to Jerusalem where now innumerable lamps were lighted in honor of the highest sabbath of the year. In the midst of all that merriment there were homes where no candles shone that evening; among the celebrating thousands there were forsaken and lonesome souls with many a bitter tear in the silence of the long night. The thoughts of the faithful women reverted to the tomb, and they formed the resolution to prepare "spices and ointments." Magdalene and Mary cannot have bought them, for they returned too late to the city; probably their share was secured by the other women who had left the hill earlier. And the preparing of the spices cannot have been done that same evening, for on the sabbath they were quiet; it must have been attended to on the next evening after six o'clock when the sabbath was over. In their opinion the burial was incomplete; the body had not been properly washed, and neither Joseph nor Nicodemus had brought ointments which also belong to a burial. But why should they buy more spices? Had not Nicodemus brought more than enough of the fragrant material? They knew that well; but does love count with pounds and coins, or is it satisfied to appear empty handed? When a great and good man, a kind benefactor is buried, and his wealthy friends send their tokens of respect in profusion, will not also the grateful poor, blessed by his benefactions, bring his humble gift of gratitude, perhaps only a few cheap flowers scarcely noticeable among the other offerings? And do they not also eloquently speak of love and respect? Those women had lost more than a good friend or great benefactor! Their hearts prompted them to do something, however little, to honor their Lord! We would be justly astonished if they had done nothing at all. They "rested the sabbath day according to the commandments," and that rest was also as valuable as a precious nard. It is significant that not only Joseph and Nicodemus exerted themselves to finish the burial before the sabbath, but that likewise these women kept the Law of God so flagrantly transgressed by the rulers of Israel. The sad experiences of that Friday, the dreary fate of Jesus, did not make these honest souls despair of truth and righteousness, of piety and religion. They knew that the godless leaders must not be confounded with the Law represented by them, and that their apparent triumph could detract not the least from the glory of God who brings all things to pass in his own chosen time. How brave were those grief-stricken friends, and how encouraging an example is their conduct to those Christians who on account of most trifling offenses within the Church sometimes lose confidence in the glorious cause of their Master! For the sake of Jesus those men and women were ready to do what all Jerusalem called defilement; and to the honor of that same Jesus they were careful to abstain from the least that might bring reproach upon the Master or upon the followers that had acquired their wisdom in his school.

And Jesus also "rested the sabbath day." He who had not where to lay his head was even in death the guest of a friend. From the manger to the grave he walked as a pilgrim whose home was not on earth. Among the Jews it was considered a disgrace not to own a grave, and the rulers may have spoken with supreme contempt of that Jesus who needed the tomb of a charitable friend. They knew not that it was the greatest glory of Jesus to call no grave his own. Only as a stranger did he visit this grand cemetery which we call world; and merely on a transient pilgrimage he went through the abode of the dead. His footsteps have blessed the fields and the sea, the vales and the mountains; now his body also sanctifies the bosom of mother earth that his friends dread not to sleep in it a while, for it has become "God's Acre" in which a precious seed, sown by God, ripens for the harvest of eternity.

That sabbath was indeed a "high day." It was the culmination of all the sabbaths of the Old Testament and the golden dawn of the glorious sabbath of the New Testament. With a parting look we greet once more the tomb in the garden and take along a gift more fragrant than Nicodemus' spices: "There remaineth therefore a rest to the people of God." Heb. 4, 9

71. THE SEAL AND THE WATCH
Matt. 27, 62-66

"Now the next day, that followed the day of preparation, the chief priests and Pharisees came together unto Pilate, saying, Sir, we remember that that deceiver said, while he was yet alive, After three days I shall rise again. Command therefore that the sepulchre be made sure until the third day, lest his disciples come by night, and steal him away, and say unto the people, He is risen from the dead: so the last error shall be worse than the first. Pilate said unto them, Ye have a watch: go your way, make it as sure as you can. So they went, and made the sepulchre sure, sealing the stone, and setting a watch."

———

He that sitteth in the heavens shall laugh: the Lord shall have them in derision! To their dismay the rulers learned that they had not so thoroughly annihilated the Nazarene as they had aimed to do. If the friends spent the night of the sabbath in restless pain, the enemies no less had their slumbers disturbed by disquieting apprehensions. In the afternoon and evening of Friday already the Sanhedrists certainly learned all the particulars of what had happened on Calvary and in Joseph's garden. There was a succession of disagreeable incidents: the speedy death of Jesus; the earthquake; the parted veil; the open tombs; and the confession of the centurion. Though the rulers themselves were not impressed by those signs, the people were, for many of them had returned in silence from Calvary and their experiences were discussed in the city. Jesus was still the main topic of conversation, and by no means did they speak contemptuously of him, as the rulers had hoped. The most startling information was that the body had been saved from disgraceful burial, and this through two prominent rulers who had openly declared their faith in Jesus. The cause of the Nazarene, instead of being crushed forever, still lived, and grew, and intruded even into the supposedly immune circle of the Sanhedrin! What will the multitudes say when they learn of Joseph's and Nicodemus' action? A feeling of insecurity seized the rulers, they realized that the victory was far from being complete, and the anxiety of the night found expression in their conduct the next morning.

"Now the next day, that followed the day of preparation, the chief priests and Pharisees came together unto Pilate." The day after the preparation was the sabbath, the "high" day. Why, then, does Matthew not simply write that they met on the "sabbath"? Why does he call it merely the "next" day, as if it had been a common work day, as if the preparation was more important than the sabbath? It has been supposed that among the earliest Christians the "preparation" was the standing term for the day of crucifixion, even as we call it "Good Friday." There is nothing to prove that so vague a designation was ever in vogue among the believers. Or it is thought that the day did not deserve the name "sabbath" because the rulers desecrated it so much. But did the lack of piety in the rulers change the nature of the sabbath? There were thousands of earnest people who observed it as a sabbath, among them the friends of the Lord. Matthew emphasizes the preparation in order to call our attention to the hypocrisy of the Sanhedrists. These men were watching that everybody in the city finished his work precisely at six o'clock; and how conscientiously the sincere Jews kept that regulation was seen in the exertions of Joseph and Nicodemus. The rulers had demanded the breaking of the bones "because it was the preparation," as if they were so careful themselves or, at least, respected the pious sentiments of the people. But now we learn that they used the preparation only for their selfish purposes, that at heart they were not afraid to transgress even the ordinances of the sabbath itself, when their interests were involved. On that high sabbath, when a solemn quiet reigned throughout the city, there was an unusual stir among the rulers. They "came together" unto Pilate. They did not march in a procession as the day before, but singly, one by one, coming from different directions and meeting in the governor's residence at an appointed hour. This betrays a previous agreement, a secret session, in which their plan of action had been decided on; and this confidential consultation must have taken place either quite early the same morning, or the night before; in either case it was held on the highest sabbath day in contradiction to the religious convictions of the Jews. That hastily called meeting was no official session of the Sanhedrin, for the three classes of priests, scribes and elders were not represented as such. Quietly, to escape public notice, the informal gathering convened, attended by "the chief priests and Pharisees." Some scribes and elders may have belonged to the Pharisees, but what business had this religious sect as such in the Sanhedrin? We surmise that the Pharisees were stirred and excited as never before in their lives as soon as they learned that one of their own number, the Pharisee Nicodemus, had taken part in the burial of Jesus. These men regarded their sect as the very citadel of orthodoxy and enmity against the Nazarene, and now one of them became a disciple of the Crucified Christ!

The Pharisees had been the first to incite the priests to hostile actions, and here they came again to spur them on. The "chief priests" were the closest adherents and colleagues of Annas and Caiaphas, and to them the apostacy of Joseph and Nicodemus must have been a severe shock. This meeting was composed of men who had distinguished themselves in their enmity against Jesus, men who could be depended on to defend the safety and honor of the Sanhedrin to the last. These were all trusted leaders determined to avenge the "treachery" of the two members and to leave nothing undone to rid the land of the Galilean heresy. Perhaps the bitterest humiliation was the circumstance that, after years of conspiracy against the living Jesus, the dead and buried Nazarene should still cause them so much trouble.

Cautiously they went their way to the procurator, as if they just happened to meet at his gate. The principal object now was not to cover their secret arrangements but the novel fact that they came "unto Pilate," into the defiling house of the Gentile. On the day before when they delivered Jesus unto him, "they themselves went not into the judgment hall, lest they should be defiled; but that they might eat the passover." When they asked for the breaking of the bones, they merely "besought" Pilate, either by sending a committee or a higher Jewish officer. Now, however, the holy priests and the immaculate Pharisees came in considerable numbers, and this entering the Gentile's house took place on the sabbath of sabbaths! What must the people think when they hear of their pious leaders profaning the sabbath and defiling themselves with a light heart—then to mingle with the worshippers as if nothing was wrong. Another example of how little they believed or practiced what they taught! And how surprising to see the conceited rulers of Israel call submissively on their great foe in his own house and on a day when all official business was suspended! Probably Joseph's bold visit had its effect, and the rulers wished to appear fully as liberal as he.

Their address contained the result of the private deliberations. "Sir, we remember that that deceiver said, while he was yet alive, After three days I will rise again. Command therefore that the sepulchre be made sure until the third day." First of all they justified their unusual visit and request by stating that they had remembered a matter of importance which tolerated no delay. Exceedingly reverential and polite was their address "Sir." That title had probably never before come over their lips, for at heart they hated and despised the Gentile. But they also knew that the dislike was mutual, and since they had come to ask a favor it was wise to make an extra effort to win his good will. Sir, "we remember": as if the thought had suddenly and spontaneously occurred to them all. Was that true? If they remembered at all that Jesus spoke of his resurrection, it must have been so remarkable a saying that they could not well forget it, for thereby he claimed to be more than the Messiah, he asserted his Sonship. They had surely often thought of it, but never believed its possibility; they considered it so baseless a boast that it was not once mentioned in their trial of the Lord. What was it that changed their opinions so quickly and made them fear the doctrine of the resurrection? We are hardly mistaken if we think of the tombs opened by the earthquake. Not that they considered it as a divine announcement of opening also the tomb of Jesus; but what, if the frightened people explained it as such? If the rulers remembered some words about the resurrection, why not also the people? Many of them had returned from Calvary in a serious mood, and it is not impossible that one or the other, when comparing the signs, realized the divinity of Jesus and, by the open tombs, was reminded of his words concerning the resurrection.

The rulers may have heard such rumors and thereupon took their precautions. Their careless "we remember" was to conceal their uneasiness at the continuing and alarming interest taken in Jesus by the populace. The annoying feature was something which "that deceiver said." So contemptible a person was the Nazarene, that they refused to utter his name. There was but one such deceiver in the land, and Pilate knew without asking to whom they referred. They called Jesus an impostor also for the benefit of the governor. If he should be disquieted by the events of yesterday, by the rumors of the people, by the report of the centurion, then the rulers are in a position to assure him that all that is superstition, that Jesus was nothing but a deceiver. Here their opinion of Joseph and Nicodemus was also implied. As Paul testifies, the apostles, like their Master, were described "as deceivers." The two wayward rulers were naught but deceived deceivers, and Pilate must not think that the whole Sanhedrin took fright at the many signs or were converted to the cause of the Nazarene. The saying remembered by them was said by the deceiver "while he was yet alive." Of course, he could not say it when he hung dead on the cross or lay in the grave; why did they mention it with such care? On the one hand they point triumphantly to the fact that the deceiver is actually dead, and that to this moment nothing has happened to indicate any resurrection; the signs and the fears of the people must not be taken seriously; and, again, they point out that Jesus made his prediction not only once or twice, but ever "while he lived," it constituted an essential part of the doctrines with which he deceived the people. That oft repeated saying consisted of the assertion, "After three days I will rise again." That sounded like a very positive assurance admitting of no doubt; and in his own power he wanted to break through the prison of death: I will rise.

2 Cor. 6, 8

Now it has been argued that Jesus never spoke of his resurrection in so explicit or intelligible a manner as to give his disciples a clear understanding of it, and much less could the rulers therefore have such an exact knowledge of that doctrine. We fail to see why the disciples or the rulers should have been ignorant on that subject. Quite frequently, and commencing at an early date, did Jesus announce his resurrection. He showed his disciples how he must go to Jerusalem, suffer many things, "and be killed, and be raised again the third day." While he yet abode in Galilee he foretold that "they shall kill him, and that the third day he shall be raised again." Only a few days before his Passion, on the way to Jerusalem, he explained how the Son of man should be delivered to the Gentiles, they "to crucify him: and the third day he shall rise again." If the disciples disliked the discussion of that subject, it was not because they failed to understand everything about the rising again, but because the resurrection was preceded by the sorrows and death so distasteful to their thoughts. And if the disciples did not preach on that theme, so that the rulers derived no information from that source, then the scribes and Pharisees had heard that prediction of Jesus himself. "But he answered and said unto them, An evil and adulterous generation seeketh after a sign; and there shall be no sign given it, but the sign of the prophet Jonas: for as Jonas was three days and three nights in the whale's belly; so shall the Son of man be three days and three nights in the heart of the earth." On no other occasion did Jesus prophesy so clearly of the miraculous manner and of the certainty of his resurrection after a space of three days. This saying was certainly never effaced from the memory of the Sanhedrin. And did not all the assembled judges hear Jesus declare in open court, in the night session on Friday, that they should see the Son of man come in the clouds of heaven?

Matt. 16, 21

Matt. 17, 23

Matt. 20, 19

Matt. 12
39, 40

What did that signify but that neither death nor grave could keep him, that the rulers were not done with him even after the crucifixion? The rulers spoke the truth, and they spoke from their own knowledge, when they said that Jesus claimed a speedy resurrection; and they condemned themselves by admitting this truth. With the claims of the Lord's resurrection in their minds, they must have known that the two witnesses swore falsely when they accused Jesus as a blasphemer of the temple because he said: "Destroy this temple, and in three days I will raise it up." The rulers well knew that in those words the Lord had spoken of the resurrection of his body, and therefore also knew that they had condemned him unjustly. Queen truth stands ever watching the unguarded moments of a guilty heart, seeking to escape from the bars and bolts of hypocrisy that try to imprison her forever in the silence of a sinful bosom!

After having thus justified their visit, the rulers submitted the request which Pilate was to grant: "Command therefore that the sepulchre be made sure until the third day." If the governor is to command, he must have an interest in the affair. As much as the rulers themselves had to fear a renewed religious commotion among the masses, so much and more could Pilate dread political disturbances. The Jewish world and the Gentile world must work together that no fraudulent resurrection can be preached to mankind! The location of the tomb was not described, they would not take the detested name of Joseph upon their lips; and Joseph, when asking for the body, may have informed Pilate of his intention to bury Jesus in his garden. The tomb was to be "made sure," guarded by soldiers "until the third day." A longer watch was not required, for if the report of the resurrection was started during these days, the soldiers were witnesses that it could not have taken place; but if the rumor was spread later than the third day, it contradicted "that deceiver" in his own clear statement that "after three days" he would rise again, and then the fraud would be obvious. Here we find plainly indicated that many Jews were thinking of the resurrection. Luke tells us that when Jesus spoke to the scribes and Pharisees about the sign of Jonas, "the people were gathered thick together." Those masses had not yet forgotten the prediction of the resurrection, and of this the rulers were aware. We must not suppose for a moment that the Sanhedrists wanted the grave watched for their own benefit; they would not believe a resurrection whether the report of it came on, after, or before the third day. However, they knew of people who would gladly believe if the third day brought such report; this precaution was to prevent that possibility. It has been thought very strange that the rulers, entertaining such serious fears, should not themselves have taken care of the body of Jesus in order to preclude a fraudulent resurrection. There was no need of it. The guarding of the tomb by soldiers was as safe as they could wish. It was now too late to claim the body, for Pilate's grant had made it Joseph's property. And why should they on Friday afternoon already think of rumors of a resurrection? They had done everything to render Jesus an abomination to the Jews; how could they foresee that the interest in him would continue so long, that the signs would impress the people so much as to make them think of the resurrection, that even rulers would publicly avow their faith in the Nazarene! Quite unexpectedly that threatening turn had come, and the rulers did their best under the circumstances. There is nothing strange in that. But it is surprising that they asked for Roman soldiers when all the rulers had their private servants, and the Sanhedrin had the officers of the court and

Luke 11, 29

the temple police at their command. They could have assembled a sufficiently strong guard of their own men if they
had so desired. While the Roman authorities did not allow
the Jews to exercise their police privileges indiscriminately,
yet the watching of the grave, so harmless in itself, would
not have been refused by Pilate, had they petitioned him
to that effect. True, the Galileans were bold people; but
if the rulers expected a raid on the tomb, the small Roman
guard stationed there could not have repulsed an assault
of many courageous disciples. And who would believe the
story of a resurrection occurring in the course of a veritable
combat! The rulers did not fear so much a forcible robbery,
as rather a secret crafty stealing of the body, and the soldiers were to be more witnesses than guards supposed to
meet an armed interference. And just for that purpose
Jewish officers and servants were least desirable. If the
people in general were so profoundly moved with the signs
on Calvary, will not the officers also be impressed at the least
unusual occurrence? Whom could the rulers trust? Two
of the enlightened counsellors had been deceived by the
Nazarene, what could be expected of the ignorant servants?
Had not some of them been sent to apprehend him, and had
they not returned without him because "never man spake John 7, 46
like this man"? The decision in favor of the Roman soldiers
tells us how insecure the rulers felt, how little they had
succeeded in disgracing the memory of Jesus among the
citizens. Pilate's men alone could be depended on to perform their duties to the letter, no matter what their private
opinions might be; that had been proved on Calvary by the
centurion and his subordinates. The Gentiles were not
preoccupied with fears or hopes of a resurrection, and they
would naturally watch every event with a critical eye and
cool judgment. Incidentally the Roman guard could teach
a lesson to Joseph and Nicodemus: they were branded not

only as traitors of the Jewish religion, but as conspirators who might assist in the stealing of the body, as dangerous characters threatening the peace of the country, as men whom Pilate had to watch.

As a reason for making this request the rulers adduced their suspicion: "Lest his disciples come by night, and steal him away, and say unto the people, He is risen from the dead: so the last error shall be worse than the first." His disciples! The rulers, then, admitted that they had not succeeded in driving away all people from the Nazarene or in killing all hopes in his cause. Despite the disgrace heaped upon Jesus, he had still men who wanted to be his disciples and to work for his glory. His disciples! While the enemies remembered the saying of Jesus concerning his resurrection and were troubled by it, those men remained in hopeless solitude. Yet we are now tempted to rejoice that they stayed away from Calvary and that their sorrow was so disconsolate; we recognize the hand of God in it rendering the charges of the rulers the more absurd and the facts of Easter the more glorious. The disciples! They must be desperate men to rob a grave and to base future claims of the Messiah on a dead person. And they must be fools to "steal" what they could have for the asking. Joseph was before the Roman law the owner of the body and in his garden it was buried; he had a right to remove it when and where he pleased. Since he had confessed himself as a believer in "that deceiver," he must be suspected of participating in the fraud, and then the disciples would not need to "steal." Did not the rulers think of that? They certainly did, and therefore we surmise that they wished to hide from Pilate their hatred against Joseph, the bitter pains caused them by his conduct. They wanted to create the impression as if they were in full accord with their fellow judge, as if his garden had been selected with their

consent, and as if they were as anxious as he that the body
be not stolen from him. In this way they could best cast
reproach upon the disciples of the Nazarene. How depraved
must those men be if they can "say unto the people, He is
risen from the dead." They will not execute the theft
merely to make other people believe that they were justified
in following their Messiah, but they will scatter the dangerous deception, leading others astray. Again we wonder
how the rulers could presume that, with their mere "saying"
that Jesus had risen, the disciples should be able to cause
a great commotion among the people and to make propa-
ganda for and with a Messiah whom nobody had seen after
his death. The statement of the rulers would have no sense
whatever if during the last few hours they had not learned
of numerous people who would willingly accept as true a
story of the resurrection. "The people," the masses, may
hear and believe; and the welfare of the nation demands
that they hear no more of the Nazarene. For if they do,
"the last error shall be worse than the first." What was
that first error which was bad enough in itself? That Jesus
called himself the Messiah? Yes; but the rulers were
speaking to Pilate who did not care for religious heresies;
to him that first error must also have been unwelcome.
The Sanhedrists referred to the Messiah King who forbade
to give tribute to Cæsar. Though Pilate found no fault in
him, the rulers insist that they were correct and truthful in
their accusations of the previous day. If the first was bad,
"the last error shall be worse." Why? Because then all
the people believing in the resurrection will be unanimous in
saying that Jesus is the Son of God, while hitherto they were
divided on that subject; and because then the movement
will not be so easily suppressed. They could crucify the
living Jesus, but what can they do to the supposedly risen
Christ who in their opinion does not exist at all? Then

they have to deal with eleven disciples and scores of believers who all proclaim that Jesus is risen! The rulers were correct: "the last error shall be worse than the first." If the doctrine of Jesus and the faith of the disciples had been from the beginning based on an error; and if then his resurrection had been a still greater error, an invention and a myth, what a carnival of fanaticism, superstition, and folly would have ensued! How quickly and deservedly the religion of the Nazarene would have died of the death it carried in its own heart. "The last error shall be worse than the first." The rulers practically described their own mistakes. Their first error was to prosecute and crucify the noblest son of their country; and their greater error was that they tried to stay the hand of God reaching down to the grave in the garden, and that they refused to accept the life of the risen Son of God. They were cast aside, and the young Church stepped forth over the ruins of their temple into the wide world.

The governor was very obliging; almost before they had uttered the last word his ready reply came: "Pilate said unto them, Ye have a watch: go your way, make it as sure as you can." This answer is somewhat peculiar, and deserves a little more attention than it generally receives. First Pilate was accommodating: ye have a watch; then he grew insulting: go your way; at last he seemed to give them a good advice: make as sure as you can. If he courteously granted the request, why should he drive them from his presence? Or if he was angry, why should he give them an advice or even the watch? Let us inquire into the meaning of the three sentences. Pilate said unto them, "Ye have a watch." Does this signify that he refused to interfere, because the matter did not concern him and the rulers had their own guards whom they could station at the tomb? But it did concern him, for the plea had been

made that the public peace and safety were in danger; and if
he refused now, why did he afterwards actually send his men
to the grave? Or did he remind them that they had a watch
already, namely the four soldiers who had guarded the
crosses? These were released the evening before, at six
o'clock, and were no longer at the disposal of the rulers.
And how could four men be expected to keep the watch for
several days! More than four men were required. Perhaps
the governor sneered at them; it gave him satisfaction to
humiliate his enemies, yesterday so overbearing, crouching
before him today! But would not his revenge and triumph
have been greater if he had sent them away without advice
and guards? Finally, it might have been indifference; he
was weary of these interviews, he took no interest in their
fears, and simply to get rid of them granted the request.
Who will believe that the highest Roman officer in the land
sends his soldiers on errands at the slightest wish of the
Jewish rulers! We have no choice left but to hear in his
words a deliberate and full compliance with their request,
spoken in the short, commanding tone of a military officer:
"Have a watch," a complete watch of four quaternions, as
many men as they need or want for the enterprise. And he
said it in angry mood, ordering them from the palace: "Go
your way." For who will seriously entertain the idea that
Pilate implored them to make haste, to go straightway to
the tomb, lest they come too late! Did the governor really
have faith in a resurrection? The thought was entirely
foreign to the Gentile. Or did he suspect the disciples of
stealing the body, then to say, He is risen? In Joseph he
had met a secret disciple, and if all were like him, they
could not be desperadoes. During the whole trial of Jesus
he had heard not a single word against the followers of
the Nazarene. And supposing they would steal the body
and spread a false rumor, why should Pilate be afraid of

that? All the years while Jesus was living there had been not the least trouble on account of him or his disciples. Pilate was not afraid. We rather notice that the rulers' talk was disgusting to him; despite the repeated slurs on "that deceiver" he was still convinced that Jesus was innocent, and he grew weary of listening to these accusers. The sooner they leave him, the more he is pleased: "Go your way." Then he gave them a good advice along: "Make it as sure as you can." Was that actually an admonition to take every possible precaution? How superfluous, since he had not the faintest misgivings concerning a real or supposed resurrection! Or did he speak as a man at his wit's end, who declared that he had done all in his power and must leave the rest to the sagacity of the rulers? But nobody had asked him to do more than furnish the guard. No: when an angry man considers a certain measure as senseless, and yet deems it wise to submit to a foolish demand, and apparently adds an advice, what is that? Nothing but sarcasm! Pilate stands there with his Roman blood aroused, chasing the rulers from him, and ironically calling after them: Yes, go and see that nothing is forgotten to keep the Nazarene in his grave. What was it that kindled his ire, and why did he, despite his anger, grant the superfluous guard? The defeat of the previous morning was still of bitter taste to him, but something also was added, and the demand of the rulers gives the explanation. The Lord had died so unusually early that Pilate himself marvelled at it; yet he had taken every precaution to ascertain his death before giving the body away. Now came these rulers and spoke of his rising again, of the disciples stealing him, of watching the tomb. He could not but take it as a distrust in himself, as he had not fully done his duty, as if it had been wrong to give the body to Joseph instead of to the rulers. Thereby the governor was forced to grant a watch in order to convince the rulers of the baselessness of their suspicions, and to protect himself against their future slanders as if he had been negligent in the crucifixion of Christ. While the Passion of the Savior brought Herod and Pilate together in friendship, it separated the governor and the rulers in bitter enmity. A chasm has opened and grows wider and wider between Judea and Rome!

The rulers did not wait for a second command to leave the presence of the ungracious procurator. "So they went, and made the sepulchre sure, sealing the stone, and setting a watch." Personally they went to Joseph's garden to station the guards and to instruct the soldiers how to act in an emergency. The sepulchre was "made sure"; they were not afraid of defiling themselves by investigating the grave and convincing themselves that the body was there, and that the body was that of the Nazarene. A weird scene to behold the arch enemies of Christ bent over his body in the tomb to assure themselves that his defeat is complete! After replacing the stone they "sealed" it by stretching a cord across its surface, attaching the ends to the rock with soft clay or wax taken along for that purpose. The "seal" used on that occasion may have been a threefold one: Pilate's official seal; the seal of the Sanhedrin; or the private seal of one of the rulers, as it was customary with rich Jews to carry the sealing ring on the finger. This private seal would overawe nobody who attempted to steal the body of the Master; its breaking would merely show that the door had been tampered with, and that would have been poor consolation if the thief of the body had escaped. The seal of the Sanhedrin could not be used, for no official resolution had been passed on this subject. And one who defies the entire supreme court and the whole religion of the Jews by stealing the dead Jesus to call him revived, will not be deterred by the insignia of the Sanhedrin. Only the fear of death was strong enough to hinder desperate men from opening the tomb. And death awaited him who violated the seal of Pilate who affixed it in the name of Cæsar! Pilate certainly did not go to the tomb nor did he entrust his seal to the rulers; but a centurion or another officer may have come with them to act in Pilate's name. The tomb was also "made sure" by setting the watch. The soldiers were not collected in one and the same spot, but distributed, watching the grave in different positions and from all directions, to frustrate any plan of robbery and to recognize and apprehend the conspirators. A veritable trap! Now since these arrangements were made in absolute secrecy, we suspect that they were intended not only, perhaps not even principally, for the disciples in general, but mainly for Joseph! Supposing what might easily have happened, that the generous man had come alone or with some friends in the late evening merely to see whether all was left in good order, and, without noticing the seal in the darkness, had pushed the stone aside, and the guards had broken forth from ambush! That would have been revenge on him as the rulers desired. The Sanhedrists could depart in peace. Had they not done all in their power to remain forever unmolested by the Nazarene?

The sun looked down on that sabbath as usual, and the stars of the night beheld the quiet tomb of Him whose eyes, by the decrees of man, should greet the light of this world no more. But the past ages and the eons to come were assembled around the rocky vault, and in the breezes of the garden we hear them whisper, What think ye: The hopes of the fathers, and the visions of the prophets, and the yearnings of the human soul, are they all in vain? And these voices are not hushed until answered by the swift, glorious light of Easter Morn.